THE 50 GREATEST PLAYERS IN DETROIT LIONS HISTORY

ALSO AVAILABLE IN THE 50 GREATEST PLAYERS SERIES

The 50 Greatest Players in Boston Celtics History
The 50 Greatest Players in Boston Red Sox History
The 50 Greatest Players in Braves History
The 50 Greatest Players in Buffalo Bills History
The 50 Greatest Players in Chicago Bears History
The 50 Greatest Players in Cincinnati Bengals History
The 50 Greatest Players in Cincinnati Reds History
The 50 Greatest Players in Cleveland Browns History
The 50 Greatest Players in Dallas Cowboys History
The 50 Greatest Players in Denver Broncos History
The 50 Greatest Players in Detroit Tigers History
The 50 Greatest Players in Green Bay Packers History
The 50 Greatest Players in Houston Astros History
The 50 Greatest Players in Kansas City Chiefs History
The 50 Greatest Players in Minnesota Vikings History
The 50 Greatest Players in New England Patriots History
The 50 Greatest Players in New York Giants History
The 50 Greatest Players in New York Yankees History
The 50 Greatest Players in Philadelphia Eagles History
The 50 Greatest Players in Philadelphia Phillies History
The 50 Greatest Players in Pittsburgh Pirates History
The 50 Greatest Players in Pittsburgh Steelers History
The 50 Greatest Players in San Francisco 49ers History
The 50 Greatest Players in St. Louis Cardinals History

THE 50 GREATEST PLAYERS IN DETROIT LIONS HISTORY

ROBERT W. COHEN

LYONS PRESS

Essex, Connecticut

An imprint of The Globe Pequot Publishing Group, Inc.
64 South Main St.
Essex, CT 06426
www.GlobePequot.com

Copyright © 2025 by Robert W. Cohen

All rights reserved. No part of this book may be reproduced in any form or by any electronic or mechanical means, including information storage and retrieval systems, without written permission from the publisher, except by a reviewer who may quote passages in a review.

British Library Cataloguing in Publication Information available

Library of Congress Cataloging-in-Publication Data available

ISBN 9781493088072 (paperback) | ISBN 9781493088089 (epub)

CONTENTS

ACKNOWLEDGMENTS   vii

INTRODUCTION   viii
    The Lion Legacy   viii
    Factors Used to Determine Rankings   xv

THE RANKINGS

1.	Barry Sanders	1
2.	Joe Schmidt	12
3.	Calvin Johnson	19
4.	Jack Christiansen	28
5.	Lou Creekmur	35
6.	Yale Lary	40
7.	Alex Karras	47
8.	Lem Barney	54
9.	Dutch Clark	62
10.	Dick LeBeau	69
11.	Charlie Sanders	76
12.	Matthew Stafford	82
13.	Bobby Layne	90
14.	Herman Moore	98
15.	Lomas Brown	104
16.	Alex Wojciechowicz	109
17.	Chris Spielman	113
18.	Wayne Walker	119
19.	Billy Sims	124
20.	Doug English	131

vi CONTENTS

21.	Robert Porcher	136
22.	Dick "Night Train" Lane	142
23.	Roger Brown	148
24.	Doak Walker	155
25.	Jason Hanson	162
26.	Jim David	169
27.	Mike Lucci	173
28.	Ndamukong Suh	178
29.	Ox Emerson	184
30.	Harley Sewell	189
31.	Al "Bubba" Baker	193
32.	John Gordy	198
33.	Gail Cogdill	202
34.	Larry Hand	209
35.	Jared Goff	213
36.	Ed Flanagan	219
37.	Bennie Blades	225
38.	Kevin Glover	230
39.	Penei Sewell	234
40.	Les Bingaman	239
41.	Jerry Ball	243
42.	Eddie Murray	248
43.	Mel Gray	253
44.	Johnnie Morton	259
45.	Amon-Ra St. Brown	264
46.	Paul Naumoff	270
47.	Aidan Hutchinson	274
48.	Frank Ragnow	279
49.	Terry Barr	284
50.	Darris McCord	289

SUMMARY AND HONORABLE MENTIONS (THE NEXT 25)	293
GLOSSARY	305
BIBLIOGRAPHY	307

ACKNOWLEDGMENTS

I wish to thank Kate Yeakley of RMYAuctions.com, George A. Kitrinos, All-Pro Reels Photography, and Mike Morbeck, each of whom generously contributed to the photographic content of this work.

INTRODUCTION

THE LION LEGACY

The history of the Detroit Lions can be traced back to the Portsmouth Spartans, a team comprised primarily of players imported from defunct independent professional and semiprofessional teams that first formed in 1929. Absorbed by the fledgling National Football League in 1930, the Spartans spent the next four years compiling an overall record of 28–16–7, before relocating from Portsmouth, Ohio, to Detroit, Michigan, and being renamed the Lions (as a tie-in to baseball's Detroit Tigers) after a group headed by George A. Richards, the owner of Detroit radio station WJR, purchased them following the conclusion of the 1933 campaign.

Competing in the NFL West, which they spent the next few seasons sharing with the Green Bay Packers, Chicago Bears, and Chicago Cardinals before being joined by the Cleveland Rams as well in 1937, the Lions finished second in the division with a record of 10–3 in 1934 while being coached by George "Potsy" Clark and playing their home games at the University of Detroit Stadium. Moving into Tiger Stadium the following year, the Lions made their first season in their new home a memorable one, posting a regular-season mark of 7–3–2 that earned them their first division title, before recording a 26–7 victory over the New York Giants in the NFL Championship Game.

Clark remained head coach of the Lions for one more season, guiding them to an 8–4 record and a third-place finish in 1936, before being replaced at the helm the following year by Dutch Clark (no relation), the league's finest all-around player, who, after starring on both sides of the ball for the 1935 championship ball club, assumed the role of player-coach in 1937. With Clark choosing to relinquish his post after directing the Lions to consecutive 7–4 records his two years in charge, four different men took

INTRODUCTION **ix**

turns coaching the team to subpar finishes from 1939 to 1942, with the 1942 squad compiling an embarrassing mark of 0–11.

Meanwhile, away from the playing field, poor health prompted George A. Richards to sell the team prior to the start of the 1940 season to 31-year-old Fred L. Mandel Jr., a member of the family that owned the Mandel Brothers Department Store of Chicago. Mandel retained ownership of the Lions until January 15, 1948, when he sold them to the Detroit Football Company, a seven-person syndicate headed by Edwin J. Anderson, who assumed the position of team president.

The Lions continued to struggle under head coaches Gus Dorais and Bo McMillin from 1943 to 1950, going a combined 32–55–2, although quarterback Frank Sinkwich gained recognition as NFL Player of the Year in 1944 by leading the team to a record of 6–3–1.

With the rival All-America Football Conference (AAFC) folding prior to the start of the 1950 season, the NFL absorbed three teams from the defunct league, prompting it to rename and realign its two divisions. While the New York Giants, Cleveland Browns, Philadelphia Eagles, Pittsburgh Steelers, Chicago Cardinals, and Washington Redskins made up the American Division, the Lions found themselves sharing the National Division with the Chicago Bears, Green Bay Packers, New York Yanks, Baltimore Colts, Los Angeles Rams, and San Francisco 49ers.

After failing to post a winning record in any of the previous five seasons, the Lions showed marked improvement under new head coach and former NFL player Buddy Parker in 1951, finishing second in their division with a mark of 7–4–1. Establishing themselves as the league's foremost team the following year, the Lions outscored their opponents by a combined margin of 344–192, posting in the process a regular-season record of 9–3 that tied them with the Rams for first place in the National Division. The Lions subsequently defeated the Rams, 31–21, in a one-game playoff to determine the division champion, before laying claim to their second league title with a 17–7 win over the Cleveland Browns in the NFL Championship Game. Equally dominant in 1953, the Lions finished first in the renamed Western Conference with a record of 10–2, before defeating Cleveland again in the NFL title game, this time by a score of 17–16. The Lions captured their third straight division title in 1954 by compiling a record of 9–2–1 during the regular season. But they subsequently suffered a humiliating 56–10 defeat at the hands of the Browns in the NFL Championship Game.

Injuries and a sense of complacency caused the Lions to suffer through a dismal 1955 campaign in which they won just three games. But they rebounded the following year to post nine victories, although they still

INTRODUCTION

finished one-half game behind the first-place Bears in the NFL West. Buddy Parker subsequently surprised everyone at the end of the year by leaving Detroit to coach the Pittsburgh Steelers. Nevertheless, the Lions performed well under former assistant George Wilson in 1957, finishing the regular season with a record of 8–4 that tied them with the 49ers for the best mark in the Western Conference. The Lions then defeated San Francisco, 31–27, in a one-game playoff to determine the conference champion, before winning their third league championship in six years by routing the Browns, 59–14, in the NFL title game.

The NFL's strongest team for much of the 1950s, the Lions possessed outstanding talent on both sides of the ball. While flamboyant quarterback Bobby Layne proved to be the team's most recognizable figure, he received a considerable amount of help on offense from the versatile Doak Walker, who excelled as both a runner and a pass receiver, and an exceptional line that included standout guard Harley Sewell and Hall of Fame tackle Lou Creekmur. Meanwhile, the Lions boasted one of the league's top-ranked defenses throughout the decade—one that featured Hall of Fame middle linebacker Joe Schmidt, hard-hitting cornerback Jim David, and perennial All-Pro safeties Jack Christiansen and Yale Lary.

With the Lions having won the 1957 NFL Championship Game with backup quarterback Tobin Rote starting for them behind center as an injured Bobby Layne watched from the sidelines, they decided to part ways with the latter during the early stages of the ensuing campaign, trading him to the Pittsburgh Steelers for fellow quarterback Earl Morrall and two future draft picks. Before leaving for Pittsburgh, though, legend has it that Layne said that the Lions would not win another championship for 50 years. Unfortunately, Layne's prediction, which subsequently became known as the "Curse of Bobby Layne," ultimately came to fruition, with the organization failing to come close to capturing another NFL title for the next half century.

After posting losing records in 1958 and 1959, the Lions experienced a moderate amount of success under head coach George Wilson the next three seasons, earning three consecutive second-place finishes in the NFL West, with their mark of 11–3 in 1962 placing them two games behind the eventual NFL champion Green Bay Packers in the final standings. However, following a pair of mediocre finishes, new Lions owner William Clay Ford Sr., who purchased a controlling interest in the team for $6 million on November 22, 1963, replaced Wilson at the helm with former Lions quarterback and Minnesota Vikings assistant coach Harry Gilmer. Gilmer ended up lasting just two seasons, guiding the Lions to an overall record of 10–16–2, before being handed his walking papers following the conclusion of the 1966 campaign.

INTRODUCTION   xi

Although mediocre play from their quarterbacks throughout the period prevented the Lions from seriously contending for the NFL title, their exceptional defense allowed them to remain competitive much of the time. Consistently ranking among the league's top teams in fewest points allowed, the Lions featured an imposing defense that included original "Fearsome Foursome" members Alex Karras, Roger Brown, Darris McCord, and Sam Williams along with the incomparable Joe Schmidt at middle linebacker and Hall of Fame cornerbacks Dick LeBeau and Dick "Night Train" Lane. In fact, the Lions' defense proved to be so dominant in 1962 that, in addition to recording an NFL-high 45 sacks, it surrendered the fewest yards and the second-fewest points of any unit in the league.

With the recently retired Joe Schmidt assuming head coaching duties prior to the start of the 1967 season, the Lions moved into the Central Division in the NFL's new four-division setup that grouped them with the Packers, Bears, and Vikings. And following the AFL–NFL merger three years later, the Lions found themselves sharing the NFC Central with the same three teams when the league adopted a two-conference format that featured three divisions in each conference.

Amid all those changes, the Lions struggled their first two seasons under Schmidt, before experiencing something of a resurgence in 1969, when they finished second in their division with a record of 9–4–1. Even better in 1970, the Lions compiled a record of 10–4 that enabled them to advance to the postseason as the NFC's first wild card playoff team. However, they lost to the Dallas Cowboys, 5–0, in the opening round, before beginning an extended period of mediocrity that lasted two decades.

Winning more games than they lost just four times from 1971 to 1990, the Lions posted as many as nine victories only twice, as Joe Schmidt (1971–1972), Don McCafferty (1973), Rick Forzano (1974–1976), Tommy Hudspeth (1976–1977), Monte Clark (1978–1984), Darryl Rogers (1985–1988), and Wayne Fontes (1988–1990) all took turns coaching the team. Experiencing a considerable amount of heartbreak as well, the Lions lost wide receiver Chuck Hughes on October 24, 1971, when he collapsed on the field and died of a massive heart attack during a home game against the Chicago Bears. And less than three years later, head coach Don McCafferty died from heart disease just before the start of 1974 training camp.

On a happier note, the Lions finished first in the NFC Central Division with a record of 9–7 in 1983. However, they lost to the San Francisco 49ers, 24–23, in the opening round of the postseason tournament when the usually reliable Eddie Murray missed a 43-yard field goal in the closing seconds.

After spending the previous 40 years playing their home games at Tiger Stadium, the Lions moved into the newly constructed Pontiac Silverdome

xii INTRODUCTION

in 1975. An 82,600-seat stadium located in the Detroit suburb of Pontiac, Michigan, the Silverdome remained home to the Lions until 2002, when they christened Ford Field in downtown Detroit.

Meanwhile, despite the Lions' struggles as a team, several outstanding players graced their roster at different times, with running back Billy Sims and tight end Charlie Sanders starring on offense and linemen Larry Hand, Doug English, and Al "Bubba" Baker; linebackers Wayne Walker, Mike Lucci, and Paul Naumoff; and Hall of Fame cornerback Lem Barney all excelling on the defensive side of the ball.

However, it took the greatest player in franchise history to finally end the lengthy malaise in which the Lions found themselves immersed. After spending his first two seasons in Detroit playing for losing teams, Barry Sanders led the Lions to five playoff appearances and two division titles from 1991 to 1997, before shocking the football world by announcing his retirement at only 31 years of age following the conclusion of the 1998 campaign. Prior to leaving the game, though, Sanders gained more than 1,000 yards on the ground 10 straight times, winning in the process four rushing titles.

Unfortunately, the Lions advanced beyond the opening round of the postseason tournament just once with Sanders, doing so in 1991, when, after laying claim to the division title by compiling a record of 12–4 under head coach Wayne Fontes during the regular season, they defeated the Dallas Cowboys, 38–6, in their first-round matchup. However, the Lions subsequently suffered a humiliating 41–10 defeat at the hands of the eventual Super Bowl champion Washington Redskins in the NFC Championship Game.

Division champions again in 1993 after going 10–6 during the regular season, the Lions lost to the Packers in the wild card round of the playoffs, dropping a 28–24 decision to their division rivals. Advancing to the playoffs as a wild card in each of the next two seasons, the Lions lost to the Packers in the opening round again in 1994, this time by a score of 16–12, before losing to the Philadelphia Eagles, 58–37, the following year.

With the Lions finishing a disappointing 5–11 in 1996, ownership replaced Wayne Fontes with former San Diego Chargers head coach Bobby Ross at the end of the year. Ross subsequently led the Lions into the playoffs as a wild card in two of the next three seasons, although they exited the postseason tournament quickly both times, losing to the Tampa Bay Buccaneers, 20–10, in the opening round in 1997, before falling to the Redskins, 27–13, in the wild card round two years later.

Although Barry Sanders remained the face of the franchise his entire time in Detroit, several other outstanding players donned the blue and silver during his period of dominance. Offensive linemen Lomas Brown

INTRODUCTION **xiii**

and Kevin Glover did an exceptional job of blocking up front for Sanders, while Herman Moore and Johnnie Morton formed one of the league's better pass-receiving tandems. Meanwhile, linemen Jerry Ball and Robert Porcher, linebacker Chris Spielman, and safety Bennie Blades all starred on the defensive side of the ball.

Following the retirement of Sanders at the end of 1998 and the resignation of Ross midway through the 2000 campaign, the Lions entered the darkest period in franchise history under Matt Millen, who assumed the dual role of team president and CEO in 2001. A former standout linebacker for the Raiders who later spent several years doing color commentary on television for NFL games, Millen nevertheless displayed an inability to properly judge talent, making numerous poor selections in the annual NFL Draft that ended up setting the franchise back for years. Faring no better with his choice of head coaches, Millen went through Marty Mornhinweg (2001–2002), Steve Mariucci (2003–2005), Dick Jauron (2005), and Rod Marinelli (2006–2008), before finally being relieved of his duties after the Lions compiled an overall record of just 31-97 during his eight years in charge, with their mark of 0–16 in the last of those campaigns making them the first team in NFL history to go winless in a 16-game season.

After the firing of Millen, new team president Tom Lewand and GM Martin Mayhew appointed former Tennessee Titans defensive coordinator Jim Schwartz head coach. But even though the Lions, who began playing their home games at Ford Field and competing in the four-team NFC North in the league's new eight-division alignment in 2002, advanced to the playoffs once in their five seasons under Schwartz, they showed little overall improvement, posting a losing record the other four years, with only quarterback Matthew Stafford and star wide receiver Calvin Johnson bringing a measure of excitement to the Motor City.

With the Lions concluding the 2013 campaign with a record of 7–9, management replaced Schwartz with Jim Caldwell, who had previously served as an assistant on the coaching staff of the Baltimore Ravens as well as head coach in both Tampa Bay and Indianapolis. Meanwhile, control of the team passed from William Clay Ford Sr. to his widow, Martha, after the longtime owner died at the age of 88 on March 9, 2014.

Performing extremely well their first year under Caldwell, the Lions advanced to the playoffs as a wild card after posting a record of 11–5 during the regular season, although they ended up losing to the Dallas Cowboys in the opening round of the postseason tournament by a score of 24–20. But after the Lions got off to a 1–7 start in 2015, they fired Tom Lewand and Martin Mayhew and replaced them with close family friend Rod Wood,

xiv   INTRODUCTION

who previously worked as the president and CEO of the Ford Estates, and former New England Patriots executive Bob Quinn.

Although the Lions rebounded somewhat the next two seasons, making the playoffs again as a wild card in 2016, they finished just 9–7 both years, leading to the firing of Caldwell following the conclusion of the 2017 campaign. The Lions subsequently took a step backward under Matt Patricia, compiling an overall record of just 14–33–1 from 2018 to 2020, before finally beginning their return to prominence shortly after new majority owner and chairperson Sheila Ford Hamp, who assumed control of the team when her mother, Martha, stepped down on June 23, 2020, hired former Rams executive Brad Holmes as executive vice president and general manager. Making his first major move a brilliant one, Holmes replaced Patricia with former New Orleans assistant head coach Dan Campbell, who has since instituted a winning culture in Detroit.

After going just 3–13–1 their first year under Campbell, the Lions posted a mark of 9–8 in 2022 by winning eight of their final 10 contests, nearly earning a trip to the playoffs in the process. Picking up right where they left off the following year, the Lions laid claim to their first division title in three decades by finishing the regular season with a record of 12–5. They subsequently defeated the Rams, 24–23, and the Tampa Bay Buccaneers, 31–23, in the playoffs, before suffering a heartbreaking 34–31 loss to the San Francisco 49ers in the NFC Championship Game after holding a 24–7 lead at halftime.

Despite being plagued by a plethora of injuries in 2024, the Lions captured their second straight division title by compiling a franchise-best regular-season record of 15–2, outscoring their opponents by a combined margin of 564–342 in the process. But with the Lions entering the post-season tournament with a depleted defense, they suffered a 45–31 loss to Washington in the divisional round.

Nevertheless, with a solid defense anchored by pass-rusher extraordinaire Aidan Hutchinson and a potent offense led by quarterback Jared Goff, running back Jahmyr Gibbs, wide receiver Amon-Ra St. Brown, tight end Sam LaPorta, and arguably the league's best line, the Lions figure to be perennial contenders in the NFC North in the years ahead. Their next division title will be their 11th. They have also won four NFL championships. Featuring a plethora of exceptional performers through the years, the Lions have inducted 21 players into their Ring of Honor (also known as the Pride of the Lions), seven of whom have had their numbers retired by the team. Meanwhile, 22 members of the Pro Football Hall of Fame spent at least one full season in Detroit, 16 of whom wore a Lions uniform during many of their peak seasons.

FACTORS USED TO DETERMINE RANKINGS

It should come as no surprise that selecting the 50 greatest players ever to perform for a team with the rich history of the Detroit Lions presented quite a challenge. Even after narrowing the field down to a mere 50 men, I still needed to devise a method of ranking the elite players who remained. Certainly, the names of Barry Sanders, Joe Schmidt, Alex Karras, Lem Barney, and Calvin Johnson would appear at or near the top of virtually everyone's list, although the order might vary somewhat from one person to the next. Several other outstanding performers have gained general recognition through the years as being among the greatest players ever to don the team's colors, with Bobby Layne, Jack Christiansen, Yale Lary, Dick LeBeau, and Matthew Stafford heading the list of other Lions icons. But how does one compare players who lined up on opposite sides of the ball with any degree of certainty? Furthermore, how does one differentiate between the pass-rushing and run-stopping skills of front-seven defenders Alex Karras and Robert Porcher and the ball-hawking skills of defensive backs Lem Barney and Dick LeBeau? And, on the offensive end, how can a direct correlation be made between the contributions made by standout lineman Lou Creekmur and skill position players such as Billy Sims and Herman Moore? After initially deciding whom to include on my list, I then needed to determine what criteria I should use to formulate my final rankings.

The first thing I decided to examine was the level of dominance a player attained during his time with the Lions. How often did he lead the league in a major statistical category? Did he ever capture league MVP honors? How many times did he earn a trip to the Pro Bowl or a spot on the All-Pro Team?

I also chose to assess the level of statistical compilation a player achieved while wearing a Lions uniform. I reviewed where he ranks among the team's all-time leaders in those statistical categories most pertinent to his position. Of course, even the method of using statistics as a measuring stick has its inherent flaws. Although the level of success a team experiences rushing and passing the ball is impacted greatly by the performance of its offensive line, there really is no way to quantifiably measure the level of play reached by each individual offensive lineman. Conversely, the play of the offensive line affects tremendously the statistics compiled by a team's quarterback

xvi INTRODUCTION

and running backs. Furthermore, the NFL did not keep an official record of defensive numbers such as tackles and quarterback sacks until the 1980s (although the Lions kept their own records prior to that, and pro football researchers have tabulated "unofficial" sack totals in recent years). In addition, when examining the statistics compiled by offensive players, the era during which a quarterback, running back, or wide receiver competed must be factored into the equation.

To illustrate my last point, rules changes instituted by the league office have opened up the game considerably since the turn of the century. Quarterbacks are accorded far more protection than ever before, and officials have also been instructed to limit the amount of contact defensive backs are allowed to make with wide receivers. As a result, the game has experienced an offensive explosion, with quarterbacks and receivers posting numbers that players from prior generations rarely even approached. That being the case, one must place the numbers that star signal-caller Matthew Stafford compiled during his time in Detroit in their proper context when comparing him to Bobby Layne. Similarly, the statistics posted by Calvin Johnson and Amon-Ra St. Brown must be viewed in moderation when comparing them to previous Lions wideouts Gail Cogdill and Terry Barr.

Other important factors I needed to consider were the overall contributions a player made to the success of the team, the degree to which he improved the fortunes of the club during his time in Detroit, and the manner in which he impacted the team both on and off the field. While the number of championships and division titles the Lions won during a player's years with the team certainly factored into the equation, I chose not to deny a top performer his rightful place on the list if his years in the Motor City happened to coincide with a lack of overall success by the club. As a result, the names of players such as Paul Naumoff and Larry Hand will appear in these rankings.

One other thing I should mention is that I considered only a player's time in Detroit when formulating my rankings. That being the case, the names of standout performers such as Dick "Night Train" Lane and Al "Bubba" Baker, both of whom had many of their finest seasons in other cities, may appear lower on this list than one might expect. Meanwhile, the names of Hall of Famers John Henry Johnson and Dick Stanfel are nowhere to be found.

Having established the guidelines to be used throughout this book, the time has come to reveal the 50 greatest players in Lions history, starting with No. 1 and working our way down to No. 50.

1

BARRY SANDERS

Although Barry Sanders received stiff competition from Joe Schmidt and Calvin Johnson for the top spot on this list, the enormous impact he made during his 10 seasons in Detroit made him the only possible choice for first place in these rankings. Among the handful of greatest running backs ever to play the game, Sanders gained more than 1,500 yards on the ground five times and amassed more than 2,000 yards from scrimmage twice, en route to winning four NFL rushing titles. One of only nine players in league history to rush for more than 2,000 yards in a season, Sanders accomplished the feat in 1997, when he won the Bert Bell Award as NFL Player of the Year for the second time. The central figure on Lions teams that won two division titles and made five playoff appearances, Sanders gained Pro Bowl and All-Pro recognition in each of his 10 seasons in the Motor City, before receiving the additional honors of being named to both the *Sporting News'* 1999 list and the NFL Network's 2010 list of the NFL's 100 Greatest Players, being awarded a berth on the NFL 100 All-Time Team in 2019, having his No. 20 retired by the Lions, and gaining induction into the Pro Football Hall of Fame in his very first year of eligibility. Yet, nearly three decades after Sanders unexpectedly announced his retirement, fans of the game continue to feel cheated that they did not get to see more of him.

Born in Wichita, Kansas, on July 16, 1968, Barry Sanders grew up in a loving but strict home, where he and his 10 siblings acquired a strong sense of responsibility at an early age. The son of a roofer and carpenter, Sanders and his older brothers often assisted their father with his work, with Mitch Albom writing in the *Detroit Free Press*, "All day they would labor, with the hammers, with the tar, sweating in the hot summer sun. You did not complain in the Sanders family. Not unless you wanted a good whupping."

Finding time for sports as well, Sanders played youth football and basketball, before eventually establishing himself as a star on the gridiron

En route to winning four NFL rushing titles, Barry Sanders gained more than 1,000 yards on the ground in each of his 10 seasons with the Lions.
Courtesy of George A. Kitrinos

at Wichita North High School, where he rushed for 1,417 yards and 17 touchdowns his senior year, earning in the process All-State and Honorable Mention All-America honors. Subsequently offered only a handful of scholarships due to his short stature, the 5'8" Sanders ultimately chose Oklahoma State University over Wichita State, Iowa State, and the University of Tulsa.

Playing behind future NFL Hall of Fame running back Thurman Thomas his first two seasons at OSU, Sanders saw a limited amount of action, gaining a total of just 928 yards on the ground and scoring only 16 touchdowns. But after replacing Thomas as the Cowboys' featured back his junior year, Sanders turned in one of the greatest single-season performances in college football history, gaining unanimous All-America recognition and winning the Heisman Trophy in 1988 by leading the nation with 2,628 rushing yards, 2,734 yards from scrimmage, 3,249 all-purpose yards, and 39 touchdowns.

Originally ineligible for the 1989 NFL Draft since he had yet to complete his senior year, Sanders faced the prospect of playing for an Oklahoma State team that had been penalized heavily by the NCAA for violating recruiting rules. But with OSU having been made ineligible to appear on television or compete in any college bowl games, NFL commissioner Pete Rozelle allowed Sanders to enter the draft, where the Lions selected him with the third overall pick.

Recalling that, with Dallas expected to take quarterback Troy Aikman with the first pick and Green Bay projected to select offensive tackle Tony Mandarich with the second pick, he had already made up his mind to claim Sanders at No. 3, former Lions head coach Wayne Fontes told the *Detroit News*, "After I saw the film [of his 1988 season], there was no question. Barry was the guy that we wanted. I was a new head coach, all these people were writing notes—he ran this fast, and he jumped this high. I looked at my scouts and said, 'Look, you have all these things about how high he jumps, how fast he runs the cones, but the guy can play. He's a football player.'"

Fontes continued, "They [the GMs of other teams] kept coming up, 'We'll give you this, we'll give you that. We'll give you a draft choice. We'll give you a player.' I had a cigar in my jacket, which is kind of my trademark, and I pulled out the cigar and said, 'You guys can go home, we're taking Barry,' and lit up my cigar. . . . I remember talking to Billy Sims before the draft, and he asked me, 'How do you like the running back?' I said, 'Billy, he's great. Billy, he's going to make people forget you.' He laughed and he said, 'I think so.' I told [Lions owner William Clay Ford] Mr. Ford exactly what Billy said, and I said, 'Mr. Ford, I know you love running backs. I know you love Billy, but this guy is going to make you forget Billy Sims.'"

Proving Fontes prophetic, Sanders performed magnificently his first year in the league, earning Pro Bowl, First-Team All-Pro, and NFL Offensive Rookie of the Year honors by ranking among the circuit leaders with 1,470 yards rushing, 1,752 yards from scrimmage, 14 rushing touchdowns, and an average of 5.3 yards per carry. Continuing to perform at an elite

THE 50 GREATEST PLAYERS IN DETROIT LIONS HISTORY

level in subsequent seasons, Sanders posted the following numbers his next several years in the league:

1990: **1,304*** yards rushing, 36 receptions, 480 receiving yards, 1,784 yards from scrimmage, **16** touchdowns.

1991: 1,548 yards rushing, 41 receptions, 307 receiving yards, 1,855 yards from scrimmage, **17** touchdowns.

1992: 1,352 yards rushing, 29 receptions, 225 receiving yards, 1,577 yards from scrimmage, 10 touchdowns.

1993: 1,115 yards rushing, 36 receptions, 205 receiving yards, 1,320 yards from scrimmage, 3 touchdowns.

1994: **1,883** yards rushing, 44 receptions, 283 receiving yards, **2,166** yards from scrimmage, 8 touchdowns.

1995: 1,500 yards rushing, 48 receptions, 398 receiving yards, 1,898 yards from scrimmage, 12 touchdowns.

1996: **1,553** yards rushing, 24 receptions, 147 receiving yards, 1,700 yards from scrimmage, 11 touchdowns.

1997: **2,053** yards rushing, 33 receptions, 305 receiving yards, **2,358** yards from scrimmage, 14 touchdowns.

1998: 1,491 yards rushing, 37 receptions, 289 receiving yards, 1,780 yards from scrimmage, 4 touchdowns.

* Note that any numbers printed in bold throughout this book indicate that the player led the NFL in that statistical category that year.

Consistently ranking among the NFL leaders in yards rushing, yards from scrimmage, and touchdowns, Sanders led the league in each of those categories on multiple occasions, earning in the process Pro Bowl and All-Pro honors each year, two NFL Offensive Player of the Year nominations, and league MVP honors in 1997, when his 2,358 yards from scrimmage set a new single-season NFL record (since broken). Sanders also finished second in the league MVP voting to 49ers quarterback Steve Young in 1994. More important, Sanders led the Lions to five playoff appearances and two division titles, with Detroit finishing first in the NFC Central Division in both 1991 and 1993.

Taking advantage of his relatively short stature, the 5'8", 203-pound Sanders ran low to the ground, making him less of a target for would-be tacklers. In discussing his running style, Sanders said, "To me, it was the only way I'd ever run. I was always the smallest guy, or the near-smallest guy out there. I was never gonna be a guy running over everyone. Dipping my shoulder was always a designed play. Just being able to run that way, run, you know, follow what you see, and follow your eyes."

Blessed with outstanding speed and tremendous elusiveness, Sanders possessed the rare ability to stop on a dime and change directions, seemingly at will, making him that much more difficult for opposing defenders to bring down in the open field, with Atlanta Falcons cornerback D. J. Johnson saying, "He makes you miss so bad, you kind of look up in the stands and wonder if anybody's looking at you. You've got 60,000 people in there, and you wonder if anyone saw you miss that tackle."

Tampa Bay Buccaneers defensive lineman Santana Dotson commented, "Barry is a phenomenal running back. He's got an engine that doesn't quit. . . . To stop him, you need all eleven defensive players . . . and then you hope that a referee gets in his way."

Capable of turning apparent losses into huge gains, Sanders drew praise for his proficiency in that area from Paul Zimmerman of *Sports Illustrated*, who wrote, "It doesn't matter where the play is blocked; he'll find his own soft spot. . . . While other people are stuck with joints, he seems to have ball bearings in his legs that give him a mechanical advantage. . . . Sanders' finest runs often occur when he takes the handoff and, with a couple of moves, turns the line of scrimmage into a broken field. . . . Nobody has ever created such turmoil at the point of attack as Sanders has."

Extremely durable, Sanders missed a total of just seven games over the course of his career, with a torn medial collateral ligament and torn posterior cruciate ligament he sustained during a 10–6 loss to the Chicago Bears on November 25, 1993, forcing him to sit out the final five contests of the regular season.

In addition to his many other outstanding qualities, Sanders became known for his humility and strong sense of propriety, which prevented him from ever engaging in any sort of self-promotion. Never one to take part in any elaborate post-touchdown celebrations, Sanders merely handed the football to the official after he crossed the opponent's goal line, put his head down, and accepted the congratulations of his teammates. Also famous for putting his team before himself, Sanders rarely spoke publicly about his individual accomplishments, once even denying a request from head coach Wayne Fontes to return to play in a game so that he could gain enough yardage on the ground to win the rushing title.

Totally unaffected by the success he experienced on the football field, Sanders once said, "Happiness does not come from football awards. It's terrible to correlate happiness with football. Happiness comes from a good

THE 50 GREATEST PLAYERS IN DETROIT LIONS HISTORY

job, being able to feed your wife and kids. I don't dream of football. I dream the American dream—two cars in a garage, be a happy father."

Yet, even though Sanders always kept football in its proper perspective, he possessed a fierce competitive spirit and a burning desire to win, both of which contributed to his decision to leave the game at only 31 years of age. Making his decision known to the public in a letter he faxed to the *Wichita Eagle*, his hometown newspaper, on July 27, 1999, Sanders wrote,

> Shortly after the end of last season, I felt that I probably would not return for the 1999–2000 season. I also felt that I should take as much time as possible to sort through my feelings and make sure that my feelings were backed with conviction. Today, I officially declare my departure from the NFL.
>
> It was a wonderful experience to play in the NFL, and I have no regrets. I truly will miss playing for the Lions. I consider the Lions' players, coaches, staff, management, and fans my family. I leave on good terms with everyone in the organization. I have enjoyed playing for two great head coaches, Wayne Fontes and Bobby Ross, who are good coaches and leaders. I am not involved in a salary dispute of any kind. If I had played this season, I would have earned a more than satisfactory salary.
>
> The reason I am retiring is simple: My desire to exit the game is greater than my desire to remain in it. I have searched my heart through and through and feel comfortable with this decision.
>
> I want to thank all of the fans and media who made playing in the NFL such a wonderful experience. I have had the pleasure of meeting many of them. Although I was not able to honor many of your requests for autographs and interviews, it was not because I overlooked the importance of those who asked.
>
> Finally, I want to thank my family and friends for their support and guidance. I wish my teammates, coaches, and the entire Lions organization all the best.

While Sanders took the high road and chose not to assign blame to anyone when he made his announcement, he later revealed his true feelings when he wrote in his autobiography *Barry Sanders: Now You See Him:*

His Story in His Own Words, "My retirement letter didn't even hint at my frustration, because I didn't want to take shots at people as I left. . . . Management had let quality players slip away. We'd been losing for years. Now we were right back where we were when I arrived. A goal that I still hadn't realized was playing in the Super Bowl, and all of the statistical achievements didn't put the team any closer to playing in the big game."

Sanders, who retired just 1,457 yards short of breaking Walter Payton's then-all-time NFL rushing record, ended his playing career with 15,269 yards rushing, 352 receptions, 2,921 receiving yards, 18,190 yards from scrimmage, 18,308 all-purpose yards, 99 rushing touchdowns, 10 touchdown receptions, and a rushing average of 5.0 yards per carry. Currently the NFL's fourth all-time leading rusher, Sanders also ranks among the league's career leaders in yards from scrimmage (7th) and all-purpose yards (11th).

Unfortunately, with Sanders having signed a six-year contract extension with the Lions worth $34.56 million two years prior to announcing his retirement, controversy ensued, with the team demanding that he return $7.37 million of the $11 million signing bonus he received at the time and Sanders subsequently refusing to do so. Eventually, an arbitrator ruled that Sanders had to repay what amounted to the final four years of the bonus. However, prior to the ruling, Sanders offered to repay the entire bonus if the Lions either released him or traded him to another team.

Other than that conflict, Sanders has maintained a low profile in retirement. The father of four children, Sanders continues to live by the same principles that have always made him a man of integrity. Eventually settling his differences with the Lions as well, Sanders returned to the organization in 2017, when he accepted the position of brand ambassador. In discussing Sanders's hiring at the time, team president Rod Wood told the *Detroit News*, "We've thankfully, the last couple years, had an unofficial relationship with him. This year, we formalized it. You described it well, it's kind of a brand ambassador. He'll be going on road trips, showing up for suite visits, he'll be at the Taste of the Lions event, and just interacting with our fans on behalf of the team."

Ranked by the NFL Network in 2007 as the most elusive runner in NFL history and as the greatest player never to play in a Super Bowl, Sanders also found himself being lauded by his former head coach Wayne Fontes, who stated, "God ain't made a better back in this lifetime. Maybe one will come along someday. But it hasn't happened yet."

Meanwhile, longtime teammate Chris Spielman stated, "Obviously, everybody knows what Barry meant to, not only our team, but to the league, and what a weapon he was. He's the GOAT—the greatest of all-time."

THE 50 GREATEST PLAYERS IN DETROIT LIONS HISTORY

CAREER HIGHLIGHTS

Best Season

There are so many great seasons from which to choose, with the 1990, 1991, 1994, 1995, and 1997 campaigns all ranking among Sanders's finest. After winning his first rushing title, amassing a career-high 480 receiving yards, and scoring a league-leading 16 touchdowns in 1990, Sanders earned a third-place finish in the NFL MVP voting and gained recognition as the NFL Player of the Year the following season by accumulating 1,855 yards from scrimmage and topping the circuit with a career-high 17 touchdowns. Sanders also performed brilliantly in both 1994 and 1995, earning a runner-up finish in the NFL MVP balloting in the first of those campaigns by leading the league with 1,883 yards rushing, 2,166 yards from scrimmage, and a rushing average of 5.7 yards per carry, before gaining 1,500 yards on the ground, amassing 1,898 yards from scrimmage, and scoring 12 touchdowns in the second. But Sanders had his finest all-around season in 1997, when he earned league MVP and NFL Offensive Player of the Year honors by establishing career-high marks with 2,053 yards rushing, 2,358 yards from scrimmage, and a rushing average of 6.1 yards per carry while also scoring 14 touchdowns.

Memorable Moments/Greatest Performances

Sanders led the Lions to a 31–24 win over the Atlanta Falcons in the final game of the 1989 regular season by rushing for 158 yards and three touchdowns, the longest of which went for 25 yards.

Sanders helped lead the Lions to a 33–24 victory over the Indianapolis Colts on September 22, 1991, by carrying the ball 30 times for 179 yards and two touchdowns.

Sanders earned NFL Offensive Player of the Week honors for the first of three times by gaining 160 yards on 27 carries and scoring three touchdowns during a 31–3 win over Tampa Bay on September 29, 1991, with the longest of his TD runs covering 69 yards.

Sanders put the finishing touches on a comeback that saw the Lions overcome a 17-point fourth-quarter deficit by scoring the go-ahead touchdown on a 15-yard run late in the final period of a 24–20 win over the Vikings on October 6, 1991. He finished the game with 116 yards rushing, nine receptions for 76 yards, and one TD.

Sanders gained recognition as NFL Offensive Player of the Week for the second time by making four receptions for 31 yards and carrying the

BARRY SANDERS 9

ball 23 times for 220 yards and four touchdowns during a 34–14 victory over the Vikings on November 24, 1991, scoring his TDs on runs of 17, 45, 4, and 9 yards.

Sanders earned the first of his 11 NFC Offensive Player of the Week nominations by gaining 187 yards on 29 carries during a 23–0 win over Tampa Bay on November 7, 1993.

Sanders earned that distinction again by carrying the ball 40 times for 194 yards during a 20–17 overtime win over the Cowboys on September 19, 1994.

Sanders rushed for 167 yards during a 21–16 win over the Bears on October 23, 1994, gaining 84 of those yards on one carry.

Sanders led the Lions to a 14–9 victory over Tampa Bay on November 13, 1994, by rushing for a career-high 237 yards, earning in the process NFC Offensive Player of the Week honors.

Sanders helped lead the Lions to a 34–31 win over the Packers on December 4, 1994, by rushing for 188 yards and one touchdown, which came on a 13-yard run.

Sanders earned NFC Offensive Player of the Week honors by rushing for 157 yards and three touchdowns during a 38–20 win over the Cleveland Browns on October 8, 1995, with the longest of his TD runs covering 75 yards.

Sanders earned that accolade again by gaining 215 yards on the ground and scoring three touchdowns during a 27–9 victory over Tampa Bay on October 12, 1997, with two of his TDs coming on runs of 80 and 82 yards.

Sanders led the Lions to a 32–10 win over Indianapolis on November 23, 1997, by carrying the ball 24 times for 216 yards and two touchdowns, one of which covered 80 yards.

Sanders followed that up four days later by rushing for 167 yards and three touchdowns during a 55–20 rout of the Bears on Thanksgiving Day 1997.

Sanders ended the 1997 campaign in style, becoming just the third player in NFL history to gain more than 2,000 yards on the ground in a single season by rushing for 184 yards and one touchdown during a 13–10 win over the Jets in the regular-season finale.

Notable Achievements

- Rushed for more than 1,000 yards 10 times, topping 1,500 yards five times and 2,000 yards once.

THE 50 GREATEST PLAYERS IN DETROIT LIONS HISTORY

- Amassed more than 1,500 yards from scrimmage nine times, topping 2,000 yards twice.
- Scored more than 10 touchdowns seven times.
- Scored more than 100 points once (102 in 1991).
- Averaged more than five yards per carry five times.
- Led NFL in rushing yards four times, yards from scrimmage twice, all-purpose yards once, rushing touchdowns once, touchdowns twice, and rushing average once.
- Finished second in NFL in rushing yards three times, yards from scrimmage three times, all-purpose yards three times, rushing touchdowns once, and rushing average twice.
- Led Lions in rushing 10 times.
- Holds Lions single-season records for most rushing yards (2,053 in 1997), yards from scrimmage (2,358 in 1997), all-purpose yards (2,358 in 1997), and rushing touchdowns (16 in 1991 [tied with Jahmyr Gibbs]).
- Holds Lions career records for most rushing attempts (3,062), rushing yards (15,269), yards from scrimmage (18,190), all-purpose yards (18,308), rushing touchdowns (99), and touchdowns (109).
- Ranks among Lions career leaders with 352 receptions (7th) and 654 points scored (4th).
- Two-time division champion (1991 and 1993).
- 11-time NFC Offensive Player of the Week.
- Three-time NFL Offensive Player of the Week.
- Six-time NFC Offensive Player of the Month.
- 1989 NFL Offensive Rookie of the Year.
- 1989 UPI, PFWA, and *Sporting News* NFL Rookie of the Year.
- Two-time Bert Bell Award winner as NFL Player of the Year (1991 and 1997).
- 1997 NFL co-MVP.
- Two-time NFL Offensive Player of the Year (1994 and 1997).
- 1998 PFWA NFL Offensive Player of the Year.
- 10-time Pro Bowl selection (1989, 1990, 1991, 1992, 1993, 1994, 1995, 1996, 1997, and 1998).
- Six-time First-Team All-Pro selection (1989, 1990, 1991, 1994, 1995, and 1997).
- Four-time Second-Team All-Pro selection (1992, 1993, 1996, and 1998).
- Eight-time First-Team All-NFC selection (1989, 1990, 1991, 1992, 1994, 1995, 1996, and 1997).
- Pro Football Hall of Fame All-1990s First Team.

- Pro Football Reference All-1990s First Team.
- Named to NFL 100 All-Time Team in 2019.
- Number 12 on the *Sporting News'* 1999 list of the 100 Greatest Players in NFL History.
- Number 17 on the NFL Network's 2010 list of the NFL's 100 Greatest Players.
- Number 20 retired by Lions.
- Named to Lions 75th Anniversary All-Time Team in 2008.
- Named to Lions All-Time Team in 2019.
- Inducted into Lions Ring of Honor in 2009.
- Inducted into Pro Football Hall of Fame in 2004.

2
JOE SCHMIDT

Recognized by many as the originator of the middle linebacker position, Joe Schmidt spent 13 seasons in Detroit serving as the centerpiece of one of the NFL's premier defenses. The defensive leader of teams that won three division titles and two league championships, Schmidt performed equally well against the run and the pass, with his superior all-around play earning him 10 Pro Bowl selections, nine All-Pro nominations, and two top-five finishes in the NFL MVP voting. A two-time National Football League Players Association (NFLPA) NFL Defensive Player of the Year, Schmidt later received the additional honors of being included on both the *Sporting News'* and the NFL Network's respective lists of the 100 Greatest Players in NFL History, having his No. 56 retired by the Lions, being named to the NFL 100 All-Time Team in 2019, and gaining induction into the Pro Football Hall of Fame.

Born in Pittsburgh, Pennsylvania, on January 19, 1932, Joseph Paul Schmidt grew up in the borough of Brentwood, where his brothers forced him to adopt an aggressive attitude on the playing field at a young age, recalling years later, "I had three older brothers, and they all played football. I was the 'baby' of the family. They knocked me around, so I sort of grew into it. We played all kind of sports, but we grew into football."

Experiencing tragedy early in life, Schmidt lost his father and two of his brothers by the time he turned 13, with one of his siblings dying while serving his country during World War II and the other losing his life after falling out of a tree near the family home.

Finding refuge in football, Schmidt began competing on the gridiron at the age of 14 for a semipro team coached by his one remaining brother. Further immersing himself in the sport at Brentwood High School, Schmidt performed well enough at fullback on offense and guard on defense to earn an athletic scholarship to the University of Pittsburgh.

Manning several different positions for the Panthers before finally finding a home at middle linebacker, Schmidt suffered a litany of injuries

Joe Schmidt helped create the position of middle linebacker.

that included two broken ribs, a separated shoulder, a wrenched knee, torn cartilage in his knee, and a concussion.

Nevertheless, after being named captain prior to the start of his senior year, Schmidt went on to gain First-Team All-America recognition from the International News Service in 1952.

With Schmidt having sustained so many injuries in college, he subsequently lasted until the seventh round of the 1953 NFL Draft, where the Lions finally selected him with the 86th overall pick. Recalling his initial reaction to being drafted by the Lions, Schmidt revealed, "I sat down and listened to Joe Tucker on the radio, and he gave a rundown of the draft. I wasn't taken until the seventh round, and then by Detroit. They'd won the championship that season, and I figured I didn't have a snowman's chance in hell of making that team."

Faring much better than he expected, Schmidt earned a starting job almost immediately on his arrival in Detroit, after which he gained Pro

Bowl and First-Team All-Pro recognition in his second season while playing outside linebacker in the team's five-man-line, two-linebacker defense that most NFL clubs employed at that time. Describing his initial role on defense, Schmidt remembered, "When I first came to Detroit, I had to play outside linebacker. So, it was a transition for me to go from middle to outside linebacker for a couple of years. In what we called 'short yardage situations,' we would go to what we called a 'goal line defense,' which was used from about the 5-yard line to the goal line. The goal-line defense had another linebacker. So, I moved from the outside to the middle linebacker. That was not a new experience for me. The other guys in the league had to be trained and moved from one position to another position."

With Lions head coach Buddy Parker choosing to install a new "4–3" defense in 1955, he moved Schmidt to middle linebacker, where he spent the remainder of his career. Performing brilliantly at that post from 1955 to 1963, Schmidt earned nine straight Pro Bowl selections and eight All-Pro nominations while also being named NFL Lineman of the Year in 1957 and NFLPA NFL Defensive Player of the Year in both 1960 and 1963.

Suggesting that many of his individual accolades could be attributed to his move inside, Schmidt stated, "The whole defensive idea was to keep the middle linebacker from getting blocked. So, if the linebacker could run and diagnose plays, he would make a lot of tackles. As a result, you get a lot of publicity."

Better able to maximize his great quickness and shrewd football instincts from his post at middle linebacker, Schmidt proved to be the key to a Lions defense that consistently ranked among the NFL's best. Very strong, the 6'1", 220-pound Schmidt tackled well and did an outstanding job of shedding blockers, making him extremely effective against the run, with Buddy Parker saying, "He was the best at his position. He had an instinct for defense that few players ever acquire. He wasn't big, as defensive players go, but he was one of the surest and hardest tacklers you'll ever see."

Meanwhile, Schmidt's foot speed and superior instincts allowed him to excel in pass coverage as well, as his career total of 24 interceptions indicates.

Praising Schmidt for his varied skill set, former journalist and Pittsburgh Steelers broadcaster Myron Cope once wrote, "Joe Schmidt of the Detroit Lions tackles harder and thinks faster than any other defenseman around. . . . It's maneuverability that counts here, and Joe has it—the fastest reactions, probably, of any linebacker in the business."

Impressed with Schmidt's fleetness afoot and high football IQ, former Lions and Cardinals defensive end Leo Sugar stated, "Joe Schmidt was just

JOE SCHMIDT **15**

fantastic. He had the quickness that let him plug holes all the time. He read the offense very well."

In discussing everything Schmidt brought to the Detroit defense, Vince Lombardi said, "He's one of the top linebackers. A great diagnostician, a great tackler, and a strong defensive leader."

When asked about the qualities that helped him attain elite status, Schmidt responded, "I think you have to look at football skills and the intuition about playing football . . . some of those things you can't teach or diagram, and I think I had that ability."

A team captain for nine seasons, Schmidt received high praise for his leadership ability from Lions defensive coordinator Buster Ramsey, who stated, "Everybody on the team respects him. And he's got to have that. At times, he has to get on their tails and ride them, and they won't take it from a man they don't respect."

Schmidt also drew plaudits from Hall of Fame quarterback and then– Minnesota Vikings head coach, Norm Van Brocklin, who said, "If I had to start a team from scratch and had my pick of players, I'd select Schmidt as the No. 1 man to form the core of my team."

Extremely durable, Schmidt started 84 straight games for the Lions from 1953 to 1959, before suffering a dislocated right shoulder during an exhibition game on September 11, 1960, that forced him to miss the first two contests of the regular season. Beginning another streak on his return to action, Schmidt started the next 38 games the Lions played at his familiar position of middle linebacker. However, he missed another four games due to injury in 1963, a season in which the league office levied a $2,000 fine against him for placing a $50 bet on the Packers to defeat the Giants in the 1962 NFL Championship Game. Sidelined for another five games in 1964 after sustaining a second shoulder dislocation, Schmidt announced his intention to retire at the end of the year. But he soon changed his mind and decided to return for one more season. Retiring for good following the conclusion of the 1965 campaign, Schmidt ended his playing career with 24 interceptions, 17 fumble recoveries, three touchdowns scored on defense, and an unknown number of tackles that likely would put him first in franchise history.

Transitioning seamlessly into a career in coaching following his playing days, Schmidt spent the 1966 season serving as an assistant on the Lions' coaching staff, before replacing Harry Gilmer as head man prior to the start of the 1967 campaign. Schmidt subsequently spent the next six seasons guiding the Lions to one playoff appearance, four winning records, and

16   THE 50 GREATEST PLAYERS IN DETROIT LIONS HISTORY

an overall mark of 43–34–7. However, due to a variety of off-field issues that included nonstop meddling, backstabbing, and politicking within the Lions' front office, Schmidt handed in his resignation on January 12, 1973, saying at the time, "I really don't enjoy coaching anymore. It got to be a burden more than a fun-loving game. I promised my family and myself when I started coaching that I would get out when it stopped being fun. Unfortunately, it's reached that point."

After retiring from football, Schmidt became a successful businessman, founding Joe Schmidt Enterprises, a Detroit-based auto supplier he operated for 30 years that sold rubber and plastic to the Big Three automakers. Schmidt lived until September 11, 2024, when he died in Palm Beach Gardens, Florida, at the age of 92.

Still regarded as one of the greatest players ever to man the position of middle linebacker, Schmidt, of whom former NFL head coach and sportscaster Jerry Glanville once said, "He, to me, is the history of the National Football League," has a biography at the Pro Football Hall of Fame that reads, "Without question, he was the first to play the [middle linebacker] position with such finesse that even the masses in the stands could see the growing value of the 'defensive quarterback.' He anticipated plays with uncanny accuracy. He was a deadly tackler. He was fast enough to evade a 250-pound guard, to follow a play along the line or to drop back to cover a pass. He was strong enough to power past a potential blocker to crumble a play. But his greatest talent may well have been his uncanny knack of knowing what the opposition was going to do."

CAREER HIGHLIGHTS

Best Season

Schmidt performed magnificently for the Lions in 1955, 1958, and 1961, leading the league with eight fumble recoveries in the first of those campaigns, recording a career-high six interceptions in the second, and picking off four passes and registering four sacks in the third, with his superb play earning him Pro Bowl, First-Team All-Pro, and team MVP honors each year. But Schmidt made his greatest overall impact in 1957, when he led the Lions to their third NFL championship in six seasons by recording an unofficial total of 157 tackles during the regular season, before intercepting two passes in the playoffs. In addition to being accorded Pro Bowl and First-Team All-Pro honors for the fourth straight time, Schmidt earned a fourth-place finish in the league MVP voting and gained recognition from the Associated Press (AP) as the NFL Lineman of the Year.

Memorable Moments/Greatest Performances

Schmidt contributed to a 27–17 win over the Baltimore Colts on October 3, 1953, by recording the first interception of his career, which he subsequently returned 39 yards.

After delivering an impassioned halftime tirade following a poor first-half performance that put the Lions in a 17-point hole in the 1957 playoff game to determine the Western Division champion, Schmidt helped lead his teammates to a come-from-behind 31–27 victory over San Francisco by returning his interception of a Y. A. Tittle pass 16 yards to the 49ers' 2-yard line, thereby setting up the final score of the contest.

Schmidt recorded a career-high three interceptions during a convincing 41–24 victory over the Los Angeles Rams on October 26, 1958, returning his three picks a total of 46 yards.

Although the Lions lost to the Eagles, 28–10, on October 16, 1960, Schmidt scored his first points as a pro when he returned his one-handed interception of a tipped Norm Van Brocklin pass 17 yards for a touchdown.

Schmidt lit the scoreboard again when he returned a fumble 14 yards for a touchdown during a 36–0 win over the Bears in the final game of the 1960 regular season.

Schmidt punctuated a 37–10 victory over the Vikings on November 19, 1961, by returning his fourth-quarter interception of a Fran Tarkenton pass eight yards for a touchdown.

Notable Achievements

- Started 84 consecutive games from 1953 to 1959.
- Scored three defensive touchdowns.
- Led NFL with eight fumble recoveries in 1955.
- Led Lions with six interceptions in 1958.
- Ranks among Lions career leaders with 17 fumble recoveries (tied for 2nd) and 24 interceptions (tied for 9th).
- Three-time division champion (1953, 1954, and 1957).
- Two-time NFL champion (1953 and 1957).
- Finished in top five of NFL MVP voting twice (1957 and 1962).
- Four-time Lions team MVP (1955, 1957, 1958, and 1961).
- 1957 NFL Lineman of the Year.

- Two-time NFLPA NFL Defensive Player of the Year (1960 and 1963).
- 10-time Pro Bowl selection (1954, 1955, 1956, 1957, 1958, 1959, 1960, 1961, 1962, and 1963).
- Eight-time First-Team All-Pro selection (1954, 1955, 1956, 1957, 1958, 1959, 1961, and 1962).
- 1960 Second-Team All-Pro selection.
- Seven-time First-Team All-Western Conference selection (1956, 1957, 1958, 1959, 1960, 1961, and 1962).
- Pro Football Hall of Fame All-1950s Team.
- Pro Football Reference All-1950s First Team.
- Named to NFL 100 All-Time Team in 2019.
- Number 65 on the *Sporting News'* 1999 list of the 100 Greatest Players in NFL History.
- Number 84 on the NFL Network's 2010 list of the NFL's 100 Greatest Players.
- Number 56 retired by Lions.
- Named to Lions 75th Anniversary All-Time Team in 2008.
- Named to Lions All-Time Team in 2019.
- Inducted into Lions Ring of Honor in 2009.
- Inducted into Pro Football Hall of Fame in 1973.

3

CALVIN JOHNSON

Referred to on one occasion by perennial Pro Bowl cornerback Richard Sherman as "arguably the best player I've ever played against," Calvin Johnson spent nine seasons in Detroit, establishing himself as easily the greatest wide receiver in team annals. A physical freak of nature, Johnson proved to be an unstoppable offensive weapon for mostly losing Lions teams, combining with Matthew Stafford to form one of the most potent quarterback–wide receiver tandems in the NFL. The franchise's career leader in receptions, receiving yards, and touchdown catches, Johnson surpassed 80 receptions four times and 1,000 receiving yards on seven separate occasions, earning in the process six Pro Bowl selections, four All-Pro nominations, a spot on the Lions All-Time Team, and a place in the Pro Football Hall of Fame. But just as Barry Sanders did almost two decades earlier, Johnson stunned the fans of Detroit when he announced his retirement while still performing at an extremely high level.

Born in Newnan, Georgia, on September 29, 1985, Calvin Johnson Jr. grew up in nearby Tyrone, a small town located some 25 miles southwest of Atlanta. The son of Arica Johnson, a public school administrator, and Calvin Johnson Sr., a freight conductor for Norfolk Southern Railway, Johnson learned at an early age to apply himself in the classroom since his parents forbade him from playing sports if he did not get As and Bs in school.

Initially prohibited from competing in football, Johnson recalled, "I was a baseball guy. Mom wouldn't let me play football when I was little because she was scared I'd get hurt. So, I finally convinced her to let me play in the 7th grade."

Always big for his age, Johnson stood 6' tall by the time he entered Sandy Creek High School. Nevertheless, he struggled at wideout his first year on the varsity football squad, remembering, "They called me butterfingers." However, following a five-inch growth spurt he experienced between his freshman and sophomore years and an increase in confidence he developed in his own abilities, Johnson emerged as a star, making well over 100

Calvin Johnson holds franchise records for most receptions, receiving yards, and touchdown catches.
Courtesy of Mike Morbeck

receptions for more than 2,300 yards and 29 touchdowns over the course of his final three seasons.

While still in high school, though, Johnson received troubling news when he visited the doctor one day, recalling, "I remember my mom took me to the doctor. He had told me I wasn't going to be able to play sports anymore, or too much longer, because of the thing I had in my knee. . . . I actually hurt all the time. If I just got touched on my knee, it would hurt so bad. I forget exactly what the doctor told me—but when you grow so fast, I guess it's something that happens."

Proving his doctor wrong, Johnson continued to compete on the gridiron, playing through the pain until it eventually dissipated. Meanwhile,

CALVIN JOHNSON **21**

after amassing 960 receiving yards and scoring 11 touchdowns his last year at Sandy Creek High, Johnson found himself being heavily recruited by several major college programs. Eventually narrowing his choices down to the University of Georgia and the Georgia Institute of Technology, Johnson decided to enroll at the latter, Georgia Tech, where he spent his college career playing for head coach Chan Gailey.

A three-year starter for the Yellow Jackets, Johnson gained First-Team All-Atlantic Coast Conference (ACC) recognition each season and earned First-Team All-America honors twice by making 178 receptions for 2,927 yards and 28 touchdowns. Particularly outstanding his junior year, Johnson won the Biletnikoff Award as the best wide receiver in college football by leading the nation with 76 receptions, 1,202 receiving yards, and 15 TD catches.

Choosing to forgo his final year of college, Johnson declared himself eligible for the 2007 NFL Draft, which he entered as one of the most highly touted prospects in years after registering a time of 4.35 seconds in the 40-yard dash and a vertical leap of 42.5" at the NFL Scouting Combine. Selected by the Lions with the second overall pick, Johnson came off the board immediately after the Oakland Raiders took LSU quarterback JaMarcus Russell at No. 1, in what proved to be a historically bad draft class for signal-callers.

The 6'5", 239-pound Johnson subsequently made an extremely favorable impression on everyone in attendance at his first pro training camp, with his rare combination of size, strength, speed, leaping ability, and body control, prompting fellow Lions wideout Roy Williams to nickname him "Megatron" after the character from the *Transformers* series.

Although Johnson ended up earning a spot on the 2007 NFL All-Rookie Team, a bone bruise in his lower back that he sustained early in the year prevented him from posting the kind of numbers Lions fans came to expect from him. Recalling the physical problems that he encountered his first year as a pro, Johnson, who finished the season with "just" 48 receptions, 756 receiving yards, and five touchdowns, revealed, "I was on meds the rest of the season. I was taking Vicodin twice a game just to get through the game. I stayed hurt the whole season, probably because I was trying to come back too soon. But I'm not going to be the kind of guy who's going to say, 'I can't do this or this because I'm hurt.'"

Fully recovered by the start of the 2008 campaign, Johnson improved on his performance dramatically, catching 78 passes, amassing 1,331 receiving yards, and making a league-leading 12 TD grabs for a Lions team that failed to win a single game during the regular season. Joined by first overall draft pick Matthew Stafford in 2009, Johnson made 67 receptions for 984 yards and five touchdowns, before beginning an exceptional six-year run during which he posted the following numbers:

2010: 77 receptions, 1,120 receiving yards, 12 touchdown receptions
2011: 96 receptions, **1,681** receiving yards, 16 touchdown receptions
2012: **122** receptions, **1,964** receiving yards, 5 touchdown receptions
2013: 84 receptions, 1,492 receiving yards, 12 touchdown receptions
2014: 71 receptions, 1,077 receiving yards, 8 touchdown receptions
2015: 88 receptions, 1,214 receiving yards, 9 touchdown receptions

In addition to leading the NFL in receptions once and receiving yards twice, Johnson finished second in the league in touchdown catches in both 2010 and 2011, with his 16 TD grabs in the second of those campaigns setting a single-season franchise record. Johnson also established a single-season NFL mark that still stands by amassing 1,964 receiving yards in 2012. Meanwhile, the 5,137 receiving yards Johnson accumulated from 2011 to 2013 represent the highest three-year total by any player in NFL history. A Pro Bowler in each of those six seasons, Johnson also gained All-Pro and First-Team All-NFC recognition four times each.

The NFL's most dominant receiver for much of the period, Johnson proved to be virtually impossible for one man to guard one-on-one, typically drawing double- or even triple-coverage, with opposing teams often assigning him a linebacker and two defensive backs. Capable of outrunning most defenders and using his huge catch radius, tremendous strength, and outstanding leaping ability to come down with the football in tight coverage, Johnson presented a unique challenge to opposing defenses, with Lions head coach Jim Schwartz stating, "There's really no book on how to stop Calvin. The big thing with Calvin is everybody's game plan is going to be to try to limit him somehow. But he's developed enough depth to his game that, if they want to take away his deep stuff, he can make them pay underneath. He's a real good run-after-the-catch guy because he's so strong. If teams want to take the underneath stuff away, we can go deep on them."

When evaluating Johnson, Chargers head coach Norv Turner said, "He's the scariest guy I've seen in a long time because he can hit the home run on any down and they throw the ball deep to him. They throw it when he's doubled. They jump and move him around. They certainly throw it to him when he's singled, and they do a great job of getting him the ball."

Chargers safety Eric Weddle added, "He is unlike any other guy in the NFL. . . . The dude is, like, unreal."

A quiet superstar whose teammates revered him for his fierce competitiveness on the playing field and humility away from it, Johnson received high praise from former Lions backup quarterback and current NFL analyst Dan Orlovsky, who called him "one of the best athletes I've ever seen in my life . . . one of the most motivated I've ever seen . . . one of the best souls I've ever been around."

Although Johnson suffered numerous injuries, he appeared in all but nine games the Lions played from 2007 to 2015, missing a career-high three contests in 2014 due to problems with his ankle. However, Johnson's physical woes began to get the best of him in 2015, when, despite starting all 16 contests, he rarely, if ever, practiced.

Later revealing that he had trouble simply getting out of bed in the morning during the latter stages of his career, Johnson said, "When you wake up in the morning, you can't walk, you're shuffling across the floor. I gotta go through a little routine when I wake up in the morning just to get everything functioning and ready to go. But the only thing is, everything just goes back to gridlock so fast once you sit down."

Choosing to end his playing career before doing further long-term damage to himself, Johnson officially announced his retirement in a statement he released on March 8, 2016, that read,

> Let me begin by apologizing for making this announcement via a statement and not in person. While I truly respect the significance of this, those who know me best will understand and not be surprised that I choose not to have a press conference for this announcement. . . . After much prayer, thought, and discussion with loved ones, I have made the difficult decision to retire from the Lions and pro football. I have played my last game of football. Let me assure you that this was not an easy or hasty decision. As I stated, I, along with those closest to me, have put a lot of time, deliberation and prayer into this decision and I truly am at peace with it. I also want you to know that I have the utmost respect and admiration for the game of football. It has provided so much for me and my family, and I will be forever grateful to the game.

Expressing her gratitude to Johnson for everything he contributed to the organization the previous nine years, Lions team owner Martha Firestone Ford subsequently said, "I want to thank Calvin for being not only a great player for the Lions but for also being the absolute best representative our team, franchise, and community could ever ask for. He was the epitome of dignity, class, humility, and excellence. Calvin was exemplary on and off the field and will always be a part of our family and our team."

Jim Schwartz also expressed his appreciation to Johnson by saying, "It was an honor to have coached Calvin and was certainly one of the highlights of my career. I have never seen a player dominate and take over a game more than him. His work ethic was unparalleled, and it was inspiring to watch. Although he was one of the best players in the game, he came to work every day as if he was trying to make the team. But as great of a player as he was, I will always remember him for being a better person and teammate. I will never forget handing him the game ball after he broke Jerry Rice's all-time single-season receiving yards record. I wish him all the best in retirement and look forward to seeing him one day in Canton."

Johnson, who made 731 receptions, amassed 11,619 receiving yards and 11,786 yards from scrimmage, caught 83 TD passes, and scored 84 touchdowns during his career, gained admittance to the Pro Football Hall of Fame in his very first year of eligibility, entering Canton in 2021. Since that time, Johnson has further elaborated on the reasons he decided to retire at only 30 years of age, saying, "You can't take Toradol and pain medicine every day. You gotta give that stuff a rest, and that was one thing I wasn't willing to do."

Johnson continued, "You love the game, but it's hard to do the things you do when you're feeling like you're a leg down all the time, literally. Or you're always beat up, even coming into the season. So, it's just not as much fun when you're down, and you've got to work your way up. And you can't really get there because you're so beat up."

Still suffering from the aftereffects of his playing days, Johnson says, "If I'm doing stuff physically, yeah, you'll feel it. I feel fine as long as I'm not running around."

With Johnson having retired with four years left on his contract, the Lions forced him to repay $1.6 million of his signing bonus, leading to a considerable amount of acrimony between the two sides. But after refusing to attend any games or partake in any events held by the Lions the first several years of his retirement, Johnson has softened his stance more recently, attending several team practices during the 2023 season and a September 17, 2023, home game against the Seattle Seahawks.

Currently in the legal cannabis business with former Lions teammate Rob Sims and a third partner, Johnson co-owns the Primitiv Group, a company in Niles, Michigan, that has partnered with Harvard University to study the effects that medical marijuana has as a potential treatment for chronic traumatic encephalopathy (CTE). Johnson, who created the Calvin Johnson Jr. Foundation during his playing days to award scholarships to graduating football players and provide financial assistance to various community organizations, continues to remain active in the Detroit and Atlanta communities, refurbishing houses in the inner city and running youth football camps. Johnson also works as a wide receiver consultant for various players and teams.

Still held in awe by those who played with and against him, Johnson received the following plaudits from former Lions teammate and current Detroit head coach Dan Campbell: "I've never seen anybody like him. I've never been around anybody like him that had the size, length, speed, ability to adjust to the football, flexibility, was hungry and just went to work like him. He had it all. He checked every box. He was just unbelievable."

CAREER HIGHLIGHTS

Best Season

It could be argued that Johnson made his greatest impact in 2011, when he helped lead the Lions to a record of 10–6 and a trip to the playoffs by finishing fourth in the NFL with 96 receptions, leading the league with 1,681 receiving yards, and placing second in the circuit with 16 TD catches. Nevertheless, the 2012 campaign is generally considered to be Johnson's signature season. En route to earning a third-place finish in the NFL Offensive Player of the Year voting, Johnson led the league with 122 receptions and 1,964 receiving yards, setting in the process a single-season league record in the second category that still stands.

Memorable Moments/Greatest Performances

Johnson scored the first touchdown of his career in his very first game as a pro when he gathered in a 16-yard pass from Jon Kitna during a 36–21 win over the Oakland Raiders in the 2007 regular-season opener.

Although the Lions lost to the Houston Texans, 28–21, on October 19, 2008, Johnson collaborated with Dan Orlovsky on a career-long 96-yard touchdown reception, finishing the game with two catches, 154 receiving yards, and that one TD.

26 THE 50 GREATEST PLAYERS IN DETROIT LIONS HISTORY

Johnson helped lead the Lions to a 38–37 win over the Browns on November 22, 2009, by making seven receptions for 161 yards and one touchdown, which came on a 75-yard connection with Matthew Stafford.

Johnson earned NFC Offensive Player of the Week honors for the first of four times by making nine receptions for 101 yards and three touchdowns during a 37–25 win over Washington on October 31, 2010.

Johnson earned that distinction again by making nine receptions for 214 yards and two touchdowns during a 28–27 win over the Raiders on December 18, 2011, with his six-yard TD grab with just 39 seconds left in regulation providing the margin of victory.

Although the Lions lost to the New Orleans Saints, 45–28, in the wild card round of the 2011 NFC playoffs, Johnson had a huge game, making 12 receptions for 211 yards and two TDs.

Johson again starred in defeat on November 11, 2012, making 12 receptions for 207 yards and one touchdown during a 34–24 loss to the Vikings.

Continuing to perform brilliantly for one of the league's worst teams, Johnson caught 13 passes, amassed 171 receiving yards, and scored one touchdown during a 35–33 loss to the Colts on December 2, 2012.

Three weeks later, Johnson made 11 receptions for 225 yards during a 31–18 loss to the Atlanta Falcons in the final game of the 2012 campaign, breaking in the process the NFL single-season record for most receiving yards, which had been held by Jerry Rice for more than two decades.

Johnson gained recognition as NFC Offensive Player of the Week by making 14 receptions, amassing a franchise-record 329 receiving yards, and scoring a touchdown during a 31–30 win over the Dallas Cowboys on October 27, 2013.

Johnson contributed to a 34–17 victory over the Bears on Thanksgiving Day 2014 by making 11 receptions for 146 yards and two touchdowns, the longest of which covered 25 yards.

Johnson earned NFC Offensive Player of the Week honors for the fourth and final time by making six receptions for 166 yards and one touchdown during a 37–34 overtime win over the Bears on October 18, 2015, with his six-yard TD grab with just 21 seconds left in regulation sending the game into overtime.

Notable Achievements

- Surpassed 80 receptions four times, topping 100 catches once.
- Surpassed 1,000 receiving yards seven times, topping 1,600 yards twice.

- Amassed more than 1,000 yards from scrimmage eight times.
- Scored more than 10 touchdowns four times.
- Led NFL in receptions once, receiving yards twice, and touchdown receptions once.
- Finished second in NFL in yards from scrimmage once and touchdown receptions twice.
- Led Lions in receptions six times and receiving yards seven times.
- Holds NFL single-season record for most receiving yards (1,964 in 2012).
- Holds Lions single-game record for most receiving yards (329 vs. Dallas on October 27, 2013).
- Holds Lions single-season records for most receiving yards (1,964 in 2012) and most touchdown receptions (16 in 2011).
- Holds Lions career records for most receptions (731), receiving yards (11,619), and touchdown receptions (83).
- Ranks among Lions career leaders with 11,786 yards from scrimmage (2nd), 11,786 all-purpose yards (2nd), 84 touchdowns (2nd), and 508 points scored (7th).
- Member of 2007 NFL All-Rookie Team.
- Finished third in 2012 Offensive Player of the Year voting.
- Four-time NFC Offensive Player of the Week.
- Two-time NFC Offensive Player of the Month.
- Six-time Lions team MVP on offense (2008, 2009, 2010, 2011, 2012, and 2013).
- Six-time Pro Bowl selection (2010, 2011, 2012, 2013, 2014, and 2015).
- Three-time First-Team All-Pro selection (2011, 2012, and 2013).
- 2010 Second-Team All-Pro selection.
- Four-time First-Team All-NFC selection (2010, 2011, 2012, and 2013).
- Pro Football Hall of Fame All-2010s Team.
- Named to Lions All-Time Team in 2019.
- Inducted into Pro Football Hall of Fame in 2021.

4

JACK CHRISTIANSEN

A tremendous force on defense and special teams, Jack Christiansen spent his entire eight-year NFL career in Detroit, making significant contributions to teams that won four division titles and three league championships. The leader of a Lions defensive secondary that became known as "Chris's Crew," Christiansen picked off at least 10 passes twice, en route to recording the fourth-most interceptions of any player in franchise history. An exceptional punt-returner as well, Christiansen returned eight punts for touchdowns, with his superior all-around play earning him five Pro Bowl selections and six First-Team All-Pro nominations. A member of the NFL 1950s All-Decade Team, Christiansen received the additional honors of being included on the *Sporting News'* 1999 list of the 100 Greatest Players in NFL History, being named to the NFL 100 All-Time Team in 2019, and gaining induction into the Pro Football Hall of Fame.

Born in Sublette, Kansas, on December 20, 1928, John LeRoy "Jack" Christiansen moved with his widowed mother and younger sister at an early age to Wray, Colorado. Placed in an orphanage with his sister after his mother remarried and relocated to Michigan, Christiansen spent much of his adolescence living at the Odd Fellows Home in Cañon City, Colorado.

Later developing into a star athlete at Cañon City High School, Christiansen excelled in football, baseball, and basketball, proving to be especially proficient on the gridiron, where he played quarterback and defensive back. However, Christiansen's high school career ended prematurely when he sustained a serious injury to his left arm while fleeing from police following a harmless prank. Struck just above the left elbow by a stray bullet meant to be only a warning to him and his friends, Christiansen had to undergo several surgeries to repair a shattered radial nerve.

With the Independent Order of Odd Fellows (IOOF) paying his tuition fees, Christiansen enrolled at Colorado A&M University (now known as Colorado State University) following his graduation from Cañon City

Jack Christiansen's superior play on defense and special teams earned him a spot on the NFL 100 All-Time Team.

High. Still recovering from the damage to his arm, Christiansen competed only in track and field as a freshman, setting a school record that stood for the next 20 years by posting a time of 47.6 seconds in the 440-yard dash. One year later, Christiansen posted personal-best times of 9.8 seconds in the 100-yard dash and 21.8 seconds in the 200.

Fully healthy by the start of his sophomore year, Christiansen resumed his career on the gridiron, performing brilliantly for the Aggies the next three seasons at safety on defense and as a kickoff- and punt-returner on special teams. A truly exceptional all-around athlete who, by the time he received his degree from Colorado A&M in 1951, had earned a total of eight varsity letters in football, track, and baseball, Christiansen won the Skyline Conference quarter-mile track championship three times and earned All-Conference honors in football twice.

Despite Christiansen's outstanding play at the collegiate level, concerns over his slender 6'1", 165-pound physique caused him to slip to the sixth round of the 1951 NFL Draft, where the Lions finally selected him with the 69th overall pick. Subsequently named Detroit's starting free safety prior to the start of the 1951 regular season, Christiansen performed well as a rookie, picking off two passes, recovering a fumble, returning four punts for touchdowns, amassing 718 all-purpose yards, and leading the NFL with an average of 19.1 yards per punt return. Christiansen followed that up with an excellent sophomore campaign, gaining First-Team All-Pro recognition for the first of six straight times by recording another two interceptions, scoring twice on punt returns, accumulating 958 all-purpose yards, and averaging a league-leading 21.5 yards per punt return for a Lions team that won the NFL championship.

Shifted to strong safety prior to the start of the 1953 campaign, Christiansen, who had added some 25 pounds of bulk onto his frame since he first arrived in Detroit, helped the Lions repeat as NFL champions by leading the league with 12 interceptions and 238 interception-return yards, with his 12 picks setting a single-season franchise record that still stands. Selected to the Pro Bowl for the first of five consecutive times, Christiansen received the additional honor of having Detroit's outstanding defensive secondary, which also included Bob Smith, Jim David, and Yale Lary, named after him for the leadership he provided to the rest of the unit.

Citing the pivotal role that Christiansen played on defense, particularly in the secondary, Lions head coach Buddy Parker stated, "He ran it, and he was the boss."

In addition to his leadership skills, Christiansen possessed soft hands, the ability to track the football well, and exceptional running speed, which he used to blanket receivers, chase down opposing ball-carriers, and elude would-be tacklers once he gained possession of the football. A tenacious defender who typically covered the opposing tight end in the predominantly man-to-man defense the Lions employed, Christiansen also proved to be a sure and fearless tackler who never hesitated to deliver hard hits to the opposition. A menace to anyone who lined up against him, Christiansen had a devious way of throwing receivers off their game, recalling, "I can remember picking up a handful of snow or mud and throwing it in the receiver's eyes. They'd holler and bitch, but we'd get away with it."

JACK CHRISTIANSEN **31**

Equally adept on special teams, Christiansen scared the opposition any time he touched the football, with former Cleveland Browns wide receiver Mac Speedie saying of his frequent foe, "We had a standard rule when we played Detroit; Don't throw in his area, and don't punt to him."

Christiansen continued to perform at an elite level for five more years, recording another 30 interceptions, two of which he returned for touchdowns, and scoring twice more on special teams from 1954 to 1958. Particularly outstanding in 1954 and 1957, Christiansen helped lead the Lions to their third consecutive division title in the first of those campaigns by finishing third in the league with eight interceptions while also placing second in the circuit with 225 punt-return yards and scoring one touchdown on defense and another on special teams. Three years later, Christiansen earned the last of his Pro Bowl and All-Pro nominations by leading the league with 10 interceptions, one of which he returned for a touchdown.

Choosing to announce his retirement at only 30 years of age after helping the Lions capture their fourth NFL championship in 1958, Christiansen ended his playing career with 46 interceptions, 717 interception-return yards, three pick-sixes, and seven fumble recoveries on defense. Occasionally used as a running back on offense, Christiansen also rushed for 148 yards and two touchdowns and gained another 32 yards on three pass receptions. Meanwhile, Christiansen amassed 1,084 punt-return yards, 1,329 kickoff-return yards, and 3,393 all-purpose yards. He also averaged 12.8 yards per punt return and 22.5 yards per kickoff return and scored eight times on special teams, with his 11 return touchdowns tying him with Lem Barney for the most in franchise history.

Following his playing days, Christiansen spent 25 years coaching at both the professional level and the college level, serving at different times as head coach of the San Francisco 49ers and the Stanford Cardinal and as an assistant on the coaching staffs of the 49ers, Kansas City Chiefs, Seattle Seahawks, and Atlanta Falcons. Retiring to private life at the end of 1983 after learning he had cancer, Christiansen lived until June 29, 1986, when he died at the age of 57 after undergoing surgery at Stanford Medical Center.

CAREER HIGHLIGHTS

Best Season

Christiansen performed brilliantly in 1954, when he earned a fifth-place finish in the UPI NFL MVP voting by ranking among the league leaders

32 THE 50 GREATEST PLAYERS IN DETROIT LIONS HISTORY

with eight interceptions and 225 punt-return yards while also scoring a pair of touchdowns. But Christiansen had his finest all-around season in 1953, when, in addition to recovering three fumbles, scoring a touchdown, and amassing 205 yards on special teams, he led the NFL with 12 interceptions and 238 interception-return yards, establishing in the process career-high marks in both categories.

Memorable Moments/Greatest Performances

Although the Lions lost to the Rams, 27–21, on October 14, 1951, Christiansen became the first player in NFL history to return two punts for touchdowns in the same game, scoring once in the second quarter on a 69-yard return and again in the final period on a 47-yard return.

Christiansen amazingly duplicated his extraordinary feat a little over one month later, scoring on punt returns of 71 and 89 yards during a 52–35 win over the Packers on November 22, 1951.

Christiansen made an impact on both defense and special teams during a 52–17 rout of the Packers on October 26, 1952, intercepting a pass and returning a punt 65 yards for a touchdown.

Christiansen apparently gave the Lions a 23–17 victory over Chicago on November 23, 1952, when he returned a punt 79 yards for a touchdown with just two minutes left in the final period. However, the Bears ended up winning the game in the closing moments on a two-yard TD pass from George Blanda to Ed Sprinkle.

Christiansen and the Lions gained a measure of revenge against their bitter rivals in the second meeting between the two teams two weeks later, with Christiansen accumulating 120 yards on special teams and carrying the ball six times for 54 yards and one touchdown during a 45–21 pasting of the Bears on December 7, 1952.

Making further contributions on offense in the final game of the 1952 regular season, Christiansen caught three passes for 32 yards and carried the ball 13 times for 94 yards and one touchdown during a 41–6 rout of the Dallas Texans, with his TD coming on a 65-yard run.

Although the Lions ended up losing to the Rams, 37–24, on November 1, 1953, Christiansen gave them an early 10–0 lead when he returned his interception of a Norm Van Brocklin pass 92 yards for a touchdown.

Christiansen helped lead the Lions to a 17–7 win over the Colts on November 7, 1953, by recording a career-high three interceptions, which he returned a total of 42 yards.

Christiansen led the Lions to a 28–24 victory over the Packers on November 25, 1954, by returning his interception of a Tobin Rote pass 30 yards for a touchdown and scoring again on a 61-yard punt return.

Excelling again on both defense and special teams during a 45–7 blowout of the Steelers on December 9, 1956, Christiansen picked off two passes and returned a punt 66 yards for a touchdown.

Christiansen contributed to a 24–14 win over the Packers on October 6, 1957, by recording two interceptions, one of which he returned 29 yards for a touchdown.

Notable Achievements

- Returned three interceptions for touchdowns.
- Returned eight punts for touchdowns.
- Recorded at least eight interceptions four times, finishing in double digits twice.
- Amassed more than 100 interception-return yards three times.
- Led NFL in interceptions twice, interception-return yards once, and punt-return average twice.
- Finished second in NFL in interceptions once and punt-return yards twice.
- Led Lions in interceptions five times.
- Holds share of Lions single-season record for most interceptions (12 in 1953).
- Holds Lions career records for most punt-return touchdowns (8) and most return touchdowns (11).
- Ranks among Lions career leaders with 46 interceptions (4th), 717 interception-return yards (5th), three touchdown interceptions (tied for 3rd), and 1,084 punt-return yards (6th).
- Holds NFL single-season record for highest punt-return average (21.5 in 1952).
- Holds NFL career record for highest punt-return average (12.8).
- Ranks fourth in NFL history with eight career punt-return touchdowns.
- Four-time division champion (1952, 1953, 1954, and 1957).
- Three-time NFL champion (1952, 1953, and 1957).
- Five-time Pro Bowl selection (1953, 1954, 1955, 1956, and 1957).
- Six-time First-Team All-Pro selection (1952, 1953, 1954, 1955, 1956, and 1957).

- 1956 First-Team All-Western Conference selection.
- Pro Football Hall of Fame All-1950s Team.
- Pro Football Reference All-1950s First Team.
- Named to NFL 100 All-Time Team in 2019.
- Number 86 on the *Sporting News*' 1999 list of the 100 Greatest Players in NFL History.
- Named to Lions 75th Anniversary All-Time Team in 2008.
- Named to Lions All-Time Team in 2019.
- Inducted into Lions Ring of Honor in 2009.
- Inducted into Pro Football Hall of Fame in 1970.

5

LOU CREEKMUR

One of the premier offensive linemen of his era, Lou Creekmur served as a key figure on Lions teams that won four division titles and three NFL championships during the 1950s. A pillar of strength on the left side of Detroit's offensive line throughout the decade, Creekmur missed just four games his entire career, appearing in 108 consecutive regular-season contests from 1950 to 1958. Performing equally well at tackle and guard, Creekmur earned eight Pro Bowl nominations and seven All-Pro selections, before being further honored by being named to the Lions All-Time Team in 2019 and gaining induction into both the team's Ring of Honor and the Pro Football Hall of Fame.

Born in Hopelawn, New Jersey, on January 22, 1927, Louis Creekmur grew up in nearby Woodbridge, where he attended Woodbridge High School. A star tackle for his high school football team, Creekmur received an athletic scholarship to the College of William & Mary, where he earned a letter as a freshman in 1944, before entering the military. Returning to William & Mary in 1947 following a two-year stint in the U.S. Army, Creekmur helped the Indians capture the Southern Conference championship his first year back, before winning the Jacobs Blocking Trophy two years later. Excelling in track and field as well, Creekmur set a school record in the shot put.

Drafted by both the Philadelphia Eagles of the NFL and the Los Angeles Dons of the AAFC when his original class graduated in 1948, Creekmur elected to stay in school so that he could earn his master's degree. With the AAFC having disbanded by the time Creekmur completed his education, the NFL, which had admitted into its ranks three teams and several players from the defunct league, placed his name in a frozen player pool from which the Lions selected him with their second pick in the 1950 NFL Draft.

Recalling the rather unusual circumstances under which he entered the league, Creekmur said, "I was thrown into the pool with such guys as Bob Hoernschemeyer, Y. A. Tittle, and all those other guys who played in the AAFC in 1949. The reason that I probably ended up in Detroit was because

Lou Creekmur excelled for the Lions at both offensive tackle and guard.

I played in the first Senior Bowl game in Jacksonville, Florida, in January 1950. [Lions head coach] Bo McMillin was coaching the North team, but I was playing on the South team. I finally got in the game on the defensive unit and had a pretty good day. Then I blocked a punt [by] going right over Doak Walker. At the end of the game, McMillin asked me if I would like to play for the Lions if they could draft me."

Joining the Lions' starting offensive unit immediately on his arrival in Detroit, Creekmur spent his first pro season playing left guard, performing so well as a rookie that he earned Pro Bowl honors for the first of eight straight times. Later identifying his initial Pro Bowl appearance as one of the greatest thrills of his career, Creekmur said, "For years, I had been reading in the papers about the great Bulldog Turner, the Bears center. And there I was, playing on the same team with him."

Creekmur remained at guard for one more year, before spending the 1952 and 1953 campaigns shifting back and forth between guard and tackle for Lions teams that captured consecutive NFL championships. While Creekmur performed equally well at both posts, he had just one complaint about head coach Buddy Parker's tendency to use him at multiple positions, saying, "If I am going to play offensive tackle, I'd like to weigh about 255 pounds. But if I'm to play guard, I should get down to 240 pounds to increase my speed. I sure wish Coach Parker would let me know in advance, so I'll know how much to eat the week before a game."

Although the 6'4" Creekmur maintained a consistent playing weight of just over 250 pounds after he moved to left tackle full-time in 1954, he also found himself being used occasionally on defense in short-yardage situations. Seeing more extensive playing time on that side of the ball in 1955, Creekmur recalled, "The Lions were 0–6, and we didn't have anyone to replace [middle guard] Les Bingaman, who had retired. That was the year that Coach Parker started experimenting with the man over the middle dropping back and covering a zone against the pass. But I just couldn't do it. I wasn't fast enough moving backward or laterally."

Aside from his brief foray into defensive line play, Creekmur continued to perform brilliantly for the Lions at left tackle throughout the 1950s, gaining All-Pro recognition seven straight times from 1951 to 1957. While Creekmur developed a reputation as one of the league's finest run-blockers and pass-protectors, he also became known for his ability to stretch the rules somewhat. Extremely adept at holding his opponent without drawing penalties, Creekmur had the ability to lock the arm of a defender under his own and then twist and twirl him to the ground without the referee noticing. Nicknamed the "Smiling Assassin," Creekmur, as did most other linemen of his day, also did an expert job of using his elbows, later admitting, "I used to throw a few. I think one of the reasons I made it to the Pro Bowl was the coaching I received from Marvin Bass when he was my line coach at William and Mary. He was a firm believer in throwing that elbow."

A true iron man, Creekmur appeared in every game the Lions played from 1950 to 1958, playing through injuries that included a crushed sternum, dislocated shoulders, and problems with both knees. But after appearing in a total of 165 consecutive contests (including the preseason and postseason), Creekmur announced his retirement following the conclusion of the 1958 campaign. He subsequently sat out the first four games of the 1959 season, before the Lions persuaded him to return to the playing field. Retiring for good at the end of the year after starting the season's final eight games at his familiar position of left tackle, Creekmur ended his career having appeared in a total of 116 regular-season contests, 107 of which he started.

38   THE 50 GREATEST PLAYERS IN DETROIT LIONS HISTORY

Following his playing days, Creekmur, who spent his offseasons working as the terminal manager for the Saginaw Transfer Company, spent several years serving as director of labor relations for Ryder Trucks, before being promoted to the position of vice president. Eventually retiring to private life, Creekmur lived until July 5, 2009, when he died from complications of dementia at the age of 82 after experiencing a gradual decline in health over the course of the previous three decades. An autopsy subsequently revealed that Creekmur, who had been suffering from memory loss, an inability to focus properly, and increasingly intense displays of anger and aggressiveness, had developed CTE.

On learning of his passing, Lions president Tom Lewand issued a statement that read, "Lou always will be remembered as one of the true standout players in Lions history. Offensive linemen often don't get the credit they deserve and, until his induction into the Hall of Fame [in 1996], that certainly was the case with Lou. If you look at the number of All-NFL and Pro Bowl teams he was selected to, and at the success of the Lions' teams when he played, you know that Lou was one of the all-time great linemen in NFL history."

Meanwhile, former Lions teammate Yale Lary stated, "Bobby [Layne] had a nickname for everyone, and Lou's was 'The Spirit.' That group in the '50s was special, and I don't think [that it] will ever be equaled. Lou was a real team player and an important part of those teams."

CAREER HIGHLIGHTS

Best Season

Creekmur gained consensus First-Team All-Pro recognition three straight times from 1951 to 1953, and any of those seasons would make a good choice. We'll opt for 1951 since, in addition to helping Detroit running backs gain a total of 1,841 yards on the ground and average a robust 4.5 yards per carry, Creekmur provided outstanding protection for Bobby Layne, who led all NFL quarterbacks with 2,403 passing yards and 26 touchdown passes.

Memorable Moments/Greatest Performances

Creekmur helped the Lions rush for 377 yards and amass 582 yards of total offense during a 49–14 manhandling of the New York Yanks on November 23, 1950.

Creekmur and his linemates continued to impose their will against the opposition in their next game, with the Lions amassing 538 yards of total offense during a 45–21 win over the Baltimore Colts on December 3, 1950.

Creekmur's superior blocking at the point of attack helped the Lions gain 205 yards on the ground and another 302 yards through the air during a 35–17 victory over Washington in the opening game of the 1951 regular season.

Creekmur and his cohorts again dominated their opponents at the line of scrimmage in the 1952 regular-season finale, with the Lions rushing for 216 yards and amassing 517 yards of total offense during a 41–6 blowout of the Dallas Texans.

Creekmur made a key play in the fourth quarter of the 1952 NFL Championship Game when, with the Lions clinging to a 14–7 lead and the Browns in possession of the football at the Detroit 10-yard line, he tackled quarterback Otto Graham for a 10-yard loss, effectively ending the Cleveland scoring threat. The Lions subsequently tacked on three more points to come away with a 17–7 victory.

Notable Achievements

- Missed just four games entire career, appearing in 108 consecutive contests from 1950 to 1958.
- Four-time division champion (1952, 1953, 1954, and 1957).
- Three-time NFL champion (1952, 1953, and 1957).
- Eight-time Pro Bowl selection (1950, 1951, 1952, 1953, 1954, 1955, 1956, and 1957).
- Six-time First-Team All-Pro selection (1951, 1952, 1953, 1954, 1956, and 1957).
- 1955 Second-Team All-Pro selection.
- Three-time First-Team All-Western Conference selection (1956, 1957, and 1958).
- Pro Football Reference All-1950s First Team.
- Named to Lions 75th Anniversary All-Time Team in 2008.
- Named to Lions All-Time Team in 2019.
- Inducted into Lions Ring of Honor in 2009.
- Inducted into Pro Football Hall of Fame in 1996.

6

YALE LARY

An outstanding defensive back who also proved to be the finest punter of his era, Yale Lary spent his entire 11-year NFL career in Detroit, making huge contributions to teams that won three division titles and three league championships. Starting at free safety most of his time in the Motor City, Lary picked off at least five passes in a season on five separate occasions, en route to recording the third-most interceptions of any player in team annals. A superior return man as well, Lary scored three times on special teams. Meanwhile, Lary posted the highest punting average of any kicker in the league three times, with his exceptional all-around play earning him nine Pro Bowl selections, six All-Pro nominations, and a place on the NFL 1950s All-Decade Team. Later named to the Lions All-Time Team as well, Lary received the additional accolades of being inducted into both the team's Ring of Honor and the Pro Football Hall of Fame.

Born in Fort Worth, Texas, on November 24, 1930, Robert Yale Lary Jr. seemed destined for a career on the gridiron when his father gifted him a football for his first Christmas. Developing his punting skills while in junior high school, Lary often spent his evenings practicing his kicks in front of his family's home, with author George Plimpton writing in his 1966 book *Paper Lion: Confessions of a Last-String Quarterback*, "The streetlights would go on, and he would punt the ball up through the cover of darkness, gone, and then 40 or 50 yards down the street, it would suddenly re-enter the streetlight's glow, startlingly white, and bounce erratically on the macadam and rock to a rest."

Establishing himself as a star in multiple sports at Fort Worth's North Side High School, Lary earned three letters each in football and baseball, two in track and field, and one in basketball. Offered an athletic scholarship to Texas A&M University, Lary continued to compete on the diamond and gridiron, excelling as an outfielder on the school's baseball team, which he helped lead to the Southwest Conference (SWC) co-championship and an appearance in the College World Series in 1951.

In addition to starring for the Lions at free safety, Yale Lary proved to be the finest punter of his era.

Even more outstanding in football, Lary starred for the Aggies on both sides of the ball for three seasons, gaining All-SWC recognition as a defensive back in both 1950 and 1951.

Seriously considering a career in baseball, Lary spent two seasons playing in the minor leagues, before choosing to focus exclusively on football shortly after the Lions selected him in the third round of the 1952 NFL Draft with the 34th overall pick. Initially tried out at running back on his arrival at his first pro training camp, the 5'11", 185-pound Lary failed to display the blocking skills necessary to man that position, recalling, "[6'4",

250-pound] Leon Hart was playing defensive end in a scrimmage, and I was supposed to block him. After making a fool of myself a couple of times, [Lions head coach] Buddy Parker suggested I give defense a try."

Subsequently inserted at right cornerback, Lary performed well as a rookie for the first of Detroit's back-to-back NFL championships ball clubs, intercepting four passes and recovering a fumble on defense while also amassing 485 yards and scoring once on special teams. Shifted to free safety prior to the start of the ensuing campaign, Lary displayed a natural affinity for the position, earning Pro Bowl honors for the first time by recording five interceptions, which he returned a total of 98 yards.

Drafted into the U.S. Army at the end of the year, Lary missed the 1954 and 1955 seasons while serving as a second lieutenant at Fort Benning in Georgia during the Korean War. Rejoining the Lions in 1956 following his discharge from the military, Lary reclaimed his starting free safety job, which he retained for the rest of his career. Excelling at that post for the next nine seasons, Lary earned eight Pro Bowl selections and six All-Pro nominations, gaining First-Team and Second-Team recognition three times each. Particularly outstanding in 1956 and 1962, Lary recorded eight interceptions, which he returned for a total of 182 yards and one touchdown, in the first of those campaigns, before picking off another eight passes and recovering three fumbles in the second.

Known for his intelligence and superior instincts, Lary also possessed the speed and quickness to serve as a roving center fielder in Detroit's defensive backfield. Also blessed with the ability to track the football well, Lary received high praise for his proficiency in that area from Baltimore Colts Hall of Fame wide receiver Raymond Berry, who told the *Fort Worth Star-Telegram*, "He was one of the defensive backs that had such a nose for the football that you had to be careful throwing around him, because if you made a mistake, the ball will be in his hands going the other direction."

In discussing his former teammate long after he left the Lions to play for the Pittsburgh Steelers, quarterback Bobby Layne stated, "If I had to pick one defensive back who had everything, it would have to be Yale. He was the smartest, and it took him a long way. But the big thing was his quickness, his ability to make a quarterback think he had an open receiver, then recover and intercept. A lot of passers would avoid his area. He didn't get the chances for interceptions some backs do."

Yet, despite the raves he received from teammates and opponents alike, Lary revealed to Brent Zwerneman in the latter's 2003 book *Game of My Life: 25 Stories of Aggie Football* that he dreaded going up against some of the taller receivers he faced in the pros, saying, "I was scared to death all the time that I was going to get beat."

Assigned punting duties after he rejoined the Lions in 1956, Lary soon established himself as the NFL's finest kicker, averaging more than 45 yards per punt five times, with his marks of 47.1, 48.4, and 48.9 yards in 1959, 1961, and 1963, respectively, placing him first in the league rankings. In addition to driving the ball far downfield, Lary got enough hang time on his kicks to allow the coverage team to do its job, with Joe Schmidt recalling, "Kicking from the end zone, Yale invariably put the ball across midfield with enough hang time to let us cover the kick. He made our defense look good because he always gave us room to work."

In addressing his role as punter, Lary, whose career average of 44.3 yards per kick ranks as the third-highest mark among punters whose careers began prior to 1960, stated, "It wasn't my primary goal to win the punting championship; my goal was to play defensive back. I started punting in junior high and continued through high school and college. Punting was my extracurricular, and I really loved it."

Extremely durable, Lary failed to start just three games his first nine years in the league, before sustaining an injury in 1963 that forced him to miss four contests. Starting all 14 games the Lions played in 1964, Lary earned Pro Bowl honors for the final time and the last of his six First-Team All-Western Conference nominations by ranking among the league leaders with six interceptions and 101 interception-return yards. Choosing to go out while still at the top of his game, Lary announced his retirement at the end of the year, saying at the time, "It's too much to move my wife and kids twice a year. It's not fair to them."

Over the course of 11 NFL seasons, Lary intercepted 50 passes, amassed 787 interception-return yards, forced eight fumbles and recovered 13 others, and scored three times on defense. Lary also returned three punts for touchdowns, accumulated 758 punt-return yards and 495 kickoff-return yards, and carried the ball 10 times for 153 yards on offense, giving him a total of 2,269 all-purpose yards. Meanwhile, Lary punted the ball 503 times for 22,279 yards, with the last figure representing the third-highest mark in franchise history.

After retiring from football, Lary, who, during his playing days, served in the Texas House of Representatives as a Democrat from 1959 to 1963, broke ground on a Ford Motor Company dealership in Fort Worth that he co-owned with a childhood friend for nearly a decade. Lary later formed an investment company with interests in real estate, oil and gas leases, and oil

44 THE 50 GREATEST PLAYERS IN DETROIT LIONS HISTORY

and natural gas production. Lary lived until May 11, 2017, when he died at his home in Fort Worth at the age of 86.

Following Lary's passing, Pro Football Hall of Fame president David Baker issued a statement that read, "Yale Lary was a true American hero. He was defined by his heart and character that made him one of the game's greatest players. Yale led by example and raised the level of all his teammates that resulted in multiple league titles for the Detroit Lions. Those same traits were on display during his service to our country as a member of the United States Army. . . . Yale Lary lived a life of character that will serve as great inspiration to generations of fans. His legacy will forever be celebrated at the Pro Football Hall of Fame in Canton, Ohio."

CAREER HIGHLIGHTS

Best Season

Lary performed magnificently in 1962, gaining consensus First-Team All-Pro recognition by picking off eight passes, recovering three fumbles, and ranking among the league leaders with an average of 45.3 yards per punt. But Lary made a slightly greater overall impact in 1956, when he earned First-Team All-Pro honors for the first time by finishing second in the league with eight interceptions, placing fourth in the circuit with 182 interception-return yards, amassing 338 all-purpose yards, recovering a fumble, and scoring once on defense.

Memorable Moments/Greatest Performances

Lary recorded the first two interceptions of his career during a 24–16 win over the Los Angeles Rams on October 19, 1952.

Lary contributed to a 43–13 thrashing of the Dallas Texans on November 16, 1952, by returning a punt 58 yards for a touchdown and intercepting a pass, which he subsequently returned 53 yards.

Lary scored again on special teams when he returned a punt 74 yards for a touchdown during a 27–17 win over the Baltimore Colts on October 3, 1953.

Lary helped lead the Lions to a 14–7 victory over the Packers on November 15, 1953, by recording three interceptions, which he returned a total of 54 yards.

Lary again picked off three passes during a 16–7 win over the Rams on October 28, 1956.

Lary scored for the first time on defense when he returned his interception of a Ted Marchibroda pass 73 yards for a touchdown during a 45–7 rout of the Steelers on December 9, 1956.

Lary intercepted Hall of Fame quarterback Norm Van Brocklin twice during a 10–7 victory over the Rams on October 13, 1957, returning one of his picks 63 yards to set up what proved to be the game-winning touchdown.

Lary's 71-yard punt return for a touchdown proved to be one of the few bright spots of a 40–14 loss to the Colts on October 19, 1958.

Lary lit the scoreboard again when he returned a fumble 28 yards for a touchdown during a 45–21 win over the Chicago Cardinals on December 6, 1959.

Lary scored the last points of his career when he returned his interception of a Johnny Unitas pass 21 yards for a touchdown during a 25–21 loss to the Colts on October 20, 1963.

Notable Achievements

- Scored three defensive touchdowns.
- Returned three punts for touchdowns.
- Recorded at least five interceptions five times.
- Amassed more than 100 interception-return yards twice.
- Recorded longest punt in NFL in 1963 (73 yards).
- Led NFL in punting average three times.
- Finished second in NFL in interceptions twice, total punting yards once, punting average once, and total punt-return yards once.
- Led Lions in interceptions four times.
- Ranks among Lions career leaders with 50 interceptions (3rd), 787 interception-return yards (2nd), 13 fumble recoveries (7th), and 22,279 total punting yards (3rd).
- Three-time division champion (1952, 1953, and 1957).
- Three-time NFL champion (1952, 1953, and 1957).
- Nine-time Pro Bowl selection (1953, 1956, 1957, 1958, 1959, 1960, 1961, 1962, and 1964).
- Three-time First-Team All-Pro selection (1956, 1958, and 1962).
- Three-time Second-Team All-Pro selection (1957, 1959, and 1963).
- Two-time Newspaper Enterprise Association Second-Team All-Pro selection (1960 and 1961).

46 THE 50 GREATEST PLAYERS IN DETROIT LIONS HISTORY

- Six-time First-Team All-Western Conference selection (1956, 1957, 1959, 1962, 1963, and 1964).
- Pro Football Hall of Fame All-1950s Team.
- Pro Football Reference All-1950 Second Team.
- Named to Lions 75th Anniversary All-Time Team in 2008.
- Named to Lions All-Time Team in 2019.
- Inducted into Lions Ring of Honor in 2009.
- Inducted into Pro Football Hall of Fame in 1979.

7

ALEX KARRAS

Identified by former Lions head coach George Wilson as the best defensive tackle he ever saw, Alex Karras spent 12 seasons in Detroit anchoring a defense that consistently ranked among the league's finest. Although somewhat undersized, Karras used his strength and quickness to excel against both the run and the pass, finishing his career with more sacks and fumble recoveries than any other player in franchise history. A four-time Pro Bowler and eight-time All-Pro, Karras also earned spots on both the NFL 1960s All-Decade Team and the Lions All-Time Team, before finally being inducted posthumously into the Pro Football Hall of Fame in 2020 after failing to gain admittance for many years due to his one-time involvement with gamblers.

Born in Gary, Indiana, on July 15, 1935, Alexander George Karras learned to play football from his older brothers in a parking lot near his home. After losing at the age of 13 his father, Dr. George Karras, a Greek immigrant who married a Canadian woman he met while pursuing his medical degree, Alex developed into an outstanding all-around athlete at Gary's Emerson High School, excelling in football, baseball, basketball, wrestling, and track and field (shot put). Especially proficient on the gridiron, Karras received scholarship offers from several colleges, before finally choosing to enroll at the University of Iowa.

Following his arrival in Iowa City, the temperamental Karras began a turbulent relationship with head football coach Forest Evashevski that caused him to quit the team multiple times. Once asked about his former head coach, Karras replied, "There is nothing I liked about Forest Evashevski. How could I begin talking about a man I totally disliked?"

Shedding some light on his former Hawkeye teammate's disdain for Evashevski, Randy Duncan said, "I think Karras hated Evy for a lot of reasons. Evy was on everybody's back, and he was on Karras's back big time. Karras was a great football player, but he didn't really like offense, and, in those days, you had to go both ways. So, he didn't block anybody. What he wanted to do was chase down quarterbacks and play defense."

Alex Karras recorded more sacks and fumble recoveries than anyone else in franchise history.

Further troubled by homesickness and struggles in the classroom, Karras, who suffered from attention deficit disorder, told the *Des Moines Register* in 1997, "I hated going to school. I liked some of the people at the University of Iowa, but I didn't go to class very often. I guess I'm about 25 years away from getting my degree. Not 25 semester hours—25 years. I don't regret not having a degree. I think it's silly to push people to go to college."

Despite the many difficulties Karras encountered during his time at Iowa, he emerged as one of the finest players in the nation, gaining consensus All-America recognition as a senior in 1957 while also winning the Outland Trophy as college football's top lineman and earning a runner-up finish in the Heisman Trophy voting.

Impressed with Karras's exceptional play at Iowa, the Lions made him the 10th overall pick of the 1958 NFL Draft when they selected him in the first round. Prior to departing for Detroit, though, Karras, who won a collegiate wrestling championship, decided to try his hand at Pro Wrestling, recalling, "Pinkie George of Des Moines signed me to my contract." While Karras remained dedicated to his primary vocation throughout his playing career, he continued to supplement his income by spending his offseasons wrestling professionally under the alias "Killer Karras."

Joining the defending NFL champion Lions prior to the start of training camp in 1958, Karras soon laid claim to the starting left tackle job, after which he went on to earn a sixth-place finish in the NFL Rookie of the Year voting. Following another strong showing in 1959, Karras began a string of three straight seasons in which he gained Pro Bowl and All-Pro recognition. A First-Team All-Pro selection in both 1960 and 1961, Karras brought down opposing quarterbacks behind the line of scrimmage nine times in the first of those campaigns, before recording another 11½ sacks in the second. Although Karras only earned Second-Team All-Pro honors in 1962, he helped lead the Lions to a regular-season record of 11–3 and a close second-place finish to Green Bay in the NFL Western Division by registering 11 sacks while also recording a safety and the first of his four career interceptions.

The most celebrated member of an exceptional defensive line nicknamed the "Fearsome Foursome" that also included massive right tackle Roger Brown and ends Darris McCord and Sam Williams, Karras combined with the former to give the Lions the finest pair of interior defensive linemen in the league. Although much smaller than Brown, the 6'2", 250-pound Karras, who rarely worked out and never lifted weights, made up for whatever he lacked in size with his quickness, intelligence, tremendous natural strength, outstanding lateral movement, and superior technique.

Employing quick, choppy steps, Karras moved extremely well in short spaces, enabling him to fight his way through traffic in the trenches, with linebacker Mike Lucci saying of his former teammate, "Many times, he was unblockable. He was quick; he had those little, short steps. . . . There was a guard from San Francisco who used to say that his hair would fall out the week before he had to play against Alex."

In describing his style of play, Karras told the *Des Moines Register* during a 1977 interview, "I was a little different than most guys at my position. I wasn't as big. The guys now don't play the lateral game I did. I'd run around the opposition, not through them. Linemen today weigh 290 and can lift houses. They play a different game, but they're damn good."

Packers Hall of Fame guard Jerry Kramer expressed his admiration for his frequent foe when he said, "Alex Karras, to me, was one of the two best football players I ever played against [with Merlin Olsen being the other]. He had great quickness. He had quick feet. He was difficult to handle. He had great upper body strength, and Alex always brought his best game to Green Bay, or against us."

Kramer added, "Alex did things that tackles of that time weren't supposed to be able to do. He was a load. But he was a load who made a lot of plays. Alex was really a handful."

Linebacker Wayne Walker, who arrived in Detroit the same year as Karras, also addressed his longtime teammate's many unique qualities when he stated, "Alex was probably the most individual man/football player ever. He was just so original. There was no one like him before, and there won't be anyone like him after. He had this Jackie Gleason–type body and, God, he could really play. He could really play. He threw offensive linemen around."

An extremely intense player who became known for his fierce competitive spirit, Karras said, "I never had to work myself up for a game. I hated everybody, even my teammates; I never talked to anybody."

In attempting to explain Karras's behavior, Dick LeBeau commented, "Alex was a competitor, first and foremost, and he wanted to win more than anything. And, once you understood that, you understood Alex."

Roger Brown said of the man who lined up immediately next to him for six seasons, "He was a ballplayer. He knew he had a job to do, and he was the kind of guy that would bring the team with him."

Also quite intelligent, Karras knew how to use his reputation to his advantage, revealing, "I was very smart. I used psychological warfare. I don't know, they got this idea that I was this ruffian, this rough-tough character, and I played that role because, when you get dubbed that role, you might as well play that role."

Discussing the contradictory nature of Karras's personality, Chicago Bears center Mike Pyle stated, "Alex Karras was two totally different people off the field and on the field. On the field, he hated anybody that had another uniform color on. Meanest man alive. But off the field, just a nice guy."

While Karras may have been a nice guy away from the playing field, he displayed poor judgment early in his career when, after purchasing a controlling interest in the Lindell A.C., one of the first sports bars in the country, he became involved with gamblers who often gathered at his establishment. Ordered by then–NFL commissioner Pete Rozelle to sever his ties with the bar, the always stubborn Karras refused to do so at first. However, he ultimately relented, agreeing to sell his interest, but only after admitting to the league that he had bet on NFL games, including some in which he played. Subsequently suspended, along with Green Bay

Packers star running back Paul Hornung, for one season, Karras sat out the entire 1963 campaign, making a substantial living by wrestling and tending bar in Detroit.

Looking back on the ordeal years later, Karras expressed his dissatisfaction with Rozelle and his decision, saying, "I don't like Pete Rozelle. I don't talk to him. I don't know if he likes that or not. I don't think he cares. He suspended me for one season for betting on games, and that was a bullshit rap."

Returning to action in 1964, Karras picked up right where he left off, earning Second-Team All-Pro honors by recording 13 sacks and two interceptions. Continuing to harbor resentment toward the league office, Karras displayed his dry wit prior to the start of one game when he declined a referee's request to call the coin toss, stating, "I'm sorry, sir, I'm not permitted to gamble."

Karras remained a force on the interior of the Lions defensive line for five more seasons, earning another Pro Bowl selection and four more All-Pro nominations by recording a total of 53½ sacks while also recovering eight fumbles. Particularly outstanding in 1965 and 1967, Karras gained Pro Bowl and First-Team All-Pro recognition in the first of those campaigns by finishing third in the league with 15 sacks, before earning Second-Team All-Pro honors in the second by registering 12½ sacks.

Hampered by a knee injury in 1970, an aging Karras recorded just two sacks and missed the first game of his career after appearing in 161 consecutive contests. Released by the Lions prior to the start of the ensuing campaign, Karras subsequently announced his retirement, ending his career with 100 sacks, 18 fumble recoveries, and four interceptions, with his sack total not including any he registered his first two years in the league.

Following his playing days, Karras began a lengthy career in acting that included a supporting role as Mongo in the 1974 western comedy *Blazing Saddles* and a starring role in the 1980s television series *Webster*. Starring alongside his real-life wife, Susan Clark, in the latter, Karras played George Papadapolis, a former football player turned sportscaster who became the adoptive father of an African American boy named Webster. Karras also spent three years in the Monday Night Football broadcasting booth, once declaring, "I'm the bridge between Howard Cosell and Frank Gifford. I'm there to have a little fun."

Plagued by poor health the last few years of his life, Karras gradually descended into dementia, prompting him and his wife to add their names to a lawsuit against the NFL for its failure to protect players from head injuries. On adding their names to the lawsuit, Karras's wife stated, "This physical beating that he took as a football player has impacted his life, and, therefore, it has impacted his family life. He is interested in making the game of football safer and hoping that other families of retired players will have a healthier and happier retirement."

Karras lived until October 10, 2012, when he died at the age of 77, with his family saying in a statement released by the Lions, "After a heroic fight with kidney disease, heart disease, dementia, and, for the last two years, stomach cancer, Alex Karras . . . died at his home in Los Angeles early this morning, surrounded by family."

On learning of his former teammate's passing, Joe Schmidt said, "He was such a strong player, dominant at times, one of the men who really raised the importance of the [defensive] tackle position. He took the position beyond the 'grunt guy' level who just played the inside run. But even with all the Pro Bowls and stuff, Alex probably still was underrated. A great player, though, really."

Some eight years later, when Karras gained induction into the Pro Football Hall of Fame through the Centennial Committee, longtime sportswriter and selection committee member Vic Carucci attempted to place the Indiana native's career in its proper perspective by saying, "He was the toughness of the Detroit Lions. I mean, he was a terror. You think of Butkus for the Bears, and you think of Karras for the Lions."

CAREER HIGHLIGHTS

Best Season

While Karras had many other outstanding seasons for the Lions, he proved to be most dominant in 1965, when he gained consensus First-Team All-Pro recognition by placing near the top of the league rankings with a career-high 15 sacks.

Memorable Moments/Greatest Performances

Karras contributed to a 29–20 victory over the Colts on September 30, 1962, by recording the first of his four career interceptions, which he subsequently returned 28 yards.

In addition to anchoring a defense that allowed just 75 yards of total offense during an 11–3 win over the Bears on October 28, 1962, Karras recorded a safety when he sacked quarterback Bill Wade in the end zone.

Karras's outstanding play at the line of scrimmage helped limit the 49ers to just 61 yards of total offense during a 26–3 Lions win on October 6, 1963.

Karras helped lead the Lions to a 24–20 win over the Vikings on October 11, 1964, by intercepting a pass and leading a defense that sacked Fran Tarkenton nine times.

Karras earned NFL Defensive Player of the Week honors by applying constant pressure to Bart Starr, whom he and his teammates sacked seven times during a 17–17 tie with the Packers in the opening game of the 1967 regular season.

Notable Achievements

- Missed just one game entire career, appearing in 161 of 162 contests.
- Finished in double digits in sacks five times.
- Finished third in NFL in sacks twice and fumble recoveries once.
- Led Lions in sacks six times.
- Holds franchise career records for most sacks (100) and most fumble recoveries (18).
- 1967 Week 1 NFL Defensive Player of the Week.
- Four-time Pro Bowl selection (1960, 1961, 1962, and 1965).
- Three-time First-Team All-Pro selection (1960, 1961, and 1965).
- Five-time Second-Team All-Pro selection (1962, 1964, 1966, 1967, and 1969).
- Four-time First-Team All-Western Conference selection (1961, 1962, 1967, and 1968).
- Pro Football Hall of Fame All-1960s Team.
- Pro Football Reference All-1960s First Team.
- Named to Lions 75th Anniversary All-Time Team in 2008.
- Named to Lions All-Time Team in 2019.
- Inducted into Lions Ring of Honor in 2018.
- Inducted into Pro Football Hall of Fame in 2020.

8
LEM BARNEY

A true "shutdown corner" before the term became a regular part of football parlance, Lem Barney spent 11 seasons in Detroit using his great speed, superior cover skills, and excellent instincts to blanket opposing wide receivers and create turnovers. Second in franchise history in both interceptions and fumble recoveries, Barney, who picked off at least five passes in a season five times, also ranks first in team annals in interception-return yards, touchdown interceptions, and TDs scored on defense. An outstanding performer on special teams as well, Barney returned two punts and one kickoff for touchdowns, with his tremendous all-around play earning him numerous individual accolades that included seven Pro Bowl selections, five All-Pro nominations, a spot on the Lions All-Time Team, and a place in the Pro Football Hall of Fame.

Born in Gulfport, Mississippi, on September 8, 1945, Lemuel Jackson Barney grew up with his parents and three sisters in the segregated South, where he proved to be extremely precocious during his formative years, remembering, "I tried to run with the older guys. I tried to be in things that were happening. . . . I'd get summer jobs like everyone else. I worked on the piers, and I carried bananas off the banana boats for $2.35 an hour."

Developing an affinity for football at an early age, Barney eventually established himself as a star on the gridiron at all-black 33rd Avenue High School, excelling as a quarterback on offense, a cornerback on defense, and a punter and kick returner on special teams.

Urged by his mother to attend college, Barney accepted an athletic scholarship to Jackson State University, a historically black school located in Jackson, Mississippi. Although quarterback remained Barney's preferred position, he knew that his most realistic path to a career in the NFL lay in defensive back, recalling, "I recognized that there was no demand for black quarterbacks in the pros back in 1967, so I asked my coach, Rod Paige, to change me into a defensive back."

Lem Barney scored more times on defense than any other player in team annals.

Performing brilliantly at cornerback for the Tigers from 1964 to 1966, Barney recorded a total of 26 interceptions, earning in the process All-Southwestern Athletic Conference honors three times. Particularly outstanding his senior year, Barney also gained All-America recognition from *Ebony* magazine and the *Pittsburgh Courier* by picking off 11 passes.

Despite Barney's small college background, the Lions selected him in the second round of the 1967 NFL Draft with the 34th overall pick on the recommendations of scouts Will Robinson and Dick "Night Train" Lane, the Hall of Fame cornerback who had retired two years earlier.

On Barney's arrival at his first pro training camp, new Lions head coach Joe Schmidt described his chances of starting as a rookie as being "pretty damn slight," telling reporters, "It takes a little longer to learn how to play cornerback than almost any other position." Before long, though, Schmidt changed his mind, especially after he watched Barney knock down a pass to

56   THE 50 GREATEST PLAYERS IN DETROIT LIONS HISTORY

standout receiver Gail Cogdill during the team's first scrimmage and jump over him to make a one-handed interception on the very next play.

Recalling the favorable impression that Barney made on him, Schmidt stated, "Right away, you could see Lem had great lateral movement, he could run, and had the gift of playing the ball and playing through the receiver. He was the whole package, and you could see right away that he could play."

Named the team's starting left cornerback prior to the start of the regular season, Barney ended up earning Pro Bowl, NFL Defensive Rookie of the Year, and unofficial Second-Team All-Pro honors from both the Newspaper Enterprise Association and the *New York Daily News* by leading the league with 10 interceptions and 232 interception-return yards. Also filling in capably for punter Pat Studstill, who suffered a season-ending injury during the early stages of the campaign, Barney posted a punting average of 37.4 yards per kick.

After spending the following offseason serving in the U.S. Navy for six months, Barney resumed his outstanding play for the Lions in 1968, gaining Pro Bowl and consensus First-Team All-Pro recognition for the first of two straight times by picking off seven passes, leading the league with five fumble recoveries, ranking among the leaders with 670 kickoff-return yards and an average of 26.8 yards per return, and scoring twice on special teams. Barney followed that up by recording eight more interceptions, recovering another two fumbles, and returning a punt for a touchdown in 1969, prompting Joe Schmidt to say, "He's unbelievable. No matter what he's asked to do for us, he does it in spectacular fashion. I wish I had two others just like him. I would play one next to him on defense, and I'd use the other on offense."

With the speedy Barney capable of running the 100-yard dash in 9.7 seconds and blessed with tremendous open-field running ability that surfaced every time he intercepted a pass, recovered a fumble, or returned a kick, reporters often asked Schmidt if he might be more valuable to the team on offense. Although the thought likely crossed Schmidt's mind at some point, he responded by saying, "The best athletes you have on the team play at cornerback. The receivers come at you one-on-one, and you just can't hide. You either make the play or you don't. It's that simple. Barney makes the plays because of his speed, his quickness, his reactions, his senses."

Commenting on his longtime teammate's great speed, former Lions middle linebacker Mike Lucci stated, "Lem backpedaled nearly as fast as going forward. He had the wonderful ability to turn his hips and run. It was pretty comforting to know that behind me I had two future Hall of Famers as our cornerbacks, Dick LeBeau and Lem Barney. Lem was special, and he still is special in many ways."

The 6', 190-pound Barney also drew praise for his superior technique and exceptional all-around ability from Hall of Fame tight end Mike Ditka, who stated, "Lem was simply one of the best cornerbacks to ever play. He covered and tackled so well. . . . He had great footwork and was instinctive, and he was able to know from studying film what the receiver was probably going to do."

Claiming that he developed his footwork while running along the Mississippi Gulf Coast, Barney said, "I would run 3½ miles to Gulfport on the hard sand where the tide comes in, then would run back on the loose sand, most of the time backpedaling."

And as for how he prepared himself for his opponent, Barney stated, "I would watch film of the previous five games and how the guys I had to cover ran their pattern in certain situations. What does he typically do on third-and-long, second-and-short, first-and-10?"

A noted gambler on defense, Barney tended to take chances that occasionally caused him to get burned by opposing wide receivers. Beaten for touchdowns twice each by Chicago's Dick Gordon and Oakland's Fred Biletnikoff in 1970, Barney failed to gain Pro Bowl recognition for the first time in his career, even though he recorded seven interceptions, two of which he returned for touchdowns. Injured for much of the ensuing campaign, Barney appeared in only nine games and picked off just three passes, prompting reports to surface that he had decided to adopt a more conservative style of play. In response, Barney stated, "It came out in the paper that I wasn't going to gamble as much as I had previously. It said I would just stick to basic defense. But I don't think I ever changed my style, and I don't think I will, either. You have to have one style and stick to it and try to improve on what you are doing."

Returning to top form in 1972, Barney began an outstanding five-year run during which he earned four Pro Bowl selections and three All-NFC nominations. But after Barney failed to garner postseason honors in 1977 and subsequently became involved in a wiretap investigation into international drug smuggling that resulted in his having to testify before a New York grand jury, the Lions placed him on the injured waiver list just prior to the start of the 1978 regular season. With no other team offering him a contract, Barney sat out the year, before announcing his retirement when the Lions officially released him in February 1979.

Over 11 NFL seasons, Barney recorded 56 interceptions, which he returned for a total of 1,077 yards and seven touchdowns; recovered 17 fumbles; amassed 1,312 punt-return yards, 1,274 kickoff-return yards, and 3,871 all-purpose yards; and scored four times on special teams.

Looking back on his career years later, Barney said, "Interceptions were my forte. I liked to think of myself as a defensive weapon turned offensive weapon. The keys were, and are, knowledge of your opponents and the guts to say that once the ball is in the air, it's as much mine as his."

Barney added, "I gave the game everything I had. Anything I could do to help win, I was willing to do, and the skills that the Lord had blessed me with, I didn't leave the game by saying I did not use them. Everything I had I gave while I was on the field."

Considered by some to be the greatest player ever to man his position, Barney, said Joe Schmidt, "was one by himself. He was phenomenal and always a threat to go all the way because he was so fast and could see the whole field and make great yardage. . . . Lem had such a natural way of conducting himself and playing; the best that's ever played, as far as I'm concerned."

Expressing similar sentiments during his speech in which he introduced Barney at the latter's 1992 Hall of Fame induction ceremony, former Lions defensive backs coach Jim David stated, "If there was ever anybody better than Lem, I never saw or heard of him. Nobody before or since measured up to him."

After retiring from football, Barney remained in the Detroit area, where he used his celebrity status to serve as an advocate for youth and civic affairs through organizations such as the United Way, the Metro Detroit Youth Foundation, and the Detroit Children's Hospital. Barney also worked as a color commentator of college football games for Black Entertainment Television and as a public relations executive for the Michigan Consolidated Gas Company. Although a 1993 arrest for drug possession tarnished his image somewhat, Barney ultimately gained acquittal and went on to become a finance director for former teammate Mel Farr at the latter's auto dealership in Detroit. Barney, who is an ordained minister, also became involved in Prison Fellowship, a nonprofit organization that purportedly uses the Christian faith to restore those affected by crime and incarceration.

Unfortunately, Barney eventually began experiencing health problems that resulted in doctors diagnosing him as being in the advanced stages of dementia due to the multiple concussions he sustained during his playing career. In discussing his longtime friend's condition, former Detroit Pistons star Dave Bing told the *Detroit News* on August 27, 2023, "Dementia has set in. But long story short, he is in Houston with his two children and his grandchildren. He's not doing well, and he's in a long-term care facility right now. . . . All we can do is hope and pray that he comes through this."

LEM BARNEY **59**

As of this writing, Barney, who is listed in court documents as a "Legally Incapacitated Individual," remains bedridden in that Houston long-term health care facility.

CAREER HIGHLIGHTS

Best Season

Although Barney also performed magnificently in each of the next two seasons, he arguably played the best ball of his career as a rookie in 1967, when, in addition to leading the NFL with 10 interceptions and 232 interception-return yards, he returned three of his picks for touchdowns.

Memorable Moments/Greatest Performances

Barney made an immediate impact in his first game as a pro, intercepting the first pass thrown in his direction and returning it 24 yards for a touchdown during a 17–17 tie with the Packers in the opening game of the 1967 regular season.

Barney recorded two interceptions in one game for the first time in his career during a 31–14 win over the Browns on September 24, 1967.

Barney scored the first points of a 24–3 victory over the Atlanta Falcons on October 22, 1967, when he returned an interception 44 yards for a touchdown.

Barney helped lead the Lions to a 14–3 win over the Vikings in the 1967 regular-season finale by recording three interceptions, one of which he returned 71 yards for a touchdown.

Barney contributed to a 42–0 rout of the Bears on September 22, 1968, by picking off another three passes.

Barney earned NFL Defensive Player of the Week honors by intercepting a Bart Starr pass and limiting star wideout Boyd Dowler to just one catch and 12 receiving yards during a 23–17 win over the Packers on September 29, 1968.

Barney tallied the only points the Lions scored during a 14–7 loss to the 49ers on October 27, 1968, when he returned a missed field goal attempt by Dennis Patera 94 yards for a touchdown.

Barney starred in defeat on November 3, 1968, intercepting a pass and returning the game's opening kickoff 98 yards for a touchdown during a 10–7 loss to the Rams.

60   THE 50 GREATEST PLAYERS IN DETROIT LIONS HISTORY

Barney again scored on special teams when he returned a punt 74 yards for a touchdown during a 24–0 win over the Giants on September 28, 1969.

Barney lit the scoreboard again when he returned his interception of a Bart Starr pass 40 yards for a touchdown during a 40–0 blowout of the Packers in the 1970 regular-season opener.

Barney followed that up the very next week by returning a punt 61 yards for a touchdown during a 38–3 win over the Bengals.

Barney earned NFL Defensive Player of the Week honors by returning his interception of a Bart Starr pass 49 yards for a touchdown during a 20–0 win over the Packers in the final game of the 1970 regular season.

Barney scored the first points of a 31–7 victory over the Houston Oilers on October 17, 1971, when he returned his interception of a Dan Pastorini pass 28 yards for a touchdown.

Barney crossed the opponent's goal line for the final time in his career when he returned an interception 24 yards for a touchdown during a 41–14 rout of the Seahawks on October 24, 1976.

Notable Achievements

- Returned seven interceptions for touchdowns.
- Returned two punts and one kickoff for touchdowns.
- Recorded at least five interceptions five times.
- Amassed more than 100 interception-return yards four times.
- Led NFL with 10 interceptions, 232 interception-return yards, and three touchdown interceptions in 1967.
- Led NFL with five fumble recoveries in 1968.
- Led NFL with two touchdown interceptions in 1970.
- Finished second in NFL in interceptions and interception-return yards once each.
- Led Lions in interceptions five times.
- Holds Lions career records for most interception-return yards (1,077), most touchdown interceptions (7), and most touchdowns scored on defense (7).
- Ranks among Lions career leaders with 56 interceptions (2nd), 17 fumble recoveries (tied for 2nd), and 1,312 punt-return yards (4th).
- Ranks eighth in NFL history in career interception-return yards.
- 1967 NFL Defensive Rookie of the Year.
- Two-time NFL Defensive Player of the Week.

- Seven-time Pro Bowl selection (1967, 1968, 1969, 1972, 1973, 1975, and 1976).
- Two-time First-Team All-Pro selection (1968 and 1969).
- Three-time Newspaper Enterprise Association Second-Team All-Pro selection (1967, 1970, and 1973).
- Two-time First-Team All-Western Conference selection (1968 and 1969).
- Two-time First-Team All-NFC selection (1972 and 1975).
- Two-time Second-Team All-NFC selection (1970 and 1973).
- Pro Football Hall of Fame All-1960s Team.
- Number 97 on the *Sporting News'* 1999 list of the 100 Greatest Players in NFL History.
- Number 20 retired by Lions.
- Named to Lions 75th Anniversary All-Time Team in 2008.
- Named to Lions All-Time Team in 2019.
- Inducted into Lions Ring of Honor in 2009.
- Inducted into Pro Football Hall of Fame in 1992.

9
DUTCH CLARK

Once hailed as "pro football's greatest player" by legendary Chicago Bears head coach George Halas, Dutch Clark proved to be the finest all-around player in the game for much of the 1930s, a decade during which he almost single-handedly established professional football in Detroit. A true "triple threat" who, in addition to calling all the signals on offense, ran with the football, delivered passes to his teammates, excelled at defensive back, punted, and assumed placekicking duties, Clark spent seven seasons starring for the Portsmouth Spartans/Detroit Lions franchise, leading the NFL in total offense once and points scored and rushing touchdowns three times each. The central figure on the Lions' 1935 NFL championship team, Clark earned six First-Team All-Pro nominations, before receiving the additional honors of being named the outstanding player of the 1930s, gaining induction into the Pro Football Hall of Fame, having his No. 7 retired by the Lions, and being awarded a spot on the NFL 100 All-Time Team in 2019.

Born in Fowler, Colorado, on October 11, 1906, Earl Harry Clark spent his early years living on a farm in nearby La Junta, before moving with his family at the age of 10 some 60 miles west to Pueblo, where his father took a job as a locomotive fireman on a steam railroad. Eventually emerging as a standout athlete at Pueblo's Central High School, Clark excelled in football, basketball, and track and field, earning All-State honors at fullback on the gridiron and center on the hardwood while also setting South Central League records in the discus and high hurdles.

Graduating from Central High in 1926 after earning a total of 16 letters and being voted class president his senior year, Clark enrolled at Colorado College, where he continued to compete in all three sports. Proving to be especially proficient in football, Clark became the first Colorado player to gain First-Team All-America recognition in his junior year of 1928, when he rushed for 1,349 yards and scored 103 points as a combination tailback, linebacker, safety, and placekicker.

Dutch Clark served as the central figure on the Lions' first NFL championship team.

Choosing to remain at Colorado College as the university's head basketball coach and assistant football coach following his graduation in 1930, Clark spent one year fulfilling that dual role, before taking a leave of absence in May 1931 to play for the NFL's Portsmouth Spartans. Excelling in his first year as a pro, Clark led the Spartans to an 11–3 record and a second-place finish in the 10-team circuit by ranking among the league leaders with nine touchdowns and 60 points scored, earning in the process First-Team All-Pro honors.

Following a similar path in 1932, Clark spent the first several months of the year coaching at his alma mater, before rejoining the Spartans in the fall. Leading Portsmouth to a record of 6–2–4, Clark again gained

First-Team All-Pro recognition by passing for 272 yards and two touchdowns, running for three scores, catching three TD passes, leading the NFL with 55 points scored and three field goals, and placing near the top of the league rankings with 461 yards rushing, 568 yards from scrimmage, 733 yards of total offense, and six touchdowns.

Rated by United Press International (UPI) sportswriter George Kirksey as "the greatest football player of the past 10 years" in December 1932, Clark nevertheless decided to sever ties with the Spartans at the end of the year following a salary dispute. He subsequently spent the first two months of 1933 reprising his role as head basketball coach at Colorado College, before announcing in March that he had accepted the position of head football coach at the Colorado School of Mines. However, Clark decided to resume his playing career one year later, when, after purchasing the Spartans, relocating them to Detroit, and renaming them the Lions, WJR Radio owner G. A. Richards coaxed him out of retirement.

Establishing himself as the Motor City's first gridiron hero in 1934, Clark led the Lions to a 10–3 record and a runner-up finish to the Chicago Bears in the NFL West Division by leading the league with 1,146 yards of total offense and eight rushing touchdowns while also ranking among the leaders with 763 rushing yards, 383 passing yards, 835 yards from scrimmage, 73 points scored, and an average of 6.2 yards per carry, with his outstanding play earning him the third of his six First-Team All-Pro nominations.

Selected by his teammates as team captain prior to the start of the ensuing campaign, Clark led the Lions to a regular-season record of 7–3–2 and their first division title by scoring a league-high six touchdowns and 55 points, before directing them to a convincing 26–7 victory over the Giants in the NFL Championship Game. Named First-Team All-Pro again at the end of the year, Clark garnered the additional accolade of being identified as the best player in the NFL by UPI, which called him the "keenest football strategist," the "most dangerous one-man threat," and "a fine drop-kicker and a deadly tackler."

Although often referred to as a quarterback since he called his team's signals, distributed the ball to his teammates, and essentially ran the Lions' offense, the 6',185-pound Clark received the official designation of tailback in each of his All-Pro selections since he technically played that position in the then-popular single-wing formation.

A tremendous open-field runner who followed his blockers well, Clark proved to be one of the league's most difficult players to bring down even though he possessed only average size and foot speed, with Red Grange calling him "the hardest man in football to tackle" and adding, "His change of pace fools the best tacklers."

Further expounding on the difficulties Clark presented to opposing defenders, Lions head coach Potsy Clark (no relation) said, "He's like a rabbit in brush. He has no set plan, no definite direction. He is an instinctive runner who cuts, pivots, slants, and reverses. When the interference gets him in the secondary, he begins his mad twists and turns. He'll get out of more holes than anybody you ever saw. Just about the time you expect to see him smothered, he's free of tacklers."

In discussing his running style, Clark, who one writer said had "the nimblest legs in football" and called "the modern back who comes nearest to perfection," stated, "Running is like driving a car. When you drive, you're looking quite a way down the street. The things that are close you take care of automatically with reflex action."

Extremely versatile, Clark also excelled at safety on defense, punted well, kicked field goals and extra points, and displayed greater accuracy as a passer than virtually any other player of his time, once completing 53.5 percent of his passes in a season when the league average barely exceeded 36 percent.

A superb field general as well, Clark became known for his intelligence and tremendous leadership ability, with Potsy Clark saying of his team's best player, "He knows what plays to call. He is one of the most intelligent men who ever played football. He knows the game thoroughly. He rarely makes a mistake. But his main asset is his ability to gain the confidence of players. He makes them absolutely believe in him. They never question any play he calls; they regard him as infallible. This confidence is not misplaced. I have never known Dutch to criticize any player. Any time a play goes wrong, he takes the entire blame, regardless of who is responsible."

Keenly aware of Clark's leadership skills, a rival coach once commented, "If Dutch stepped on the field with Red Grange, Jim Thorpe, and George Gipp, Dutch would be the general."

Although the Lions failed to repeat as NFL champions in 1936, Clark performed brilliantly, earning First-Team All-Pro honors for the fifth time by leading the league with seven rushing touchdowns and 73 points scored while also ranking among the leaders with 1,095 yards of total offense, 633 yards from scrimmage, and a rushing average of 5.1 yards per carry. By serving as the centerpiece of an offense that set a league rushing record (2,885 yards) that stood for 36 years, Clark also gained recognition as the NFL's most valuable player from UPI, which cited his talents as "the smartest

66 THE 50 GREATEST PLAYERS IN DETROIT LIONS HISTORY

quarterback in football" and his skills as a ball-carrier, passer, drop-kicker, and defensive player.

With Potsy Clark handing in his resignation at the end of 1936 to accept the head coaching job with the Brooklyn Dodgers, Clark added coaching duties to his list of responsibilities. He subsequently spent the next two seasons serving the Lions as player-coach, before announcing his retirement following the conclusion of the 1938 campaign with career totals of 2,772 rushing yards, 36 rushing touchdowns, 28 receptions, 341 receiving yards, six TD catches, 3,113 yards from scrimmage, 1,507 passing yards, 11 TD passes, 42 touchdowns, and 369 points scored; a rushing average of 4.6 yards per carry; and a 45.6 pass-completion percentage.

After retiring as an active player, Clark spent four years coaching the Cleveland Rams, leading them to an overall record of just 16–26–2, before leaving the game and returning to Pueblo, where he took a job as an insurance salesman. Excluding a brief tour of military duty during World War II, Clark continued to work in the insurance business until 1949, when he accepted the position of backfield coach for the Los Angeles Dons of the AAFC. After one year in that post, Clark spent the next four seasons coaching and serving as athletic director at the University of Detroit, before retiring from football altogether to become a sales representative for an engineering firm in Detroit. After living in the Detroit suburb of Royal Oak, Michigan, for more than two decades, Clark moved with his wife to Cañon City, Colorado, where he died from cancer at the age of 71 on August 5, 1978.

A member of the Pro Football Hall of Fame's inaugural class of 1963, Clark earlier found himself being named the outstanding football player of the 1930s by the AP, which, on according him that honor in 1940, noted, "He could do everything. An accurate punter, a great drop-kicker, a sure tackler, and a skillful, hard blocker, he was also one of the National League's better passers and had few equals as a runner. As a quarterback, he was virtually a coach on the field."

CAREER HIGHLIGHTS

Best Season

It could be argued that Clark played his best football for the Lions in 1934, when he established career-high marks with 763 yards rushing, 835 yards from scrimmage, 1,146 yards of total offense, eight touchdowns, 73 points scored, and a rushing average of 6.2 yards per carry. But Clark gained recognition from UPI as the league's most valuable player in 1936, when, while serving as general of an offense that set an NFL single-season rushing record that lasted until 1972, he gained 628 yards on the ground, amassed 633 yards from scrimmage and 1,095 yards of total offense, scored seven touchdowns and a league-leading 73 points, threw for a career-best 467 yards and four touchdowns, and completed a staggering (for that era) 53.5 percent of his passes.

Memorable Moments/Greatest Performances

Just three days after scoring a pair of touchdowns during a 19–0 victory over the Frankford Yellow Jackets, Clark led the Spartans to a 19–0 win over the Brooklyn Dodgers on October 18, 1931, by running for another three TDs.

Clark staked the Spartans to an early 7–0 lead in their 13–6 win over the Staten Island Stapletons on October 20, 1932, by scoring a touchdown on a 74-yard run.

Clark proved to be the difference in a 17–7 win over the Brooklyn Dodgers on November 6, 1932, successfully converting a 25-yard field goal attempt and gathering in a 65-yard touchdown pass from John Cavosie.

Clark led the Lions to a 28–0 win over the Dodgers on October 22, 1934, by carrying the ball 10 times for 97 yards and three touchdowns, the longest of which came on a 72-yard run.

Just six days later, on October 28, 1934, Clark led the Lions to a 38–0 rout of the Cincinnati Reds by gaining 194 yards on 16 carries and scoring two touchdowns, one of which came on a career-long 82-yard scamper.

Clark contributed to a 40–7 thrashing of the Pittsburgh Pirates on November 4, 1934, by gaining 110 yards on only nine carries and scoring a touchdown on a 45-yard run.

Despite gaining only 42 yards from scrimmage, Clark considered the Lions' 14–2 victory over the Chicago Bears on Thanksgiving Day 1935 to be the most memorable game of his career. After giving the Lions a 7–0 first-quarter lead by gathering in a 12-yard TD pass from Bill Shepherd, Clark scored their other touchdown in the third period when he ran 22 yards to paydirt after being on the receiving end of a lateral.

Clark helped lead the Lions to a 26–7 victory over the Giants in the 1935 NFL Championship Game by carrying the ball seven times for 80 yards and one touchdown, which came on a sensational 40-yard, first-quarter run.

THE 50 GREATEST PLAYERS IN DETROIT LIONS HISTORY

Clark led the Lions to a 13–7 win over the Bears on November 26, 1936, by throwing for 57 yards and carrying the ball 12 times for 118 yards and one touchdown, which came on a 51-yard run in the fourth quarter that provided the margin of victory.

Notable Achievements

- Averaged more than five yards per carry twice.
- Led NFL in total offense once, points scored three times, rushing touchdowns three times, and touchdowns once.
- Finished second in NFL in yards from scrimmage twice, all-purpose yards twice, total offense twice, points scored once, rushing touchdowns twice, touchdowns three times, and yards per rushing attempt three times.
- Ranks among Lions career leaders with 36 rushing touchdowns (3rd), 42 touchdowns (5th), and 369 points scored (9th).
- 1935 division champion.
- 1935 NFL champion.
- Six-time First-Team All-Pro selection (1931, 1932, 1934, 1935, 1936, and 1937).
- Named best player in NFL by UPI in both 1935 and 1936.
- Named outstanding player of the 1930s by the AP.
- Named to NFL 75th Anniversary All-Time Team in 1994.
- Named to NFL 100 All-Time Team in 2019.
- Number 7 retired by Lions.
- Named to Lions 75th Anniversary All-Time Team in 2008.
- Named to Lions All-Time Team in 2019.
- Inducted into Lions Ring of Honor in 2009.
- Inducted into Pro Football Hall of Fame in 1963.

10
DICK LEBEAU

art of the Lions' "4 Ls" defensive secondary that also included Gary Lowe and Hall of Famers Yale Lary and Dick "Night Train" Lane, Dick LeBeau spent his entire 14-year NFL career in Detroit, recording more interceptions than any other player in franchise history. Known for his intelligence and outstanding cover skills, LeBeau, who started at right cornerback most of his time in the Motor City, picked off at least five passes in a season seven times, earning in the process three Pro Bowl selections and two All-Pro nominations. An extremely durable player who missed just one game from 1960 to 1972, LeBeau proved to be a sure tackler as well, with his superb all-around play earning him a spot on the Lions All-Time Team in 2019 and a place in the Pro Football Hall of Fame.

Born in the small town of London, Ohio, on September 9, 1937, Charles Richard LeBeau grew up some 30 miles southwest of Columbus, where he starred in football and basketball at London High School. A quarterback and defensive back on the gridiron, LeBeau performed so well at both posts that he received an athletic scholarship to Ohio State University. Although LeBeau continued to excel on both sides of the ball in college under the tutelage of legendary head coach Woody Hayes, he gradually transitioned to running back on offense, where his strong play helped the Buckeyes capture the 1957 national championship.

Selected by Cleveland in the fifth round of the 1959 NFL Draft with the 58th overall pick, LeBeau arrived at his first pro training camp believing that he had an excellent chance to earn a roster spot as a member of the team's defensive secondary. However, the Browns waived him just days prior to the start of the regular season, prompting him to sign with the Lions as a free agent. LeBeau subsequently spent the first half of his rookie campaign on Detroit's taxi squad, before being promoted to the active roster in week 7. Starting at free safety and playing on special teams the rest of the year, LeBeau acquitted himself well, causing head coach George Wilson to name him the team's starting right cornerback prior to the start of the 1960 season.

Dick LeBeau recorded the most interceptions of any player in team annals.

Beginning a five-year stint during which he manned that post for the Lions, LeBeau contributed to one of the league's top-ranked defenses by registering four interceptions, which he returned a total of 58 yards. LeBeau followed that up with three more solid seasons, picking off a total of 12 passes and scoring three times on defense, before gaining Pro Bowl and All-Pro recognition for the first time in 1964. Moving to the left side of the Lions' defense in 1965, LeBeau had one of his finest seasons, earning Pro Bowl and All-Pro honors again by finishing second in the league with seven interceptions, before returning to his more familiar position of right cornerback the following year, when he garnered his third consecutive Pro Bowl selection.

Combining with Dick "Night Train" Lane his first few years in Detroit to give the Lions the finest cornerback tandem in the league, LeBeau proved to be nearly the equal of his Hall of Fame teammate in terms of his pass-coverage skills. Recalling the speedy LeBeau's ability to blanket his man downfield, former Lions receiver Pat Studstill, who later played against him as a member of the Rams, stated, "He was one guy I just didn't enjoy running patterns against, because he could cover you. For some reason, I couldn't beat him. I could beat Lem Barney, but I couldn't beat Dick Le-Beau. He always had me covered like a glove."

Although the 6'1" LeBeau weighed only 185 pounds, he did an excellent job of bringing down opposing ball-carriers, with Studstill remembering, "I saw Dick hit some people. I saw him tackle Jim Brown. I saw him tackle [Alan] Ameche. I saw him tackle some of the big guys. Dick was a hitter, he didn't care. He wasn't afraid to stick his nose in there. He wasn't a dirty player, but he'd hit you."

A superb ball-hawk, LeBeau received praise for his ability to follow the flight of the football from Bengals president Mike Brown (the son of then–Cleveland Browns head coach Paul Brown), who recalled, "He was a corner who could play the ball. When the ball was in the air, he had as much of a chance of getting it as the receiver did. He could judge its flight; it was easy for him."

In discussing everything LeBeau brought to the Detroit defense, Fran Tarkenton stated, "He was a great, great, great cornerback, and he played on the most dominating defense of the 1960s. In fact, that Lions defensive team in the 60s was the best defense I played against other than the Pittsburgh Steelers in their glory days. I mean, they had an All-Pro at every position, and LeBeau was one of them. . . . They were a nasty, nasty defense, a horror story. And Dick LeBeau was a great cornerback on a great defensive team. They were a nightmare."

Tarkenton continued, "Dick was a great cover guy. But he was also a great tackler. He had all the tools for being physical, for being fast, and for being able to cover, and having instincts. He knew how to play. He wasn't a whole lot of fun to play against."

A true student of the game, LeBeau became known for his ability to learn the tendencies of his opponents by breaking down film and reading scouting reports, with Pat Studstill saying, "Dick was astute when it came to football. He studied the game and came up with solutions when he was playing. A lot of coaches would ask him questions."

Joe Schmidt remembered, "I called the defensive signals, and Dick dropped information to me in the game that was helpful to me and helped our defense. And he had that information because he studied more

THE 50 GREATEST PLAYERS IN DETROIT LIONS HISTORY

than anybody else on the team. . . . As a player, he was always prepared, always knew what to do."

Lions Hall of Fame tight end Charlie Sanders also spoke highly of his former teammate, saying, "People would try to pick on him because, at 6'1", 185 pounds, he didn't have all the physical attributes that most guys had in the secondary. But the fact that he was as smart as he was and studied as much as he did, that's what made him excel—that's why he had the numbers. He was ahead of the quarterback."

Meanwhile, Lem Barney, who spent six seasons starting alongside LeBeau in the Lions' defensive secondary, credited his longtime teammate for much of the success he experienced during his career, telling the *New York Times*, "Dick taught me to be able to understand what offensive coordinators would try to do to you as a defensive back. Dick was a very astute defensive ballplayer, and with his insight and his intuition, he was almost like a coach out there playing."

Continuing to perform at an elite level for the Lions at right cornerback for five more seasons, LeBeau picked off another 30 passes from 1967 and 1971, bringing his career total to 62. Particularly outstanding in 1970, LeBeau gained unofficial Second-Team All-Pro recognition from the Pro Football Writers by finishing second in the league with a career-high nine interceptions. But after picking off six more passes the following year, LeBeau moved to free safety, where he spent the 1972 campaign sharing playing time with Al Randolph, before announcing his retirement at the end of the year. Over the course of 14 NFL seasons, LeBeau recorded 62 interceptions, amassed 762 interception-return yards, recovered nine fumbles, registered one and a half sacks, and scored four times on defense. LeBeau also appeared in 178 out of 179 games from 1960 to 1972, at one point putting together a string of 171 consecutive starts that set an NFL record for cornerbacks that Ronde Barber eventually broke.

Suggesting that LeBeau's consecutive starts streak revealed a lot about him as a player, Ron Borges of the *Boston Herald* wrote, "You don't start 171 straight games at cornerback if you can't play better than your average duck. You can say all you want about playing with other good guys, but it is undeniable you can't play that many games at that position if you can't play."

Most proud of that mark, LeBeau once stated, "My consecutive games played record—I think that says I was a guy who would come to work and play every week and didn't have to be in perfect health to play. I'm very proud of that. In fact, that's the only thing from playing I ever talk about."

Following his playing days, LeBeau embarked on a lengthy career in coaching that saw him serve as special teams coach for the Eagles

(1973–1975); defensive backs coach for the Packers (1976–1979), Bengals (1980–1983), and Steelers (1992–1994); defensive coordinator for the Bengals (1984–1991 and 1997–2000), Steelers (1995–1996 and 2004–2014), and Titans (2015–2017); assistant head coach of the Bills (2003); and head coach of the Bengals (2000–2002). Considered an "innovator" and a "defensive football genius," LeBeau created the famous "zone blitz" scheme during his time in Cincinnati.

Beloved by all his players, LeBeau received high praise from former Bengals linebacker Brian Simmons, who said, "He's proud of his career, and he deserves to be. But if you look at everything he's accomplished in this game, to go along with his playing, there aren't many people that have done as much as he has."

Although LeBeau's coaching career took him to many different cities, he still looks back fondly at his early years in Detroit, remembering, "It was a great time to be in Detroit, and a great time in my life. Motown was coming on, songs were playing. The American automobile was absolutely king of the world. Everybody in Detroit was working assembly lines around the clock, and everybody had money. I have great memories of being there, playing for the Lions. I made a lot of lifelong friends there. It was great."

LeBeau, who is approaching his 88th birthday as of this writing, also continues to hold a soft spot in his heart for the Lions, saying shortly before he retired from coaching, "I'll always have a lot of Honolulu blue and silver in me. You don't play for somebody for 14 years and not have it continue to be a part of your life as long as you're on the planet, and it's always a little surrealistic to be standing on one sideline and see the blue and silver guys on the other side. It was more so shortly after I retired [as a player], but it's still there a little bit. Yeah, I'll admit that."

CAREER HIGHLIGHTS

Best Season

Although LeBeau recorded a career-high nine interceptions in 1970, he earned his only two All-Pro nominations in 1964 and 1965. With LeBeau's seven picks, 84 interception-return yards, two fumble recoveries, and one touchdown in the second of those campaigns gaining him Second-Team All-Pro recognition from both the AP and the Newspaper Enterprise Association, we'll identify the 1965 season as the finest of his career.

74 THE 50 GREATEST PLAYERS IN DETROIT LIONS HISTORY

Memorable Moments/Greatest Performances

LeBeau recorded his first interception as a pro when he picked off a Johnny Unitas pass during a 30–17 win over the Colts on October 23, 1960.

LeBeau helped lead the Lions to a 37–23 victory over the Vikings on December 9, 1962, by returning a fumble 26 yards for a touchdown and recording two interceptions, one of which he returned 31 yards for a second TD.

LeBeau contributed to a 23–2 win over the Rams in the opening game of the 1963 regular season by returning an interception 70 yards for a touchdown.

LeBeau recorded two interceptions during a 45–7 pasting of the 49ers on November 3, 1963, returning his two picks a total of 55 yards.

LeBeau made a key play during the Lions' 35–28 win over the Eagles in the 1965 regular-season finale when he returned his interception of a Norm Snead pass 30 yards for a touchdown.

LeBeau contributed to a 28–14 victory over the Bears on October 5, 1970, by recording a pair of interceptions, which he returned a total of 43 yards.

LeBeau picked off another two passes during a 20–0 shutout of the Packers in the 1970 regular-season finale.

LeBeau recorded the final interception of his Hall of Fame career during a 28–3 win over the Bears on November 21, 1971, subsequently returning the ball 40 yards.

Notable Achievements

- Missed just one game from 1960 to 1972, at one point appearing in 171 consecutive contests.
- Scored four defensive touchdowns.
- Recorded at least five interceptions seven times.
- Amassed 158 interception-return yards in 1963.
- Finished second in NFL in interceptions twice.
- Led Lions in interceptions four times.
- Holds Lions career record for most interceptions (62).
- Ranks among Lions career leaders with 762 interception-return yards (3rd), three touchdown interceptions (tied for 3rd), 14 seasons played (3rd), and 185 games played (7th).
- Ranks 10th in NFL history in career interceptions.
- Three-time Pro Bowl selection (1964, 1965, and 1966).

- Two-time Second-Team All-Pro selection (1964 and 1965).
- 1966 Newspaper Enterprise Association Second-Team All-Pro selection.
- 1965 First-Team All-Western Conference selection.
- 1971 Second-Team All-NFC selection.
- Pro Football Reference All-1990s Second Team.
- Named to Lions 75th Anniversary All-Time Team in 2008.
- Named to Lions All-Time Team in 2019.
- Inducted into Lions Ring of Honor in 2010.
- Inducted into Pro Football Hall of Fame in 2010.

11

CHARLIE SANDERS

One of the NFL's first great pass-receiving tight ends, Charlie Sanders helped revolutionize his position with his ability to consistently contribute to his team's offense as more than just a blocker. Starting at tight end for the Lions from 1968 to 1977, Sanders led the team in receptions five times and receiving yards three times, en route to establishing himself as the franchise's career leader in the first category at the time of his retirement. An outstanding blocker as well, Sanders garnered seven Pro Bowl selections and three All-Pro nominations with his exceptional all-around play, before being further honored by being named to the Lions All-Time Team in 2019 and inducted into the Pro Football Hall of Fame.

Born in Richlands, North Carolina, on August 25, 1946, Charles Alvin Sanders grew up hardly knowing his mother, who passed away shortly after he turned two years of age. With Sanders's father serving in the U.S. Army, his aunt raised him in rural North Carolina, where he learned the value of hard work early in life, recalling, "The country, as I refer to it, is a place where a kid could be judged, his character could be judged, by how fast he was able to work alongside the adults."

Developing into a standout athlete at James Benson Dudley High School in Greensboro, Sanders starred in baseball, basketball, and football, performing so well in the last two sports that he received an athletic scholarship to the University of Minnesota. Continuing to excel on the court and gridiron in college, Sanders proved to be especially proficient in football, earning All-Big Ten honors at tight end as a senior in 1967 after playing on defense his first two seasons.

Selected by the Lions in the third round of the 1968 NFL Draft with the 74th overall pick, Sanders initially had reservations about going to Detroit, recalling, "I had come from the south, with the sit-ins, the segregation, and the racial turmoil. Of course, with the riots [in Detroit] having gone on, the first thing that popped into my mind was 'here we go again.'

Charlie Sanders helped revolutionize the position of tight end.

It wasn't something that I really wanted to be a part of again, or really have my family be involved in."

As a result, Sanders briefly considered playing for the Toronto Argonauts of the Canadian Football League, before ultimately signing with the Lions when general manager Russ Thomas offered him an extra $1,000 a year. An immediate starter on his arrival in the Motor City, Sanders earned Pro Bowl honors and a fourth-place finish in the NFL Offensive Rookie of the Year voting in 1968 by making 40 receptions for 533 yards and one touchdown. Sanders followed that up by averaging 38 receptions, 567 receiving yards, and five TD catches the next three seasons, earning in the process Pro Bowl, All-Pro, and First-Team All-NFC honors each year.

A trailblazer of sorts at the tight end position, Sanders significantly expanded the role of players who manned that post. Instead of functioning primarily as an in-line blocker who occasionally caught short passes just beyond the line of scrimmage, Sanders proved to be a serious downfield threat who kept defensive coordinators awake at night. A matchup nightmare, the 6'4", 225-pound Sanders possessed too much size for opposing defensive backs to guard one-on-one and too much speed for linebackers to cover, causing opposing teams to often double-team or even triple-team him.

Known for his acrobatic receptions, Sanders employed a unique catching style that included reaching out for the football until his entire body was almost parallel to the ground. He then collided with the turf just as the ball settled into his hands. In discussing his unusual manner of gathering in the football, Sanders said, "I would find myself in awkward positions. But I never thought about where my body was on the field. The only thing that was important to me was catching the football."

Former Lions quarterback Greg Landry said of his longtime teammate, "He's one of the few receivers I've ever seen who, when the ball comes to him, loses perspective of where he is. It wasn't until the ball was caught that he realized he might be parallel to the ground or that he was going to do a cartwheel. A lot of players wouldn't make the catches he did, but Charlie had that concentration."

After calling his former Lions teammate "just a tremendously great athlete," Lem Barney spoke of the confidence Sanders had in his own abilities, saying, "He was always a believer that we could win. He always thought if he could get the quarterback to throw it to him, he was going to catch it. He made some acrobatic catches. I'm telling you, one-legged, one arm in the air, floating through the air almost like Superman. If you threw it to him, he was going to find a way to catch it."

Barney added, "Without question, he's the greatest route-running tight end ever in the league and the greatest blocking tight end ever in the league."

Greg Landry also addressed Sanders's superior blocking ability when he stated, "He could hook people, hook linebackers, or hook defensive ends because he was so strong. He had strong legs, and he was strong in his arms, and he was a great blocker."

Sanders's physical style of play caused him to engage in many battles through the years with Chicago Bears middle linebacker Dick Butkus, whom he once described as a "maladjusted kid." When reminded of that quote years later, Sanders laughed and replied, "I was trying to be polite. . . . I often said during those years that Butkus would hit his own mother and not be happy unless her head was rolling on the field."

Limited to just nine games in 1972 by a fractured shoulder he sustained during the preseason, Sanders made only 27 receptions for 416 yards and two touchdowns. Although Sanders started every game the Lions played the following year, he posted similar numbers, concluding the campaign with 28 catches, 433 receiving yards, and two TDs. Returning to top form in 1974, Sanders earned Pro Bowl honors by making 42 receptions for 532 yards and three touchdowns. After gaining Pro Bowl recognition in each of the next two seasons as well, Sanders suffered a serious knee injury in a preseason game against the Atlanta Falcons in 1977 that forced him to retire at the end of the year. Over 10 NFL seasons, Sanders made 336 receptions, amassed 4,817 receiving yards, and caught 31 touchdown passes.

Inducted into the Pro Football Hall of Fame in 2007, Sanders received high praise at the induction ceremonies from his presenter, Lions chairman William Clay Ford Sr., who said of his longtime friend, "Charlie is what you look for today in a tight end. He was a pioneer at that position. You knew he was Hall of Fame material. He looked that way right off the bat."

Remaining with the organization long after his playing days ended, Sanders spent seven years working as a color analyst on the team's radio broadcasts and another eight coaching Lions wide receivers, before joining the team's scouting department. Promoted to the position of assistant director of player personnel in 2000, Sanders remained in that post until July 2, 2015, when he died from cancer at the age of 68.

On learning of his passing, Lions team president Tom Lewand issued a statement that read, "Today we lost one of the greatest Detroit Lions of all time. Charlie was a special person to the entire Lions family for nearly a half century. While never forgetting his North Carolina roots, 'Satch' became the consummate Detroit Lion on and off the field. He was a perfect ambassador for our organization and, more important, was a true friend, colleague, and mentor to so many of us."

In addressing the unselfish nature of Sanders—who, in addition to contributing to the greater Detroit community via the Lions' community relations department, the March of Dimes, and the United Way, launched the foundation Have a Heart, Save a Life in 2012 following the tragic death of high school basketball player Wes Leonard due to cardiac failure—former Detroit Pistons star and close personal friend Dave Bing stated, "Charlie did things not to bring attention to himself, but because it was the right thing to do. Helping those not as fortunate as he was."

Meanwhile, Herman Moore, who played under Sanders during the latter's tenure as Lions wide receivers coach, said of his one-time mentor, "The world lost a great man today, but Heaven gained another Angel!"

80   THE 50 GREATEST PLAYERS IN DETROIT LIONS HISTORY

CAREER HIGHLIGHTS

Best Season

Sanders had his finest statistical season in 1969, when, in addition to catching three touchdown passes, he established career-high marks with 42 receptions and 656 receiving yards. But he made a greater overall impact in 1970, when he helped the Lions advance to the playoffs by making 40 receptions for 544 yards and six touchdowns, earning in the process Pro Bowl honors, the first of his two straight First-Team All-Pro nominations, and a fifth-place finish in the NFL MVP voting.

Memorable Moments/Greatest Performances

Sanders scored the first touchdown of his career when he gathered in a 13-yard pass from Bill Munson during a 20–20 tie with the Saints on November 24, 1968.

Sanders starred in defeat in the final game of the 1968 regular season, making a career-high 10 receptions for 133 yards during a 14–3 loss to Washington.

Sanders helped the Lions forge a 14–14 tie with the Packers on November 1, 1971, by collaborating with quarterback Greg Landry on a 49-yard scoring play.

Sanders scored what proved to be the game-winning touchdown of a 24–20 victory over the Denver Broncos the following week, when he gathered in a five-yard pass from Landry in the fourth quarter.

Sanders contributed to a 32–21 win over the Kansas City Chiefs on November 25, 1971, by making five receptions for 90 yards and one touchdown.

Sanders helped lead the Lions to a 34–17 victory over the Rams in the final game of the 1972 regular season by making six receptions for 76 yards and two touchdowns.

Sanders starred during a 19–17 win over the Packers on October 27, 1974, making seven receptions for a career-high 146 yards and one touchdown, which came on an 11-yard connection with Bill Munson.

Notable Achievements

- Led Lions in receptions five times and receiving yards three times.
- Ranks among Lions career leaders with 336 receptions (8th), 4,817 receiving yards (7th), and 31 touchdown receptions (9th).
- 1970 Lions team MVP on offense.
- Finished tied for fifth in 1970 NFL MVP voting.
- Seven-time Pro Bowl selection (1968, 1969, 1970, 1971, 1974, 1975, and 1976).
- Two-time First-Team All-Pro selection (1970 and 1971).
- 1969 Second-Team All-Pro selection.
- Three-time First-Team All-NFC selection (1969, 1970, and 1971).
- Three-time Second-Team All-NFC selection (1974, 1975, and 1976).
- Named to Lions 75th Anniversary All-Time Team in 2008.
- Named to Lions All-Time Team in 2019.
- Inducted into Lions Ring of Honor in 2009.
- Inducted into Pro Football Hall of Fame in 2007.

12

MATTHEW STAFFORD

Some might argue that Bobby Layne's tremendous leadership ability and key role on Lions teams that won three NFL championships earned him a higher place on this list than Matthew Stafford. But Layne had the good fortune of being surrounded by superior talent and an outstanding defense most of his time in Detroit. Meanwhile, the Lions consistently fielded a porous defense and one of the league's least talented squads during Stafford's 12 seasons in the Motor City. And while Layne lacked elite passing skills, Stafford excelled in that regard, annually ranking among the league's top quarterbacks in most statistical categories. Factoring everything into the equation, I elected to place Stafford just ahead of Layne in these rankings.

Known for his strong throwing arm, mental and physical toughness, and commitment to his teammates, Matthew Stafford established himself as easily the most prolific passer and one of the most beloved players in franchise history during his time in Detroit. The Lions' primary signal-caller from 2009 to 2020, Stafford completed more passes for more yards and touchdowns than anyone else in team annals, throwing for more than 4,000 yards eight times while also tossing more than 30 TD passes twice. A member of the Lions All-Time Team, Stafford led Detroit to three playoff appearances, before departing for Los Angeles, where he won the Super Bowl in his first year with the Rams.

Born in Tampa, Florida, on February 7, 1988, John Matthew Stafford spent his early years living in Dunwoody, Georgia, before moving with his family at the age of three to Dallas, Texas, when his father obtained his graduate degree from the University of Georgia. A fan of the Dallas Cowboys during his youth, Stafford grew up close friends with Clayton Kershaw, with whom he played on the same youth soccer, baseball, basketball, and football teams. But while Kershaw eventually began to gravitate more toward baseball after the two enrolled at Highland Park High School,

Matthew Stafford holds franchise records for most pass completions, passing yards, and touchdown passes.
Courtesy of Mike Morbeck

Stafford chose to focus exclusively on football at the end of his sophomore year after excelling as both a quarterback on the gridiron and a pitcher on the diamond for two seasons.

Recalling his initial impression of Stafford, Highland Park head football coach Randy Allen said, "I heard about this seventh-grader who could throw the ball 70 yards in the air. He was going to be a great quarterback. He was already 6' tall. The first time I saw him throw was out in front of our house. He was throwing the ball out in the street. You could just tell he was going to be a great football player and a great quarterback."

Ending his high school career in style, Stafford led Highland Park to a perfect 15–0 record and the UIL 4A Division I State Championship in 2005 by throwing for 4,013 yards and 38 touchdowns, earning in the process *Parade* magazine All-America and EA Sports National Player of

84 THE 50 GREATEST PLAYERS IN DETROIT LIONS HISTORY

the Year honors. Regarded as a five-star recruit by Rivals.com, Stafford received several scholarship offers, before finally choosing to enroll at the University of Georgia.

A three-year starter for the Bulldogs, Stafford threw for 1,749 yards and seven touchdowns as a freshman, before leading Georgia to an 11–2 record and a No. 2 ranking in the final AP poll his sophomore year by passing for 2,523 yards and 19 touchdowns. Taking his game up a notch his junior year, Stafford led the Southeastern Conference (SEC) with 3,459 passing yards and completed a school-record 25 touchdown passes, after which he chose to skip his final season and declare himself eligible for the 2009 NFL Draft.

Selected by the Lions with the first overall pick, Stafford joined a team in Detroit that had failed to win a single game the previous season. Although the Lions ended up posting only two victories in 2009, Stafford, who passed for 2,267 yards, threw 13 touchdown passes and 20 interceptions, and completed 53.3 percent of his passes in his 10 starts as a rookie, gave an early indication of his tremendous resolve during a come-from-behind 38–37 victory over Cleveland in Week 11, when, just one play after separating his shoulder, he ignored the advice of team doctors and returned to the field to throw a game-winning one-yard TD pass as time expired in regulation.

Reinjuring his right shoulder during the early stages of the 2010 campaign, Stafford appeared in only three games, before undergoing season-ending surgery to repair an acromioclavicular joint and shave a clavicle. Fully healed by the start of the 2011 campaign, Stafford began a string of eight straight seasons in which he started every game the Lions played, posting the following numbers during that time:

2011: 5,038 yards passing, 41 TD passes, 16 interceptions, 63.5 completion percentage, 97.2 passer rating
2012: 4,967 yards passing, 20 TD passes, 17 interceptions, 59.8 completion percentage, 79.8 passer rating
2013: 4,650 yards passing, 29 TD passes, 19 interceptions, 58.5 completion percentage, 84.2 passer rating
2014: 4,257 yards passing, 22 TD passes, 12 interceptions, 60.3 completion percentage, 85.7 passer rating
2015: 4,262 yards passing, 32 TD passes, 13 interceptions, 67.2 completion percentage, 97.0 passer rating
2016: 4,327 yards passing, 24 TD passes, 10 interceptions, 65.3 completion percentage, 93.3 passer rating

2017: 4,446 yards passing, 29 TD passes, 10 interceptions, 65.7 completion percentage, 99.3 passer rating

2018: 3,777 yards passing, 21 TD passes, 11 interceptions, 66.1 completion percentage, 89.9 passer rating

Consistently ranking among the league leaders in pass completions, passing yards, and touchdown passes, Stafford earned NFL Comeback Player of the Year honors in 2011, when, in addition to setting single-season franchise records for most passing yards and TD passes, he became just the fourth quarterback in NFL history to throw for more than 5,000 yards in a season. A Pro Bowler in 2014, Stafford established a new single-season NFL mark two years later by leading the Lions to eight fourth-quarter comebacks. More importantly, the Lions advanced to the postseason three times, making the playoffs as a wild card in 2011, 2014, and 2016.

Blessed with a powerful throwing arm, the 6'3", 220-pound Stafford had the ability to complete passes few other quarterbacks in the league would even attempt. Equally effective at throwing the deep ball or hitting his receivers on short or intermediate routes, Stafford proved to be one of the league's finest pure passers, with one anonymous NFC executive stating after the Lions posted a losing record one year, "He plays in Detroit, so he's not in a position to maximize his ability. He's a major talent who'd probably be a top-five quarterback with an established franchise. He can score from anywhere on the field."

Although not much of a scrambler, Stafford also moved well in the pocket and had the ability to tuck the ball away, gaining almost 1,200 yards on the ground and rushing for 14 scores during his time in Detroit.

Revered by his teammates for his toughness and dedication to them, Stafford took the field for 136 consecutive contests, playing through injuries that included battered ribs, broken fingers, a sore ankle, and an aching back. When asked why he elected to play in a meaningless game at the end of one season, a bruised and battered Stafford responded, "Because I'm the quarterback of the Detroit Lions. And it's Sunday. I've got a bunch of teammates out there who are working their asses off. They fight to be available. And they fight to get out there and help us win. If there's any way I can play, I'm never going to not play. . . . I feel like I owe it to those guys. I owe it to the game. I owe it to this organization . . . everybody. If I'm good enough to play, healthy enough to play, my ass is going to be out there. I felt I was good enough to play Sunday, and I wanted to be out there."

Responding in kind, Stafford's teammates gave everything they had to him, with Lions tight end T. J. Hockenson stating, "He's probably the best dude, the best player, I've ever been around. Everybody on our team respects that guy. Like, everybody loves him."

Meanwhile, when asked why he wanted to remain in Detroit after he re-signed with the Lions, Calvin Johnson pointed to Stafford and said, "Who'd want to leave that?"

Also beloved by the fans of the Motor City for his willingness to give back to the community, Stafford and his wife, Kelly, donated $1 million to the S.A.Y. Detroit Play Center in 2015 and another $1 million a few years later for the purpose of funding an educational center in Detroit. And without much fanfare, Stafford and his wife started a tradition of choosing families in need over the Christmas holidays, purchasing all their gifts for them, and stopping by to spend the day with them.

Stafford's consecutive games played streak finally ended in 2019, when he missed the second half of the season with nondisplaced fractures in his upper thoracic spine. Returning to action the following year, Stafford had a solid season, completing 64.2 percent of his passes, throwing for 4,084 yards and 26 touchdowns, and posting a passer rating of 96.3. But with the Lions finishing the regular season just 5–11, they hired a new general manager (Brad Holmes) and a new head coach (Dan Campbell) the following offseason. Not wishing to play through another rebuild, Stafford, who had always maintained that he expected to end his career in Detroit, asked to be traded to a contending team. Granting Stafford's request, the Lions dealt him to the Los Angeles Rams for quarterback Jared Goff, a third-round pick in the 2021 NFL Draft, and a first-round selection in each of the subsequent two drafts.

Speaking with Mitch Albom of the *Detroit Free Press* some months later, Stafford expressed his frustration with the never-ending cycle that developed in Detroit during his time there, saying, "In my mind, I felt like I was going to be able to help us go win six, seven, eight games, because I wasn't gonna let us lose more than that, you know? But I probably wasn't good enough [by myself] to help us win *more* than that. And maybe we don't ever get those top picks that we needed."

Stafford, who left Detroit with career totals of 3,898 pass completions, 45,109 passing yards, 282 touchdown passes, and 144 interceptions; a pass-completion percentage of 62.6; and a passer rating of 89.9, struggled at times his first year in Los Angeles, throwing a league-high 17 interceptions. Nevertheless, he led the Rams to a first-place finish in the NFC West by passing for 4,886 yards and 41 touchdowns. Stafford subsequently performed well during the postseason, directing the Rams to playoff wins over Arizona, Tampa Bay, and San Francisco, before guiding them to a 23–20 victory over the Cincinnati Bengals in Super Bowl LVI.

Injured for much of 2022, Stafford appeared in only nine games, limiting him to just 2,087 passing yards and 10 TD passes. Healthy for most of the ensuing campaign, Stafford earned his second Pro Bowl nomination by amassing 3,965 passing yards and throwing 24 touchdown passes for a Rams team that ended up losing to the Lions in the wild card round of the playoffs by a score of 24–23. Stafford followed that up by throwing for 3,762 yards and 20 touchdowns in 2024, giving him career totals of 59,809 passing yards and 377 touchdown passes heading into the 2025 campaign. Stafford has also thrown 188 interceptions, completed 63.4 percent of his passes, and compiled a passer rating of 91.2 over the course of his career.

Although Stafford has spent the last four seasons playing on the West Coast, he still holds the city of Detroit close to his heart, saying, "I had a lot of experiences there over 12 years. All my daughters were born there. My wife and I went through things there that the team and the city, the town, everybody supported. So, I have nothing but great memories there. Obviously didn't get it done on the field as much as I wish we could have, but the people that I was lucky enough to know and grow with are people that I'm still close with today and mean a lot to me."

LIONS CAREER HIGHLIGHTS

Best Season

Stafford earned his lone Pro Bowl nomination as a member of the Lions in 2014, when he helped lead them to an 11–5 record and a berth in the playoffs by throwing for 4,257 yards and 22 touchdowns. Stafford also performed extremely well in 2015 and 2017, passing for 4,262 yards and 32 touchdowns, completing 67.2 percent of his passes, and posting a passer rating of 97.0 in the first of those campaigns, before throwing for 4,446 yards and 29 touchdowns, completing 65.7 percent of his passes, and compiling a passer rating of 99.3 in the second. But Stafford had his finest all-around season in 2011, when he led the Lions to a record of 10–6 and their first playoff appearance in more than a decade by ranking among the league leaders with 5,038 passing yards, 41 touchdown passes, a 63.5 pass-completion percentage, and a 97.2 passer rating.

88 THE 50 GREATEST PLAYERS IN DETROIT LIONS HISTORY

Memorable Moments/Greatest Performances

Stafford earned NFL Offensive Player of the Week honors for the only time as a member of the Lions by leading them to a 38–37 victory over the Browns on November 22, 2009, helping them overcome in the process a 21-point second-quarter deficit. Stafford, who finished the game with 422 yards passing and five touchdown throws, completed the comeback by hitting Brandon Pettigrew with a game-winning one-yard TD toss as time expired in regulation, just one play after having his left shoulder separated on a vicious hit.

Stafford displayed his mettle again during a 26–23 overtime win over the Vikings on September 25, 2011, when, despite being sacked five times, he threw for 378 yards and two touchdowns.

Stafford led the Lions to a 49–35 win over the Carolina Panthers on November 20, 2011, by passing for 335 yards and five touchdowns, the longest of which went 28 yards to Kevin Smith.

Stafford led the Lions to a dramatic 28–27 victory over the Oakland Raiders on December 18, 2011, by throwing for 391 yards and four touchdowns, two of which came in the game's final five minutes, with his six-yard toss to Calvin Johnson with just 39 seconds left on the clock providing the winning margin.

Although the Lions lost to the Packers, 45–41, in the final game of the 2011 regular season, Stafford threw for a career-high 520 yards and five touchdowns.

Stafford starred in defeat again on November 22, 2012, passing for 441 yards and two touchdowns during a 34–31 overtime loss to the Houston Texans.

In addition to throwing for 488 yards and one touchdown during a 31–30 victory over the Cowboys on October 27, 2013, Stafford scored the game-winning TD on a one-yard plunge with just 12 seconds left in regulation.

Stafford provided further heroics on November 9, 2014, when his 11-yard touchdown pass to Theo Riddick with just 29 seconds left in the final period gave the Lions a 20–16 win over Miami.

Stafford led the Lions to a 34–17 victory over the Bears on Thanksgiving Day 2014 by completing 34 of 45 pass attempts for 390 yards and two touchdowns.

Stafford had another big day against the Bears on October 18, 2015, throwing for 405 yards and four touchdowns during a 37–34 overtime win.

Stafford celebrated Thanksgiving Day 2015 by throwing for 337 yards and five touchdowns during a 45–14 victory over the Eagles, with three of his TD passes going to Calvin Johnson.

Stafford gave the Lions a 22–16 overtime win over the Vikings on November 6, 2016, by completing a 28-yard touchdown pass to Golden Tate nearly seven minutes into overtime.

Stafford gave the Lions a dramatic 23–22 victory over the Atlanta Falcons on October 25, 2020, when he hit T. J. Hockenson with an 11-yard TD pass as time expired in regulation.

En route to erasing a 10-point fourth-quarter deficit by leading the Lions on two scoring drives in the game's final five minutes, Stafford threw for 402 yards and three touchdowns during a 34–30 win over the Bears on December 6, 2020.

Notable Achievements

- Passed for more than 4,000 yards eight times, topping 5,000 yards once.
- Threw more than 30 touchdown passes twice, topping the 40 mark once.
- Completed more than 65 percent of passes four times.
- Posted passer rating above 90.0 seven times, finishing with a mark above 100.0 once.
- Posted touchdown-to-interception ratio of better than 2–1 seven times.
- Led NFL in pass completions once.
- Finished second in NFL in pass completions once and passing yards once.
- Holds Lions single-season records for most passing yards (5,038 in 2011) and most touchdown passes (41 in 2011).
- Holds Lions career records for most pass completions (3,898), passing yards (45,109), and touchdown passes (282).
- 2009 Week 11 NFL Offensive Player of the Week.
- 2011 NFL Comeback Player of the Year.
- 2011 NFL Alumni Quarterback of the Year.
- 2014 Pro Bowl selection.
- Named to Lions All-Time Team in 2019.

13

BOBBY LAYNE

A Hall of Fame quarterback whose numbers fail to do him justice, Bobby Layne spent parts of nine seasons in Detroit, serving as the central figure on teams that won four division titles and three NFL championships. A tremendous leader of men, Layne, who started behind center for the Lions from 1950 to 1957, earned the respect and admiration of his teammates with his fierce competitive spirit and quest for perfection. A solid passer as well, Layne led all NFL signal-callers in passing yards twice and touchdown passes once, with his strong play and superior leadership ability earning him four Pro Bowl selections, three All-Pro nominations, a place on the NFL 1950s All-Decade Team, a No. 52 ranking on the *Sporting News'* 1999 list of the 100 Greatest Players in NFL History, and a bust in Canton. Yet, despite his many accomplishments, Layne is remembered as much as anything for his colorful lifestyle, which ultimately led to his early passing.

Born in Santa Anna, Texas, on December 19, 1926, Robert Lawrence Layne spent his early years living on a farm in nearby Coleman County, before moving at the age of eight some 140 miles northeast, to the city of Fort Worth, to live with relatives after his father died of a heart attack. Eventually adopted by his aunt and uncle, Layne later moved with them to Highland Park, Texas, where he established himself as a star athlete at Highland Park High School. A member of the school's baseball, basketball, football, and track teams, Layne excelled in all four sports, earning All-State honors in both football and basketball his senior year while also performing so well as a pitcher on the diamond that he received a baseball scholarship to the University of Texas.

Continuing to excel on the mound in college, Layne compiled an overall record of 35–3 for the Longhorns, earning in the process All-SWC honors four straight times. Nearly choosing a different career path than the one he ultimately elected to pursue, Layne recalled years later, "When I went to Texas, all I wanted to do at first was play baseball."

Bobby Layne helped lead the Lions to four division titles and three NFL championships.
Courtesy of RMYAuctions.com

In the end, though, Layne's four All-Conference selections and two All-America nominations at quarterback convinced him that his future lay in football. Particularly outstanding his senior year, Layne, who acquired the nickname the "Blonde Bomber," gained consensus All-America recognition and earned a sixth-place finish in the Heisman Trophy voting.

Selected by the Steelers with the third overall pick of the 1948 NFL Draft, Layne balked at the idea of playing for a team that ran the single-wing offense, causing Pittsburgh to trade him to the Chicago Bears. But with the start of the football season still months away, Layne accepted an offer to play for the Lubbock Hubbers, a minor-league baseball team that competed in the West Texas–New Mexico League, explaining years later, "The only reason I did that was that some sportswriter said I couldn't compete with the pros, so that my record at Texas wasn't that big a deal. So, I just wanted to go out and show I could do it."

After a few months in the minors, Layne left baseball for good and joined the Bears, with whom he spent his first NFL season serving as a backup to Hall of Fame quarterback Sid Luckman. Not wishing to sit on the bench for another year, Layne requested a trade to another team, prompting George Halas to deal him to the New York Bulldogs for a first-round draft pick. Layne subsequently spent the 1949 season starting for the Bulldogs behind center, before being dealt to the Lions prior to the start of the ensuing campaign.

Making a huge impact on his arrival in Detroit, Layne led a team that had compiled an overall record of just 10–37 the previous four seasons to a mark of 6–6 in 1950 by leading the league with 2,323 yards passing and ranking among the leaders with 16 touchdown passes while also rushing for 250 yards and four TDs. Improving on those numbers in 1951, Layne gained Pro Bowl recognition for the first time by leading all NFL signal-callers with 2,403 yards passing and 26 touchdown passes, with his strong performance helping the Lions post a record of 7–4–1 that earned them a second-place finish in the NFL National Division.

Although Layne posted relatively modest numbers the next three seasons, throwing for more than 2,000 yards just once and completing a total of only 49 touchdown passes, he earned two Pro Bowl selections, two All-Pro nominations, and one top-five finish in the NFL MVP voting by leading the Lions to three straight division titles and back-to-back NFL championships in 1952 and 1953.

The most prominent figure on each of those championship teams, Layne served as the unquestioned leader of squads that also included fellow Hall of Famers Lou Creekmur, Dick Stanfel, Jack Christiansen, Yale Lary, and former high school teammate Doak Walker. Exhibiting a will to win second to none, Layne, who once said, "I wanted to win. That's all I wanted to do was to win a championship," demanded perfection from himself as well as his teammates, with Walker saying, "He demanded only the best and would accept only the best. Here is a man who was a general on the field and off the field in every way. He was the greatest two-minute quarterback I have ever seen."

Lou Creekmur, who spent most of his career protecting Layne's blindside, said of his longtime teammate, "Bobby Layne was probably the greatest leader that I've ever been around. If you were in a war, he'd be like a Napoleon. He could just lead the troops to any victory that he wanted to lead them to."

Creekmur also discussed Layne's fiery temperament and confrontational nature when he said, "If you ever missed a block, Layne made sure everybody knew about it. Guys on the field, guys on the bench, everybody in the stadium knew it. He'd call you right out of the huddle. He would stand there, raving at you and shaking a finger in your face, and you wanted to punch him. A couple of times, we had to grab people to keep them from hitting Bobby."

Former Lions teammate LaVern Torgeson added, "I've seen him chase teammates out of the huddle, send 'em to the sideline if they missed a block."

Meanwhile, New York Giants Hall of Fame linebacker Sam Huff stated, "Most quarterbacks are quiet, kind of laid back and easy going. They let their performance act as leadership. Bobby had the competitive spirit of a linebacker."

Extremely confident in his own abilities, Layne once proclaimed, "I never really lost a game in my career, sometimes I just ran out of time."

Although the 6'1", 200-pound Layne did not possess ideal size, a particularly strong throwing arm, or tremendous accuracy on his passes, his many intangible qualities enabled him to rise to the upper echelon of NFL quarterbacks, with former 49ers head coach Red Hickey commenting, "Layne, as bad as he looked throwing the ball, was a winner. You'd work him out and you wouldn't want him, but you'd want him in your huddle. Players feel that way about a quarterback. When a leader's in there, they'll perform."

In addition to his leadership ability, Layne became known for his exuberant lifestyle away from the playing field, which included womanizing, drinking to excess, and staying out until all hours of the evening. In discussing Layne's partying ways, LaVern Torgeson, who roomed with him for one season, claimed that he remained his roommate only "until about Tuesday each week," adding, "He'd have left me far behind by then. Some players could function that way; I couldn't."

Describing what a night on the town with Layne was like, Joe Schmidt recalled, "It was like walking into a room with Babe Ruth—everybody knew him, tables down front, drinks for everyone, and big tips to the musicians. You'd have a good time but pay for it the next day."

While Layne's raucous behavior only added to his mystique, he maintained that teammates, opponents, and reporters greatly exaggerated his excesses, suggesting, "I don't think there's any way possible I could have played for 15 years if I had done all the things I'm supposed to have done. If you ever get your name in the paper with that kind of reputation, it's going to continue. Other pro athletes did the same things I did. I was just too open with mine."

Layne remained Detroit's full-time starter behind center for two more seasons, leading all NFL quarterbacks with a 53.0 pass-completion percentage in 1955, before earning Pro Bowl and First-Team All-Pro honors the following year by directing the Lions to a regular-season record of 9–3. But after sharing playing time with Tobin Rote for much of 1957, Layne sustained a season-ending injury in week 11, when he broke his leg in three places during a 20–7 win over the Cleveland Browns. And with Rote subsequently leading the Lions to the NFL championship, ownership decided to trade Layne to the Pittsburgh Steelers for quarterback Earl Morrall and two draft picks during the early stages of the ensuing campaign.

Upset over the loss of their leader, Layne's teammates wondered why the front office had elected to part ways with him, with Alex Karras remembering, "My reaction, like everyone else, was 'why?' No one could give us a real explanation, and that disturbed a lot of us. Once he was gone, the team just wasn't what it used to be. It must have been something he must have done that wasn't good for the NFL."

While rumors abounded that Layne had been exiled from Detroit because he had become involved in organized gambling, he refuted those reports, saying, "I know I've been accused of betting on games, especially when my team loses, but I take it with a grain of salt. Losing gamblers grumble no matter what happens. First of all, I would have to be crazy to endanger my livelihood for a few thousand dollars . . . but I owe a lot to football, and to jeopardize my reputation would be ridiculous. Even if I had been betting, it would have come out in the open long ago."

Angry over the team's decision to send him elsewhere, Layne supposedly put a curse on the organization on his way out the door, saying that the Lions would not win a championship for another 50 years. When asked about his parting shot years later, Layne said, "We had been very successful in Detroit. . . . I really didn't know what to think. I tried what they referred to as a hex."

Although Layne's son, Alan, told the *Detroit Free Press* in 2017 that he never heard his father say a bad word about the Lions, he revealed that his mother told him that the curse was real.

Layne, who, during his time in the Motor City, passed for 15,710 yards and 118 touchdowns, threw 142 interceptions, completed 49 percent of his passes, posted a passer rating of 63.7, ran for 1,793 yards and 13 touchdowns, and successfully converted 18 of the 26 field goals he attempted in his two years as the team's primary placekicker, ended up spending the next five seasons starting at quarterback for the Steelers, earning two more Pro Bowl selections and another two All-Pro nominations, before announcing his retirement following the conclusion of the 1962 campaign. Over parts of 15 NFL seasons, Layne passed for 26,768 yards, threw 196 touchdown passes and 243 interceptions, completed 49 percent of his passes, posted

BOBBY LAYNE **95**

a passer rating of 63.4, ran for 2,451 yards and 25 touchdowns, and successfully converted 34 of his 50 field goal attempts. At the time of his retirement, Layne ranked first in NFL history in career pass attempts, completions, passing yards, touchdown passes, and interceptions.

Following his playing days, Layne remained in the game for five more years, serving as quarterbacks coach for the Steelers from 1963 to 1965 and as a scout for the Dallas Cowboys from 1966 to 1967, before becoming a businessman in his home state of Texas, where his business ventures included farms, bowling alleys, real estate, oil, and the stock market. Layne lived until December 1, 1986, when, following an extended battle with cancer, he died of cardiac arrest at the age of 59, with doctors subsequently attributing his health issues to a chronic liver ailment brought on by years of alcohol abuse.

Some years earlier, Layne told writer Mickey Herskowitz in his book *The Golden Age of Pro Football: A Remembrance of Pro Football in the 1950s*, "I'll tell you what I really miss. What I miss is the guys. That's what I miss more than anything. I miss going to training camp. I miss the road trips and the card games. . . . I miss the fellowship. The locker room, the places where it was a pleasure to be. The practice sessions. I miss the bar where we'd go for a beer after practice. . . . I miss the ball games. I mean, when you've got a whole team looking forward to everything, when you've got guys showing up for practice early and staying late—well, you've got something there. We had that perfect thing for a while."

LIONS CAREER HIGHLIGHTS

Best Season

Layne gained First-Team All-Pro recognition in both 1952 and 1956 by leading the Lions to identical 9–3 records and the NFL championship in the first of those campaigns. But Layne posted the best overall numbers of his career in 1951, when, in addition to leading the league with 152 pass completions, 2,403 passing yards, and 26 touchdown passes, he ranked among the circuit leaders with a 67.6 passer rating.

Memorable Moments/Greatest Performances

Layne led the Lions to a 45–21 victory over the Baltimore Colts on December 3, 1950, by throwing for 341 yards and three touchdowns, the longest of which went 82 yards to Cloyce Box.

Layne helped the Lions begin the 1951 campaign on a positive note by passing for 310 yards and two touchdowns while also running for 47 yards and one TD during a 35–17 win over Washington in the opening game of the regular season.

Layne led the Lions to a 41–28 victory over the Bears on November 11, 1951, by throwing for 259 yards and four touchdowns, connecting twice with Leon Hart and once each with Dorne Dibble and Pat Harder.

Less than two weeks later, on November 22, 1951, Layne led the Lions to a 52–35 win over the Packers by passing for 296 yards and four touchdowns, the longest of which went 35 yards to Doak Walker.

Layne posted nearly identical numbers during a 45–21 victory over the Bears on December 7, 1952, once again throwing for 296 yards and four touchdowns, with three of his TD passes going to Cloyce Box.

Layne had a big day against the Steelers in week 1 of the 1953 regular season, passing for 364 yards and two touchdowns during a 38–21 Lions win, with the longest of his TD passes going 49 yards to Leon Hart.

Layne gave the Lions a 17–16 victory over the Browns in the 1953 NFL Championship Game when he delivered a 33-yard touchdown pass to Jim Doran in the final minutes.

After replacing an ineffective Tobin Rote behind center late in the third quarter, Layne led the Lions to a come-from-behind 31–27 win over the Baltimore Colts on October 20, 1957, by guiding them on three touchdown drives in the final period, with his 29-yard TD pass to Howard "Hopalong" Cassady with just 46 seconds left in regulation providing the margin of victory.

Notable Achievements

- Missed just one game from 1950 to 1957, appearing in 95 of 96 contests.
- Passed for more than 2,000 yards three times.
- Threw more than 20 touchdown passes once (26 in 1951).
- Led NFL in pass completions once, pass-completion percentage once, passing yards twice, touchdown passes once, points scored once, and field goal percentage once.
- Finished second in NFL in pass completions and passing yards once each.
- Ranks among Lions career leaders with 1,074 pass completions (3rd), 15,710 passing yards (3rd), and 118 touchdown passes (2nd).
- Four-time division champion (1952, 1953, 1954, and 1957).
- Three-time NFL champion (1952, 1953, and 1957).

- Four-time Pro Bowl selection (1951, 1952, 1953, and 1956).
- Two-time First-Team All-Pro selection (1952 and 1956).
- 1954 Second-Team All-Pro selection.
- 1956 First-Team All-Western Conference selection.
- Pro Football Hall of Fame All-1950s Team.
- Pro Football Reference All-1950s Second Team.
- Number 52 on the *Sporting News'* 1999 list of the 100 Greatest Players in NFL History.
- Number 22 retired by Lions.
- Named to Lions 75th Anniversary All-Time Team in 2008.
- Named to Lions All-Time Team in 2019.
- Inducted into Lions Ring of Honor in 2009.
- Inducted into Pro Football Hall of Fame in 1967.

14
HERMAN MOORE

The second-leading receiver in Lions history, Herman Moore proved to be one of the NFL's most dynamic wideouts for much of the 1990s. Just the second player ever to surpass 100 receptions in three consecutive seasons, Moore accomplished the feat in the middle of an exceptional seven-year run during which he also amassed more than 1,000 receiving yards four straight times. A member of teams that won two division titles and made six playoff appearances, Moore earned four Pro Bowl selections and three First-Team All-Pro nominations during his 11 seasons in Detroit, before being further honored by being named to the Lions All-Time Team in 2019 and gaining induction into the team's Ring of Honor.

Born in Danville, Virginia, on October 20, 1969, Herman Joseph Moore received his introduction to football at the age of six in a local pee-wee league, where he learned a valuable life lesson. The smallest boy on his team, Moore grew increasingly frustrated with his lack of success, causing him to rip off his pads during practice one day and inform his coach that he no longer wished to play. Subsequently admonished by his mother, who told him that he should never quit anything he started, Moore stated years later, "That proved to be one of the best messages ever. I said, 'Momma, I promise I'll never quit again.'"

Living up to his vow, Moore continued to compete on the gridiron, eventually landing a spot on the George Washington High School football team. However, he failed to distinguish himself, serving the squad primarily as a placekicker and part-time tight end and wide receiver. Far more successful in track and field, Moore excelled in the high jump, once leaping more than 7'.

Offered an athletic scholarship to the University of Virginia, Moore had to spend the summer following his high school graduation working hard to improve his grades in order to become eligible to compete in any varsity sports. Having done so, Moore made both the football and the track and field teams as a freshman, catching 24 passes, amassing 466 receiving yards,

Herman Moore ranks second in franchise history in receptions, receiving yards, and touchdown catches.
Courtesy of George A. Kitrinos

and scoring four touchdowns as a starting wide receiver while also setting a school record by high jumping 7'2½" at the ACC indoor track meet.

Choosing to focus more on further developing his football skills as his college career progressed, Moore gradually emerged as one of the finest receivers in the nation, making 36 receptions for 848 yards and 10 touchdowns as a sophomore, before gaining consensus First-Team All-America recognition his junior year by catching 54 passes and leading the ACC with 1,190 receiving yards and 13 touchdown receptions.

100   THE 50 GREATEST PLAYERS IN DETROIT LIONS HISTORY

Making excellent use of his size and outstanding leaping ability, the 6'4", 210-pound Moore presented an inviting target to Cavaliers quarterback Shawn Moore (no relation), who stated, "All I have to do is get it near Herman and he'll go get it."

Meanwhile, after studying films of Virgina games prior to his team's meeting with the Cavaliers, Notre Dame head coach Lou Holtz said of Moore, "He's as good a big receiver as I've seen in a long, long time."

Choosing to forgo his final year of college, Moore declared himself eligible for the 1991 NFL Draft, where the Lions selected him in the first round with the 10th overall pick. Moore subsequently spent most of his rookie campaign sitting on the bench, making just 11 receptions for 135 yards, with his frequent struggles to hold on to the football causing many to wonder if the Lions had made a mistake by spending such a high draft pick on him. However, Moore, who had worn contact lenses in college but discarded them once he turned pro, began to fulfill his enormous potential after he underwent an eye exam prior to the start of his second season that revealed his problems lay in his vision.

Despite being limited by injuries to just 12 games in 1992, Moore made 51 receptions, amassed a team-high 966 receiving yards, and scored four touchdowns. Improving on those numbers slightly in 1993, Moore helped the Lions capture the NFC Central Division title by leading the team with 61 receptions, 935 receiving yards, and six TD catches, before establishing himself as one the NFL's most productive wideouts by posting the following numbers over the course of the next five seasons:

1994: 72 receptions, 1,173 receiving yards, 11 touchdown receptions
1995: **123** receptions, 1,686 receiving yards, 14 touchdown receptions
1996: 106 receptions, 1,296 receiving yards, 9 touchdown receptions
1997: **104** receptions, 1,293 receiving yards, 8 touchdown receptions
1998: 82 receptions, 983 receiving yards, 5 touchdown receptions

In addition to leading the NFL in receptions twice, Moore consistently placed near the top of the league rankings in receiving yards and touchdown catches as well, earning in the process four Pro Bowl selections and three All-Pro nominations. By surpassing 100 receptions in three straight seasons, Moore joined Jerry Rice (1994–1996) on a then-extremely exclusive list of players to accomplish the feat. Meanwhile, Moore combined with fellow Lions wideout Brett Perriman in 1995 to set an NFL single-season record for most total catches (231) and receiving yards (3,174) by two teammates.

Although Moore, who posted a time of 4.6 seconds in the 40-yard dash at the NFL Scouting Combine, possessed decent speed, he relied much more on his size and exceptional leaping ability to get the best of his defender. Downplaying his lack of high-end speed, Moore stated, "It's something that gets you respect, but now I think it's not necessary. What's really important is an awareness of where everyone is. I can sense where the defenders are. . . . You know, I've never really been hit hard."

Blessed with outstanding instincts and the ability to read his quarterback's mind, Moore developed a particularly strong connection with Scott Mitchell, with whom he experienced his greatest success. In recalling the synergetic nature of their relationship, Mitchell said, "We had an amazing chemistry on the field, and it was really fun to experience. It's really the guys that you play with more than anything. We would look at each other on the field and, in that moment, I just knew where he was going to go. I knew what he expected, and he knew the same thing. And, so often, we were able to connect and make a lot of big plays just having that relationship."

Unfortunately, Moore's days as an elite receiver ended in 1999, when he suffered the first in a series of injuries that caused him to experience a precipitous decline in production. Plagued by a knee injury that limited him to just eight games, Moore made only 16 receptions for 197 yards and two touchdowns. Moore subsequently spent the 2000 season playing with an ailing shoulder, making 40 receptions for 434 yards and three TDs, before appearing in only three games the following year after tearing an abdominal muscle. Released by the Lions following the conclusion of the 2001 campaign, Moore ended his 11-year stint in Detroit with 670 receptions, 9,174 receiving yards, and 62 touchdown catches, all of which represented franchise records at the time. After being released by the Lions, Moore signed with the Giants, with whom he appeared in just one game in 2002, before announcing his retirement.

Returning to the Detroit area following his playing days, Moore founded Team 84, a marketing and advertising enterprise that has now spent more than a decade serving as a holding company for many different types of businesses that provide various services to companies across the globe. Moore, whose father died from prostate cancer in 1999, has also been involved with Game On Cancer, an organization that helps raise money for cancer treatment and research.

THE 50 GREATEST PLAYERS IN DETROIT LIONS HISTORY

LIONS CAREER HIGHLIGHTS

Best Season

Moore posted the best numbers of his career in 1995, when he earned the first of his three straight First-Team All-Pro nominations and a fourth-place finish in the NFL Offensive Player of the Year voting by making a league-leading and single-season franchise record 123 receptions while also ranking among the circuit leaders with 1,686 receiving yards and 14 touchdown receptions.

Memorable Moments/Greatest Performances

Moore contributed to a 38–6 win over the Cowboys in the divisional round of the 1991 playoffs by making six receptions for 87 yards and one touchdown, which represented his first as a pro.

Moore went over 100 receiving yards for the first time in his career during a 38–7 win over Tampa Bay on October 25, 1992, finishing the game with three catches for 108 yards and one touchdown, which came on a 63-yard connection with Rodney Peete.

Moore collaborated with Peete on a career-long 93-yard touchdown reception during a 30–27 win over the Vikings on October 31, 1993.

Moore helped lead the Lions to a 28–25 overtime victory over the Giants on October 30, 1994, by making nine receptions for 106 yards and two touchdowns.

Moore torched the Buffalo defensive secondary for seven catches, 169 receiving yards, and one touchdown during a 35–21 win over the Bills on Thanksgiving Day 1994.

Moore earned NFL Offensive Player of the Week honors by making six receptions for 147 yards and three touchdowns during a 24–16 win over the Packers on October 29, 1995, with the longest of his TDs coming on a 69-yard connection with Scott Mitchell.

Although the Lions lost to Atlanta, 34–22, the following week, Moore had another big game, making nine receptions for 176 yards.

Moore gained recognition as NFC Offensive Player of the Week by making 14 receptions for 183 yards and one touchdown during a 27–7 win over the Bears on December 4, 1995, scoring his TD on a 46-yard pass from Scott Mitchell.

Moore earned that distinction again by making 10 receptions for 130 yards and one touchdown during a 38–15 victory over the Vikings on November 16, 1997.

Moore continued to be a thorn in the side of the Vikings the next time the two teams met on December 14, 1997, giving the Lions a 14–13 win over their division rivals by gathering in a one-yard TD pass from Scott Mitchell with just three seconds left in regulation.

Notable Achievements

- Surpassed 100 receptions three times.
- Surpassed 1,000 receiving yards four times, topping 1,500 yards once.
- Scored more than 10 touchdowns twice.
- Led NFL in receptions twice.
- Finished second in NFL in receptions once and yards per reception once.
- Led Lions in receptions and receiving yards six times each.
- Holds Lions single-season record for most receptions (123 in 1995).
- Ranks among Lions career leaders with 670 receptions (2nd), 9,174 receiving yards (2nd), 9,174 yards from scrimmage (3rd), 9,174 all-purpose yards (3rd), 62 touchdown receptions (2nd), 62 touchdowns (3rd), and 376 points scored (8th).
- Two-time division champion (1991 and 1993).
- 1995 Week 9 NFL Offensive Player of the Week.
- Two-time NFC Offensive Player of the Week.
- Finished fourth in 1995 NFL Offensive Player of the Year voting.
- Four-time Pro Bowl selection (1994, 1995, 1996, and 1997).
- Three-time First-Team All-Pro selection (1995, 1996, and 1997).
- Three-time First-Team All-NFC selection (1995, 1996, and 1997).
- Named to Lions 75th Anniversary All-Time Team in 2008.
- Named to Lions All-Time Team in 2019.
- Inducted into Lions Ring of Honor in 2018.

15
LOMAS BROWN

Known for his consistency and longevity, Lomas Brown spent 11 of his 18 NFL seasons in Detroit, serving as a pivotal piece of an offensive line that helped Barry Sanders realize his greatness. The Lions' starting left tackle from 1985 to 1995, Brown proved to be a huge contributor to teams that made four playoff appearances and won two division titles, creating gaping holes through which Sanders could run while also providing excellent pass-protection for the plethora of signal-callers that lined up behind center for the blue and silver. A six-time Pro Bowler who missed just nine non-strike games the Lions played during his 11 years in the Motor City, Brown also earned three All-Pro nominations and three First-Team All-NFC selections, before being further honored by being named to the Lions All-Time Team in 2019 and gaining induction into the team's Ring of Honor in 2023.

Born in Miami, Florida, on March 30. 1963, Lomas Brown Jr. displayed little interest in football during his formative years, preferring instead to develop his skills as a musician. Originally a trombone player for the band at Miami Springs High School, Brown had no intention of actively participating on the gridiron until the school's principal, having taken note of his size and athletic ability, strongly encouraged him to join the varsity team.

Eventually emerging as a standout two-way lineman, Brown performed so well that he received scholarship offers from several major college programs, including the University of Pittsburgh, Miami University, and the University of Florida. After initially committing to Pittsburgh, Brown changed his mind when his father suffered a heart attack on the night of his final high school game, recalling, "Right then, I decided to stay closer. I wanted to stay closer to home because of his health. I had to leave Miami because I started to run with the wrong group of kids there, and I knew if I stayed down in Miami, I would get myself in trouble. When the University of Florida came calling, I figured that was a great spot. It was five hours from home. It was far enough from home to keep the troublemakers away from me, but it was close enough that, if I had to get home, I could get there."

Lomas Brown earned six Pro Bowl and three All-Pro nominations during his time in Detroit.

A four-year starter for the Gators at offensive tackle, Brown earned numerous individual accolades while playing under head coach Charley Pell. In addition to gaining All-SEC recognition twice, Brown, who served as the anchor of an offensive line that became known as the "Great Wall of Florida," earned consensus First-Team All-America honors and won the Jacobs Blocking Trophy as the SEC's top blocker as a senior in 1984.

In expressing his admiration for his star lineman at one point during the 1983 campaign, Pell told the *Miami News*, "When we think about the potential of Lomas Brown, he must be projected as the type of player who one day could be looking back at a professional career where he's been an All-Pro for a decade or so. He's that good."

106   THE 50 GREATEST PLAYERS IN DETROIT LIONS HISTORY

Similarly impressed with Brown, the Lions made him the sixth overall pick of the 1985 NFL Draft when they selected him early in the first round. Immediately inserted at left tackle on his arrival in Detroit, Brown started all 16 games the Lions played at that post, earning a spot on the NFL All-Rookie Team with his strong play. Although Brown continued to perform well for the Lions at left tackle the next four seasons, their failures as a team prevented him from garnering any sort of postseason honors. All that changed, though, in 1990, when second-year running back Barry Sanders won the first of his four NFL rushing titles. With Sanders gaining 1,470 yards on the ground, Brown finally received the credit he deserved for his exceptional blocking up front, gaining Pro Bowl recognition for the first time.

A Pro Bowler in each of the next five seasons as well, Brown also earned All-Pro honors three times by helping Sanders rush for more than 1,500 yards on three separate occasions. Meanwhile, the Lions gradually emerged as a force to be reckoned with, winning two division titles and advancing to the playoffs four times from 1991 to 1995.

An excellent run blocker, the 6'4", 282-pound Brown possessed the size and strength to outmuscle his man at the point of attack and the quickness to lead Lions runners downfield. Outstanding in pass-protection as well, Brown did an expert job of protecting the blind side of quarterbacks Eric Hipple, Chuck Long, Rusty Hilger, Bob Gagliano, Rodney Peete, Andre Ware, Erik Kramer, and Scott Mitchell while being left on an island against many of the NFL's top pass-rushers in the run-and-shoot offense the Lions employed much of his time in the Motor City.

A team leader both on and off the field, Brown earned the respect and admiration of his teammates with his strong work ethic and quest for perfection, with Bennie Blades stating, "Lomas gets the best out of you. One of the toughest people I've ever played with."

Herman Moore also spoke of the demands Brown made on himself and his teammates, recalling, "You think about the gritty guys like Lomas—we held one another accountable for high standards, and you had to go out and do your best."

Nevertheless, the always outspoken Brown occasionally got himself into trouble by saying too much, as he did when he guaranteed a victory over the Philadelphia Eagles prior to their 1995 playoff game matchup. Using Brown's quotes as bulletin-board material, the Eagles subsequently scored 51 of the game's first 58 points, en route to recording a 58–37 win.

Leaving Detroit on that sour note, Brown signed with the Arizona Cardinals when he became a free agent following the conclusion of the 1995 campaign. Brown, who, in his 11 seasons with the Lions, started 163 out of the 164 contests in which he appeared, ended up spending three years in

Arizona, earning one more Pro Bowl selection, before splitting his final four seasons between the Cleveland Browns, New York Giants, and Tampa Bay Buccaneers. Choosing to announce his retirement after winning a Super Bowl as a backup with Tampa Bay in 2002, Brown ended his career having appeared in a total of 263 games, 251 of which he started.

Following his playing days, Brown began a career in broadcasting that started with an eight-year stint as an analyst at ESPN. However, Brown's stay at that network ended shortly after he admitted during a 2012 interview that he once purposely let Green Bay defensive end Sean Jones sack Scott Mitchell in the hope that the struggling quarterback might suffer an injury that would force him to leave the game. On learning of his former teammate's comments, a stunned Mitchell, who sustained a broken finger on the play, stated, "I had Lomas in my home. . . . I'm dumbfounded that he would do such a thing. . . . For him to allow someone to take a shot at a teammate, that's crazy."

Appearing on an episode of ESPN's *First Take* less than a week later, Brown expressed remorse for his actions, saying, "It's one play out of the 18,000 that I regret. . . . I'm not going to retract. I'm not going to sit here and make excuses. . . . The one thing I can say is I should have been more tactful at how I said that. That was wrong on my part. I should have humbly said that. It came off as boastful, and I shouldn't have said it that way. I said it, I can't take it back, but I shouldn't have said it the way I said it."

Mitchell eventually forgave Brown, with both men indicating after reviewing footage of the play in question that the latter did not actually miss his block. But Brown's image remained tarnished somewhat, perhaps even more so after he admitted that he may have fabricated the story to further his career with ESPN, stating, "I blanked out. . . . I started ranting and raving about what I did. . . . Until I saw the play, I actually thought I did it."

Relieved of his duties shortly thereafter, Brown subsequently reinvented himself as a business entrepreneur, becoming the CEO of LBJB Sports, a sports marketing firm in Detroit he founded more than a decade ago. The philanthropic Brown, who, while still playing in the NFL, started the Lomas Brown Jr. Foundation, which provides financial assistance to students seeking to further their education, also hosts free football camps in Detroit for local high school students and contributes to several other charitable causes. Brown also serves as the color analyst for Lions broadcasts on WJR Radio, a position he has held since 2018.

Looking back fondly on the 11 years he spent in Detroit, Brown says, "We never got to the Super Bowl with the Lions, but we still bleed Honolulu Blue and Silver. We appreciate the journey. It was hard times, but when I look back, I appreciate it."

108   THE 50 GREATEST PLAYERS IN DETROIT LIONS HISTORY

LIONS CAREER HIGHLIGHTS

Best Season

Brown had arguably the finest season of his career in 1995, when he earned his lone First-Team All-Pro nomination by helping the Lions lead the NFL in total yards gained on offense and place second in the circuit in points scored (436).

Memorable Moments/Greatest Performances

Brown helped the Lions amass a season-high 421 yards of total offense during a 40–27 win over the Denver Broncos on November 22, 1990, with 248 of those yards coming through the air and the other 173 on the ground.

The strong play of Brown and his linemates enabled the Lions to amass 402 yards of total offense and not allow a single sack of quarterback Rodney Peete during a 33–24 win over the Indianapolis Colts on September 22, 1991.

Brown's superior blocking helped the Lions gain 395 yards through the air and amass 534 yards of total offense during a 44–38 win over the Minnesota Vikings on November 23, 1995.

Notable Achievements

- Missed just nine non-strike games in 11 seasons, starting 163 of 173 contests.
- Two-time division champion (1991 and 1993).
- Member of 1985 NFL All-Rookie Team.
- Six-time Pro Bowl selection (1990, 1991, 1992, 1993, 1994, and 1995).
- 1995 First-Team All-Pro selection.
- Two-time Second-Team All-Pro selection. (1991 and 1994).
- Two-time Newspaper Enterprise Association Second-Team All-Pro selection (1989 and 1990).
- Three-time First-Team All-NFC selection (1990, 1994, and 1995).
- Named to Lions 75th Anniversary All-Time Team in 2008.
- Named to Lions All-Time Team in 2019.
- Inducted into Lions Ring of Honor in 2023.

16
ALEX WOJCIECHOWICZ

A fixture in the Lions' lineup on both sides of the ball for nearly a decade, Alex Wojciechowicz proved to be one of the few bright spots on mostly mediocre teams. A 60-minute player who manned center on offense and linebacker on defense, Wojciechowicz excelled at both posts, with his outstanding all-around play earning him First-Team All-Pro honors twice, a spot on the NFL 1940s All-Decade Team, and a bust in Canton. Extremely durable, Wojciechowicz missed just two games during his time in Detroit, before spending most of his last five NFL seasons in Philadelphia, where he helped lead the Eagles to three division titles and two league championships.

Born in South River, New Jersey, on August 12, 1915, Alexander Francis Wojciechowicz received his introduction to organized sports at South River High School, where, in addition to playing center for the school's football team, he excelled on the diamond at catcher. Although baseball had always been Wojciechowicz's first love, his desire to receive a college education caused him to eventually focus primarily on further developing his skills on the gridiron. Offered football scholarships to Villanova, Dartmouth, and Fordham University as graduation neared, Wojciechowicz ultimately chose to enroll at Fordham due to its Catholic orientation and relatively close proximity to his home.

A member of Fordham's football team from 1935 to 1937, Wojciechowicz started for the Rams at center all three years, anchoring an offensive line known as the "Seven Blocks of Granite" that also included future Hall of Fame head coach Vince Lombardi. Named a First-Team All-American at center in both 1936 and 1937, Wojciechowicz received high praise from Rams head coach Jim Crowley, who called him "one of the greatest defensive centers" and noted that he "seldom made a bad pass from center." A standout linebacker as well, Wojciechowicz helped the Rams compile a record of 7–0–1 his senior year that earned them a No. 3 ranking in the final AP poll by serving as the centerpiece of a defense that surrendered just 16 points all season.

Alex Wojciechowicz starred for the Lions on both offense and defense.

Selected by the Lions in the first round of the 1938 NFL Draft, with the sixth overall pick, Wojciechowicz earned a starting job on both sides of the ball immediately on his arrival in Detroit. As he had done in college, Wojciechowicz played center on offense and linebacker on defense, doing so for Lions teams that posted just four winning records over the course of the next eight seasons. Yet, even though he often found himself surrounded by mediocrity, Wojciechowicz continued to perform at an extremely high level.

Although generally ranked behind future Hall of Fame centers Mel Hein and Clyde "Bulldog" Turner, the 5'11", 217-pound Wojciechowicz excelled at that post, where he used his brute strength and quick feet to outmuscle and outmaneuver his opponent. An exceptional linebacker as well, Wojciechowicz used his speed to track down opposing ball-carriers and his powerful arms and vice-like hands to bring them to the ground. A two-time

First-Team All-Pro selection, Wojciechowicz received that accolade for the first time in 1939, before being similarly honored in 1944, when he finished second in the league with seven interceptions, which represented a Lions single-season record at the time.

A popular player who often brought comic relief to his teammates with his sense of humor, Wojciechowicz proved to be an outstanding team leader who served as one of the central figures on Lions teams that posted consecutive runner-up finishes in the NFL Western Division in the war years of 1944 and 1945. A true iron man who hardly ever left the playing field, Wojciechowicz missed just one game in 1941 and another in 1943, appearing in 83 of 85 contests from 1938 to 1945.

Despite his many contributions to the Lions through the years, Wojciechowicz suffered the indignity of being released with three other linemen by head coach Gus Dorais during the early stages of the 1946 campaign following a humiliating 34–14 loss to the Chicago Cardinals that dropped the team's record to 0–3.

Commenting on his coach's decision afterward, Wojciechowicz said, "This day had to come, and I can't say I'm not disappointed that it happened now. This is going to be a long, hard season for the Lions."

Proving Wojciechowicz's words prophetic, the Lions went on to compile a record of 1–10 that represented the league's worst mark. Meanwhile, Wojciechowicz joined the Philadelphia Eagles, who, over the course of the next five seasons, won three division titles and two NFL championships.

Serving as an integral member of those Eagles championship teams, Wojciechowicz gradually assumed the role of a defensive specialist around whom head coach Earle "Greasy" Neale built his defense. After continuing to function as a two-way player through the end of 1946, Wojciechowicz spent the remainder of his career playing linebacker exclusively, before announcing his retirement following the conclusion of the 1950 campaign with a career total of 19 interceptions, 14 of which he recorded as a member of the Lions.

Following his playing days, Wojciechowicz returned to his home state of New Jersey, where he spent several years working as a real estate appraiser and broker. Wojciechowicz later helped found the NFL Alumni Association, of which he became president in 1968, the same year that he gained induction into the Pro Football Hall of Fame. In his role as president, Wojciechowicz negotiated with owners for the creation of a pension plan to benefit the game's retired players, with his son recalling, "He worked hard to establish the indigent players' fund and establish pensions."

Wojciechowicz lived until July 13, 1992, when he died in his hometown of South River, New Jersey, at the age of 76.

THE 50 GREATEST PLAYERS IN DETROIT LIONS HISTORY

LIONS CAREER HIGHLIGHTS

Best Season

Although Wojciechowicz also gained First-Team All-Pro recognition in 1939, he made his greatest overall impact in 1944, when, in addition to registering a career-high seven interceptions, he helped lead the Lions to a regular-season record of 6–3–1 and their highest point total (216) his entire time in Detroit.

Memorable Moments/Greatest Performances

Wojciechowicz scored the only points of his career when he returned an interception 11 yards for a touchdown during a 23–14 win over the Packers on October 20, 1940.

Wojciechowicz excelled on both sides of the ball during a 21–0 win over Philadelphia on November 17, 1940, helping the Lions rush for 266 yards and amass a total of 397 yards on offense while also contributing to a defense that held the Eagles to minus 23 yards rushing.

Wojciechowicz helped lead the Lions to a 19–14 win over the Brooklyn Tigers on October 8, 1944, by recording two interceptions, which he returned a total of 24 yards.

In addition to anchoring an offensive line that helped the Lions amass 417 yards of total offense during a 38–7 win over the Boston Yanks in the final game of the 1944 regular season, Wojciechowicz picked off two passes on defense.

Notable Achievements

- Missed just two games from 1938 to 1945, appearing in 83 of 85 contests.
- Scored one defensive touchdown.
- Finished second in NFL with seven interceptions in 1944.
- Two-time First-Team All-Pro selection (1939 and 1944).
- Pro Football Hall of Fame All-1940s Team.
- Named to Lions 75th Anniversary All-Time Team in 2008.
- Named to Lions All-Time Team in 2019.
- Inducted into Lions Ring of Honor in 2009.
- Inducted into Pro Football Hall of Fame in 1968.

17

CHRIS SPIELMAN

An intense competitor who rarely thought of anything but football during his playing days, Chris Spielman spent eight seasons in Detroit serving as the cornerstone of the Lions' defense from his inside linebacker position. The franchise's career leader in tackles (since the Lions began recording tackles statistically in 1973), Spielman led the club in that category seven times, registering more than 100 stops in each of his eight seasons in the Motor City. A key member of teams that won two division titles and made four playoff appearances, Spielman earned four Pro Bowl selections, three All-Pro nominations, and an eventual place on the Lions All-Time Team, before departing for Buffalo, where he spent the last two years of his NFL career.

Born in Canton, Ohio, on October 11, 1965, Charles Christopher Spielman grew up in a blue-collar neighborhood located in the city that serves as home to the Pro Football Hall of Fame. With a high school football coach for a father, Spielman developed a love for the game at an early age, remembering, "Something about the game—really everything about it—fascinated me. The sights, the sounds, the smells, the mouth guards, the helmets, the uniforms, the camaraderie, the contact. I connected with all of it."

Displaying an unusually high level of intensity almost as soon as he began competing on the gridiron, the nine-year-old Spielman tackled his opponents so hard in Midget League ball that some suggested he play with and against children older than himself. And later, Canton Lehman Junior High School coach Mike Patton did not allow Spielman to hit his teammates during the week of practice.

Beginning to make a name for himself at Massillon Washington High School in nearby Massillon, Spielman earned First-Team All-Ohio honors as a junior by leading the Tigers to a berth in the state championship game, which they lost, 35–14, to Cincinnati Moeller. A rare three-year starter, Spielman also gained First-Team All-Ohio recognition his senior year with his superb play at linebacker on defense, at running back on offense, and

Chris Spielman recorded more tackles than anyone else in team annals.

as both a punter and a return man on special teams. Identified by *Parade* magazine as the best linebacker in the country, rated by Street and Smith Publications as one of the top 15 high school players in the nation, and accorded First-Team All-America honors at linebacker by *USA Today*, Spielman excelled in the classroom as well, winning the Dial Award as the national high school scholar-athlete of the year.

Recalling everything Spielman contributed to Massillon High on the football field, Canton McKinley head coach Thom McDaniels stated, "He played the game better than any player I ever coached against. I don't know if he was the best player, but he played the game better than everyone else."

Offered the opportunity to attend either the University of Michigan or Ohio State University on a football scholarship, Spielman initially expressed an interest in playing for the Wolverines, before his father, a lifelong fan of the Buckeyes, rejected that idea. Recounting the story of how he ended up choosing Ohio State over its bitter rival in the HBO documentary *Michigan vs. Ohio State: The Rivalry,* Spielman remembered, "My dad said, 'Okay, where are you going to go?' I said, 'Dad, I want to go to Michigan.' And he said, 'You *traitor*! I'll tell you where you're going. You're going right down 71 South, and you're going to play for the Ohio State Buckeyes. . . . Better not go there [Michigan]. Don't ever come home if you do.'"

Heeding his father's words, Spielman enrolled at Ohio State, where he spent three seasons starting for the Buckeyes at linebacker. A two-time All-American who won the Lombardi Award as the nation's top lineman or linebacker his senior year, Spielman later received high praise from head coach Earle Bruce, who said, "Chris taught me what intensity looked like in football. He had fun, but football was his consuming passion. He always has and always will set a standard for pure love of the game."

Despite his exceptional play, the 6', 234-pound Spielman, who posted a time of 4.86 seconds in the 40-yard dash at the NFL Scouting Combine, did not possess the measurables necessary to be considered an elite pro prospect, causing him to fall to the second round of the 1988 NFL Draft, where the Lions selected him with the 29th overall pick.

Expressing his disdain for the rating system employed by pro scouts, Spielman said at the time, "I'm tired of hearing questions about my height and speed. I'm a football player, not a basketball player."

Meanwhile, former Ohio State teammate and NFL offensive lineman Jim Lachey recalled, "When he went in the second round, he already had a chip on his shoulder, but then it turned into a boulder. I mean, he was ready to go out there and prove to everybody that he was the best linebacker in that class, if not the league."

Laying claim to the starting left-inside linebacker job in the Lions' 3–4 defense immediately on his arrival in Detroit, Spielman performed exceptionally well in his first pro season, earning a runner-up finish in the 1988 NFL Defensive Rookie of the Year voting by recording a team-high 153 tackles. Amassing well over 100 tackles in each of the next three seasons as well, Spielman gained Pro Bowl recognition each year and garnered his lone First-Team All-Pro nomination in 1991, when he helped lead the Lions to a record of 12–4 and their first division title in nearly a decade.

Spielman, who gradually increased his playing weight to 247 pounds during his first few years in the league, proved to be a sure tackler and extremely hard hitter who thoroughly enjoyed the physicality of the game, as former Lions head coach Wayne Fontes acknowledged when he said, "All he wanted to do was play football and knock you down. He threw his body around when he got to piles like it was a duffle bag. He had no regard for his body."

116   THE 50 GREATEST PLAYERS IN DETROIT LIONS HISTORY

Outstanding against the run, Spielman excelled at filling holes and pursuing ball-carriers, even though he lacked elite speed. Solid in pass coverage as well, Spielman used his superior instincts and knowledge of opposing offenses to do an effective job of covering tight ends and backs coming out of the backfield.

Known more than anything, though, for his leadership ability, toughness, and tremendous intensity, Spielman, who served as the Lions' defensive captain most of his time in Detroit, impressed everyone around him with his determination and dedication to his profession, with Lomas Brown describing his longtime teammate as "a straight throwback—Dick Butkus, Ray Nitschke. That was this guy. He was cut out of that mold."

Brown then added, "Football was his life. He was consumed with football. He's in there watching film on his off day. Spielman didn't have an off day."

Giving credence to Brown's words, Spielman said, "My only goal ever since I walked into this league that supersedes any other goal is to win the Super Bowl. That's all that I think about."

Spielman also made an extremely favorable impression on former Cincinnati Bengals and Tampa Bay Buccaneers head coach Sam Wyche, who said of him, "He's just a raw-boned, pure football player. He could have played in the forties, the fifties, or the nineties."

Continuing to perform at an elite level for the Lions at left-inside linebacker from 1992 to 1994, Spielman earned another Pro Bowl selection and a pair of Second-Team All-Pro nominations by registering more than 140 tackles in each of those seasons, with his 195 stops in 1994 setting a single-season franchise record that still stands. Moved to middle linebacker when the Lions switched to a 4–3 defense in 1995, Spielman performed equally well at that post, earning All-NFC honors for the third and final time in his career by making 137 tackles, forcing two fumbles and recovering three others, picking off a pass, and recording a sack. But with the Lions refusing to meet his financial demands when he became a free agent at the end of the year, Spielman chose to sign with the Buffalo Bills.

Spielman, who left Detroit with career totals of 1,138 tackles, 12 forced fumbles, 17 fumble recoveries, 10½ sacks, four interceptions, and one touchdown, ended up spending two seasons in Buffalo, recording another 225 tackles, before sustaining a serious back injury midway through the 1997 campaign that essentially ended his playing career. Although Spielman attempted a comeback with the Cleveland Browns two years later, he suffered a neck injury prior to the start of the regular season that forced him to announce his retirement.

CHRIS SPIELMAN **117**

Following his playing days, Spielman entered the field of broadcasting, working at Fox Sports for two years, before joining ESPN in 2001. After working primarily on ESPN's *College Football Saturday* for the next 15 years, Spielman returned to Fox in 2016 as a color commentator for NFL games. Spielman also spent seven years serving as an analyst for Lions preseason games, before rejoining the organization in a front-office capacity as a special assistant to president and CEO Rod Wood. While serving in that position, Spielman has played an integral role in the hirings of executive vice president and general manager Brad Holmes and head coach Dan Campbell.

On a more personal note, Spielman suffered a tragic loss on November 19, 2009, when, after surviving four bouts of breast cancer, his first wife and the mother of his four children, Stefanie, passed away after the disease returned for the fifth time. Spielman, who, after his wife lost her hair while undergoing treatment, shaved his head in a show of solidarity, has since been extremely active in raising funds for breast cancer research. He has also remarried and currently resides with his second wife and two adopted daughters in Upper Arlington, a suburb of Columbus, Ohio.

LIONS CAREER HIGHLIGHTS

Best Season

Spielman earned First-Team All-Pro honors for the only time in 1991 by recording 126 tackles, forcing three fumbles and recovering three others, and registering one sack for the NFC Central Division champions. But Spielman proved to be a bit more dominant in 1994, when, en route to gaining Second-Team All-Pro recognition, he led all NFL players with 195 tackles and 124 solo stops and forced three fumbles and recovered three others, one of which he returned 25 yards for the only touchdown of his career.

Memorable Moments/Greatest Performances

Spielman earned NFC Defensive Player of the Week honors by recording a sack and recovering a fumble during a 21–14 win over the Atlanta Falcons on September 16, 1990.

En route to gaining recognition as NFL Defensive Player of the Week, Spielman recorded the first interception of his career during a 27–10 win over the Saints on October 28, 1990.

THE 50 GREATEST PLAYERS IN DETROIT LIONS HISTORY

Spielman contributed to a 34–14 victory over the Vikings on November 24, 1991, by recording a sack and recovering a fumble.

Spielman's 17 combined tackles and six solo stops helped lead the Lions to a 20–17 overtime victory over the Dallas Cowboys on September 19, 1994.

Spielman earned NFL Defensive Player of the Week honors by making eight tackles and returning a fumble 25 yards for a touchdown during a 21–16 win over the Bears on October 23, 1994.

Notable Achievements

- Missed just four games in eight seasons, starting 124 of 128 contests.
- Scored one defensive touchdown.
- Recorded more than 100 tackles eight straight times.
- Led NFL with 195 combined tackles and 124 solo stops in 1994.
- Finished third in NFL in combined tackles twice.
- Led Lions in tackles seven straight times.
- Holds franchise single-season record for most tackles (195 in 1994).
- Holds franchise career record for most tackles (1,138).
- Ranks among Lions career leaders with 12 forced fumbles (tied for 3rd) and 17 fumble recoveries (tied for 2nd).
- Two-time division champion (1991 and 1993).
- Member of Pro Football Writers Association 1988 NFL All-Rookie Team.
- Finished second in 1988 NFL Defensive Rookie of the Year voting.
- Three-time NFL Defensive Player of the Week.
- Two-time NFC Defensive Player of the Week.
- Two-time Lions team MVP on defense (1993 and 1994).
- Four-time Pro Bowl selection (1989, 1990, 1991, and 1994).
- 1991 First-Team All-Pro selection.
- Two-time Second-Team All-Pro selection (1992 and 1994).
- 1994 First-Team All-NFC selection.
- Two-time Second-Team All-NFC selection (1989 and 1995).
- Named to Lions 75th Anniversary All-Time Team in 2008.
- Named to Lions All-Time Team in 2019.
- Inducted into Lions Ring of Honor in 2021.

18

WAYNE WALKER

The Lions' starter at right-outside linebacker from 1960 to 1972, Wayne Walker spent 15 seasons in Detroit, appearing in a total of 200 games, placing him fourth in team annals. A durable player who missed just one game his entire career, Walker proved to be a stout run defender who excelled even more in pass coverage, with his solid all-around play gaining him Pro Bowl and All-Pro recognition three times each. Doubling as the Lions' place-kicker much of his time in the Motor City, Walker, who ranks among the franchise's career leaders in points scored, later received the additional honor of being named to the Lions 75th Anniversary All-Time Team in 2008.

Born in Boise, Idaho, on September 30, 1936, Wayne Harrison Walker first began to make a name for himself at Boise High School, where he starred in both baseball and football. A two-way standout on the grid-iron, Walker also performed so well on the diamond that he received an offer to turn pro. Choosing instead to pursue a career in football, Walker enrolled at the University of Idaho, where he spent three seasons excelling at linebacker on defense and center on offense under Vandals head coach Skip Stahley while serving as a linemate of future Green Bay Packers Hall of Fame guard Jerry Kramer.

Having earned Second-Team All-Pacific Coast honors as a senior in 1957, Walker entered the 1958 NFL Draft, where the Lions selected him in the fourth round with the 45th overall pick. Joining a Lions team coming off their third NFL championship in six seasons, Walker spent his first year in Detroit playing mostly on special teams, although he managed to score twice on defense in limited duty.

Somewhat overwhelmed by his surroundings the first time he walked into Briggs Stadium for a Saturday night exhibition game against the Giants, Walker recalled, "Growing up, I was a big baseball fan, so I knew about the ballpark. I remember getting off the bus and going through the tunnel and onto the field. To a kid from Boise, it was like seeing the seventh wonder of the world. It was just what a ballpark was supposed to look like."

Wayne Walker missed just one game during his 15 seasons in Detroit.

After assuming a backup role on defense for one more year, Walker joined the starting unit in 1960, beginning in the process a 13-year run during which he started all but a handful of games. Performing well for a Lions team that finished second to the Green Bay Packers in the NFL Western Division for the first of three straight times, Walker gained unofficial Second-Team All-Pro recognition from the *New York Daily News* by intercepting a pass, recording a safety, recovering four fumbles, and registering seven sacks. Walker followed that up with two more solid seasons, before earning three straight trips to the Pro Bowl and two All-Pro nominations from 1963 to 1965 by providing consistently excellent play for one of the league's top-ranked defenses.

Playing alongside Hall of Fame middle linebacker Joe Schmidt, the 6'2", 225-pound Walker helped anchor a defense that also included "Fearsome Foursome" members Alex Karras, Roger Brown, Darris McCord, and Sam Williams and a secondary that featured Yale Lary, Dick LeBeau, and

Dick "Night Train" Lane. Although often overlooked in favor of some of his more celebrated teammates, Walker proved to be invaluable to the Lions, plugging holes at the line of scrimmage, pursuing ball-carriers from sideline to sideline, and doing an expert job of covering tight ends and backs coming out of the backfield. In addition to his duties on defense, Walker spent seven seasons serving as the Lions' primary placekicker, before finally stepping aside for kicking specialist Errol Mann in 1969.

Steady and dependable, Walker performed his job without much fanfare, rarely drawing attention to himself. Nevertheless, his teammates knew how much he contributed to the success the Lions experienced on defense, with Dick LeBeau stating, "Wayne Walker was a great football player." After gaining All-Pro recognition for the third straight time in 1966, Walker remained a fixture on the right side of the Lions' defense for six more years, before announcing his retirement following the conclusion of the 1972 campaign.

In addition to appearing in a then-franchise record 200 games, Walker recorded 14 interceptions, amassed 163 interception-return yards, recovered 15 fumbles, registered 38½ sacks and one safety, scored twice on defense, successfully converted 53 out of 131 field goal attempts and 172 out of 175 extra-point attempts, and scored a total of 345 points.

Looking back on his playing career years later, Walker said, "I've told my grandkids this: I was proud of the fact that I could actually tell people—and say it and know that it's the truth—I never took a game off. I never took a play off. I never took a practice off—and I really don't even remember taking a play off in practice. I went every day as hard as I could."

Following his retirement as an active player, Walker spent 20 years serving as the sports director for KPIX-TV, the CBS affiliate in San Francisco. Walker also served as an analyst for regional NFL games for CBS and as a color commentator for San Francisco 49ers and Oakland A's games for several years.

Developing a pristine reputation during his years in broadcasting, Walker received the following words of praise from KTVU sports anchor Joe Fonzi, who worked with him for more than a decade at KPIX: "I don't know that you could really properly explain to people who were not there how big of a deal Wayne was as a sports personality in the Bay Area. . . . There was a point where Wayne was pretty much the voice of record when it came to Bay Area sports."

Meanwhile, Joe Montana said of Walker, "He was the best. He did things the right way that allowed him to get answers and trust from players that no one else could."

122   THE 50 GREATEST PLAYERS IN DETROIT LIONS HISTORY

Choosing to retire from broadcasting in 1998, Walker returned to his home state of Idaho, where, after surviving a bout with throat cancer some years earlier, he announced in 2015 that he had been stricken with Parkinson's disease. Walker passed away a little less than two years later, dying from complications of the illness at the age of 80 on May 19, 2017.

On learning of his former teammate's passing, Joe Schmidt told the *Detroit Free Press*, "It was a real shock to hear that Wayne passed away because I just spoke with him on the phone two days ago. We had a great time reminiscing about our playing days stories, and stories from the old Lindell AC bar downtown. We had some good laughs. Wayne was a good football player, intelligent, well read, and he had a great sense of humor. It really grabs you when you lose your teammate and friend. Just like it did when we lost Yale Lary."

Some years earlier, Walker discussed what playing in Detroit meant to him when he told that same publication, "Basically, I grew up in Detroit, just loved this area. I was only 21 when I got drafted here. I mean, what does anybody know when you're 21, when you look back? And the '60s were a sensational, exciting time to be here. Those are all clear, fond memories you don't leave behind."

CAREER HIGHLIGHTS

Best Season

Although Walker recorded a career-high seven sacks in 1960 and established career-best marks in field goals made (14) and field goal percentage (56.0) in 1964, he earned his lone First-Team All-Pro nomination in 1965, when he registered two interceptions and four and a half sacks.

Memorable Moments/Greatest Performances

Walker scored the first points of his career when he returned an interception 33 yards for a touchdown during a 41–24 win over the Los Angeles Rams on October 26, 1958.

Walker crossed the opponent's goal line again on December 7, 1958, when he returned a fumble 34 yards for a touchdown during a 19–17 loss to the Giants.

Walker contributed to a 36–0 shutout of the Bears in the final game of the 1960 regular season by tackling running back John Adams in the end zone for a safety.

Walker had a huge hand in the Lions' 11–3 win over the Bears on October 28, 1962, successfully converting field goal attempts of 17, 43, and 38 yards.

Walker kicked a career-high four field goals during a 26–17 win over the 49ers in the opening game of the 1964 regular season, with the longest of his kicks traveling 31 yards.

Notable Achievements

- Missed just one game from 1960 to 1972, appearing in 179 of 180 contests.
- Scored two defensive touchdowns.
- Recorded seven sacks and recovered four fumbles in 1960.
- Ranks among Lions career leaders with 15 fumble recoveries (5th), 345 points scored (10th), and 200 games played (4th).
- Lions team MVP on defense in 1968.
- Three-time Pro Bowl selection (1963, 1964, and 1965).
- 1965 First-Team All-Pro selection.
- Two-time Second-Team All-Pro selection (1964 and 1966).
- Three-time First-Team All-Western Conference selection (1964, 1965, and 1966).
- Pro Football Reference All-1960s First Team.
- Named to Lions 75th Anniversary All-Time Team in 2008.

19

BILLY SIMS

A tremendously gifted running back who combined great power with outstanding speed, Billy Sims appeared destined for the Pro Football Hall of Fame before suffering a catastrophic knee injury that brought his career to a premature end. Nevertheless, the former Heisman Trophy winner accomplished enough during his four-plus seasons in Detroit to earn a prominent place in these rankings. The second-leading rusher in franchise history, Sims gained more than 1,000 yards on the ground three times and amassed more than 1,800 yards from scrimmage twice, en route to earning three Pro Bowl selections and two All-Pro nominations. The 1980 NFL Rookie of the Year, Sims performed so well during his relatively brief stint in the Motor City that he later received the additional honors of having his No. 20 retired by the organization and being named to the Lions All-Time Team in 2019. Still, we are left to wonder what might have been.

Born in St. Louis, Missouri, on September 18, 1955, Billy Ray Sims grew up rooting for the St. Louis Cardinals and hoping to play in the major leagues one day himself, recalling, "I thought I'd be the next Bob Gibson. In St. Louis, most black kids played baseball. I wore No. 20 because of Lou Brock."

Changing his priorities after he moved to tiny Hooks, Texas, to live with his grandmother while in the eighth grade, Sims naturally began to gravitate more toward football, later saying, "Football was king. Everybody played football."

Although Sims never competed in organized football until his first year at Hooks High School, he displayed a natural affinity for the sport, exhibiting such prowess on the gridiron before long that people came from miles around to watch him play. Commenting on his childhood friend's rare skill set and the excitement he created, Patrick James remembered, "Like a man playing with boys, he was just that much better than everybody. He didn't just outrun everybody, he just went around them or over them, whatever it took. . . . Ten thousand people would show up at a stadium that would hold two or three thousand. Everybody wanted to see something special,

Billy Sims ranks second to Barry Sanders in franchise history in rushing.
Courtesy of RMYAuctions.com

and he definitely was. . . . On Friday nights, every coach that was anybody would be in Hooks. I mean, it's like the who's who of coaches showed up just to see this guy."

Establishing himself as the finest running back in the state, Sims finished his high school career with an incredible 7,733 rushing yards, earning in the process a pair of All-State selections, All-America and All-South honors his senior year, and the attention of University of Oklahoma head football coach Barry Switzer, who recalled, "I spent more time recruiting Billy than any other player I've ever recruited."

With Switzer ultimately getting his man, Sims embarked on an extremely successful college career that started slowly but ended in glorious fashion. After barely playing as a freshman, Sims sustained an injury in the opening game of his sophomore year that forced him to miss the rest of the season. A despondent Sims subsequently quit football and returned home, only to be coaxed back to Norman by Switzer.

Granted another year of eligibility because of his earlier misfortune, Sims rushed for 413 yards and six touchdowns in 1977, before having his season derailed by another injury. Fully healthy by the start of the 1978 campaign, Sims performed magnificently as a junior, winning the Heisman Trophy by leading the nation with 1,762 yards rushing and 20 TDs. Sims followed that up by gaining 1,506 yards on the ground and scoring 23 touchdowns his senior year, earning in the process a runner-up finish to University of Southern California (USC) running back Charles White in the Heisman balloting.

Later expressing his admiration for his two-time All-American running back, who, in his five seasons at Norman, rushed for 4,118 yards and 50 touchdowns, Barry Switzer stated, "Billy had it all. Billy had the strength, the size, the great speed, and the running ability, plus the mental and physical toughness. He just was the biggest, the strongest, the fastest of all the backs I ever had, so that made him the best."

Despite Sims's extraordinary play his last two seasons at Oklahoma, some pro scouts expressed concerns over his frequent fumbles and inability to establish himself as a reliable receiver out of the backfield heading into the 1980 NFL Draft. But even though he made just two receptions in his five years as part of the Sooners' run-based offense, Sims quickly convinced quarterback Gary Danielson that he had the ability to catch passes out of the backfield after the Lions selected him with the first overall pick of the draft, with the Detroit signal-caller saying, "In camp, I could tell right away that he was a natural receiver. Sometimes when we run our seven-on-seven passing drills in practice, you see a guy catching the ball, but it's not natural. He's fighting it. With Billy, it's very smooth and easy."

Meanwhile, Barry Switzer responded to those who criticized Sims for his tendency to occasionally cough up the football in college by stating, "He fumbled because he got hit from so many different directions. That's when fumbles usually come. Guys who never fumble are usually the ones who go down on the first hit."

Making an enormous impact his first year in Detroit, Sims helped a team that won just two games the previous season compile a record of 9–7 by ranking among the league leaders with 1,303 yards rushing and 1,924 yards from scrimmage while also topping the circuit with 13 rushing

BILLY SIMS **127**

touchdowns and 16 TDs. In addition to being named NFL Rookie of the Year, Sims gained Pro Bowl, Second-Team All-Pro, and First-Team All-NFC recognition. Equally effective in 1981, Sims again earned Pro Bowl, Second-Team All-Pro, and First-Team All-NFC honors by placing near the top of the league rankings with 1,437 yards rushing, 1,888 yards from scrimmage, 13 rushing touchdowns, 15 TDs, and a rushing average of 4.9 yards per carry.

Extremely fast, Sims, who posted a time of 4.45 seconds in the 40-yard dash at the NFL Scouting Combine, possessed so much more speed than any other previous Lions running back that offensive tackle Karl Baldischwiler claimed that he and his linemates had to adjust their blocking style somewhat to account for his quickness, saying, "We had to learn a technique for his speed; he was so fast and would get there so quickly. He had something that only came through in a game when everything meant something."

Very strong as well, the 5'11", 212-pound Sims rarely went down on first contact, usually requiring two or three men to bring him to the turf, with former Lions quarterback Eric Hipple stating, "Billy was a workhorse. Billy was always going to get positive yardage, no matter what."

Claiming that Sims proved to be particularly effective in short-yardage situations, Hipple added, "One yard, two yards, or three yards, he was gonna leap over the top."

Although a players' strike shortened the 1982 season to just nine games, Sims still managed to gain 639 yards on the ground, amass 981 yards from scrimmage, and score four touchdowns, earning in the process Pro Bowl and All-NFC honors for the third straight time. But with Sims's agent, Jerry Argovitz, assuming control of the Houston Gamblers of the United States Football League (USFL) prior to the start of the ensuing campaign and secretly signing his client to a five-year, $3.5 million deal with the Gamblers, Sims appeared to be on the verge of leaving Detroit until he inked a new five-year, $4.5 million contract extension with the Lions a few months later. With both teams claiming his services, the matter wound up in court, where a federal judge ruled in favor of the Lions.

Returning to the Motor City in 1983, Sims had another outstanding season, leading the Lions to their first division title in 26 years by rushing for 1,040 yards, gaining another 419 yards on 42 pass receptions, and scoring seven touchdowns despite missing three games due to injury. Continuing to perform at an elite level through the first half of the 1984 campaign, Sims appeared to be well on his way to gaining more than 1,000 yards on the ground for the fourth time in five seasons. But after rushing for 687 yards, amassing 926 yards from scrimmage, and scoring five touchdowns through mid-October, Sims sustained a devastating injury to his right knee during a 16–14 win over the Vikings in week 8 that ultimately ended his playing career.

The fateful play occurred during the third quarter of the contest, when, in attempting to cut back to the left after taking a handoff, Sims caught his foot in the turf while simultaneously being hit by Minnesota linebacker Walker Lee Ashley. Once he hit the ground, Sims grabbed his right knee and didn't get up, recalling years later, "I knew once that happened, I had never felt pain like that in my life. I'm like, 'Oh, man.' It was so bad, I just let the ball loose. Forget this ball. I was grabbing my knee."

Lost for the rest of the season after undergoing surgery the very next day, Sims subsequently spent the next two years trying to rehabilitate his knee, before realizing that the damage that had been done made it impossible for him to return to action. However, after retiring prior to the start of the 1987 campaign, Sims announced to the press in 1989 that he had made a full recovery and intended to play again. But by that time, the Lions had drafted Barry Sanders and had no need of a running back who had not seen the playing field in four years, prompting Sims to retire for good.

Sims, who, over parts of five seasons with the Lions, rushed for 5,106 yards and 42 touchdowns, made 186 receptions for 2,072 yards and 5 TDs, amassed 7,178 yards from scrimmage, and averaged 4.5 yards per carry, received a $1.9 million insurance settlement from Lloyd's of London following his retirement that, coupled with the income he earned during his playing career, seemed to set him up financially for years to come. But Sims, unfortunately, lost his accumulated wealth through a series of failed business ventures that included a nightclub, a radio station, a dry cleaner, and a car parts manufacturer. Forced to file for bankruptcy in 1990, Sims sold his Heisman Trophy and spent some time in jail for failure to make child support payments.

Sims continued to struggle financially until 2004, when he partnered with an Oklahoma businessman to open the first Billy Sims Barbecue restaurant, which has since developed into a successful restaurant chain that has locations in several states. Sims later started the Billy Sims Foundation, which helps students in Oklahoma attend college.

Looking back on the star-crossed nature of his former Lions teammate's career, Rob Rubick stated, "He'd be in Canton. No doubt he would have been in the Hall of Fame. Look at the numbers. Look at his numbers in his first, what'd he play, four years? Five years? Look at his numbers. His numbers were as good as anyone in that era in his first five years."

Yet Sims, who is 69 years old as of this writing, expresses no regrets over how his career ended, saying, "I was blessed to play those five years. I was a lot older as a rookie than most guys. As a running back, I didn't have long to play. If I could play five years, that was a blessing. I played four-and-a-half."

CAREER HIGHLIGHTS

Best Season

Sims performed magnificently in each of his first two NFL seasons, and either of those campaigns would make an excellent choice here. Although Sims gained 134 more yards on the ground in 1981 (1,437 [1980: 1,303]), I opted to go with 1980 since he posted slightly better overall numbers, finishing the season with more receptions (51 [28]), receiving yards (621 [451]), yards from scrimmage (1,924 [1,888]), and touchdowns (16 [15]).

Memorable Moments/Greatest Performances

Sims performed brilliantly in his first game as a pro, rushing for 153 yards, gaining another 64 yards on two pass receptions, and scoring three touchdowns during a 41–20 win over the Los Angeles Rams in the 1980 regular-season opener.

Continuing his exceptional play in week 2, Sims earned NFL Offensive Player of the Week honors by rushing for 134 yards, making two receptions for 94 yards, and scoring two touchdowns during a 29–7 win over the Packers, with one of his TDs coming on a career-long 87-yard catch-and-run.

Sims helped lead the Lions to a 27–7 victory over the Vikings on September 28, 1980, by gaining 157 yards on 27 carries.

Almost exactly one year later, on September 27, 1981, Sims rushed for 133 yards and one touchdown during a 16–0 shutout of the Oakland Raiders.

Sims starred in defeat on October 11, 1981, rushing for 185 yards and two touchdowns during a 27–21 loss to the Denver Broncos.

Sims had a big game against Dallas on November 15, 1981, gaining 119 yards on the ground and scoring two touchdowns during a 27–24 Lions win, with one of his TDs coming on an 81-yard catch-and-run.

Sims led the Lions to a 19–14 victory over the Rams on September 19, 1982, by amassing 222 yards from scrimmage, gaining 119 of those yards on the ground and the other 103 on five pass receptions.

130   THE 50 GREATEST PLAYERS IN DETROIT LIONS HISTORY

Sims earned NFL Offensive Player of the Week honors by carrying the ball 36 times for 189 yards and making five receptions for 47 yards during a 23–20 overtime win over the Packers on November 20, 1983.

Sims led the Lions to another overtime win on September 9, 1984, by rushing for 140 yards and one touchdown during a 27–24 victory over the Atlanta Falcons.

Notable Achievements

- Rushed for more than 1,000 yards three times.
- Surpassed 50 receptions and 600 receiving yards once each.
- Amassed more than 1,800 yards from scrimmage twice.
- Scored at least 15 touchdowns twice.
- Averaged more than five yards per carry once.
- Led NFL with 13 rushing touchdowns and 16 touchdowns in 1980.
- Finished second in NFL in yards from scrimmage, rushing touchdowns, and average yards per carry once each.
- Finished third in NFL in rushing yards and all-purpose yards once each.
- Led Lions in rushing five times, receptions twice, and receiving yards once.
- Ranks among Lions career leaders with 5,106 rushing yards (2nd), 7,178 yards from scrimmage (4th), 7,178 all-purpose yards (5th), 42 rushing touchdowns (2nd), and 47 touchdowns (4th).
- 1983 division champion.
- Member of 1980 NFL All-Rookie Team.
- 1980 NFL Offensive Rookie of the Year.
- 1980 NFL Rookie of the Year.
- Two-time NFL Offensive Player of the Week.
- Three-time Pro Bowl selection (1980, 1981, and 1982).
- Two-time Second-Team All-Pro selection (1980 and 1981).
- Two-time First-Team All-NFC selection (1980 and 1981).
- 1982 Second-Team All-NFC selection.
- Number 20 retired by Lions.
- Named to Lions 75th Anniversary All-Time Team in 2008.
- Named to Lions All-Time Team in 2019.

20
DOUG ENGLISH

The heart and soul of a formidable defensive front that became known as the "Silver Rush," Doug English spent 10 seasons in Detroit providing stout run defense and a strong inside pass rush for mostly losing Lions teams. The Lions' primary starter at right tackle from 1977 to 1984, English recorded more than 100 tackles and 10 sacks once each, earning in the process team MVP honors on defense twice. A four-time Pro Bowler and four-time All-Pro, English received the additional honor of being named to the Lions All-Time Team in 2019, accomplishing all he did after briefly retiring for one season in the middle of his career.

Born in Dallas, Texas, on August 25, 1953, Lowell Douglas English first began to make a name for himself on the gridiron at Bryan Adams High School, where, after gaining far more recognition in track and field for the success he experienced as a discus-thrower, he finally earned a starting spot on the varsity football squad his senior year. Emerging as one of the finest two-way linemen in the state, English earned All-District and honorable mention All-America honors from *Coach & Athlete* magazine for his outstanding play on both sides of the ball.

Recruited to play football at the University of Texas by Longhorns defensive line coach Pat Patterson, who later described him as "all Adam's apple and elbows," English continued his progression into an elite player with the help of a weight-training program and offensive lineman Jerry Sisemore, the future Philadelphia Eagles Pro Bowler, against whom he practiced each day. A two-time All-SWC selection, English proved to be especially outstanding as a senior in 1974, when he also earned First-Team All-America honors.

Selected by the Lions in the second round of the 1975 NFL Draft with the 38th overall pick, English spent his first two seasons in Detroit playing mostly on special teams and seeing limited duty on defense, before laying claim to the starting right tackle job in 1977. Performing well in his first year as a full-time starter, English finished second on the team with eight

Doug English earned Pro Bowl and All-Pro honors four times each.

sacks, before gaining Pro Bowl and Second-Team All-NFC recognition the following season by bringing down opposing quarterbacks behind the line of scrimmage seven times. Solid again in 1979, English earned team MVP honors on defense by registering 122 tackles and six and a half sacks while also recording a safety and recovering two fumbles.

Despite English's strong play in each of the previous three seasons, the Lions' horrendous 2–14 record in 1979 left him feeling so disheartened that he decided to quit football. Recalling his emotions at the time, English later said, "I thought I'd had enough after that 2–14 season. There just wasn't enough money in it for me to go through that stuff again."

Immersing himself in his outside interests, the 27-year-old English spent the 1980 campaign dabbling in the oil business, before electing to return to action at the end of the year after a Lions team led by rookie running back Billy Sims compiled a regular-season record of 9–7 in his absence.

Returning to the Lions with a different attitude, English stated, "I'm extremely happy to be back. The year off was the most important experience of my life. It has been extremely beneficial to me. It enhances your outlook.

DOUG ENGLISH **133**

I'm a year older, too. I saw a side of the front office and the coaches that I didn't see before. I wasn't a subordinate."

Meanwhile, Lions head coach Monte Clark said, "I couldn't be happier. I feel like we've just acquired another No. 1 draft choice. But this one has experience and leadership ability. We missed him last year."

Reclaiming his starting right tackle job, English spent the next two seasons playing between left tackle William Gay and right end Al "Bubba" Baker on an outstanding defensive line that also included left end Dave Pureifory. The emotional leader of the group, English used his experience and wisdom to counsel the other members of the unit both on and off the playing field. A Pro Bowl and All-Pro selection in each of those two seasons, English recorded nine sacks in 1981, before registering another four and a half sacks during the strike-shortened 1982 campaign.

Continuing to excel following the departures of Baker and Pureifory, English gained All-Pro recognition in both 1983 and 1984 by bringing down opposing quarterbacks behind the line of scrimmage a total of 18 times, with his career-high 13 sacks in the first of those seasons placing him among the league leaders. But after being moved to nose tackle by first-year Lions head coach Darryl Rogers in the team's new 3–4 defensive scheme in 1985, English sustained a serious neck and spinal injury in week 10 that brought both his season and his career to a premature end. Over parts of 10 NFL seasons, English recorded 55½ sacks and an unknown number of tackles, recovered nine fumbles, and registered four safeties, tying him with Ted Hendricks, Jared Allen, and Justin Houston for the most in NFL history.

Recalling how his physical stature came to be viewed differently over the course of his playing career, English stated, "I came into the league at 6–5, 260. I was known as a big player, a giant. Eleven years later, I left at 6–6, 265. I was known as a small player."

Following his playing days, English returned to his home state of Texas, where he became co-owner of the supplier logistics company Pro Line Warehouse and Distribution. Since retiring from football, English has also taken part in a variety of businesses and given of himself to several charitable causes, including serving as president of the Lone Star Paralysis Foundation, which seeks to cure spinal cord paralysis. Through his association with the nonprofit foundation, the agency has raised close to $3 million toward research of paralysis from spinal cord injuries through celebrity golf tournaments.

Claiming that the year he spent away from football in the middle of his playing career helped him develop the mindset and ability to eventually pursue such philanthropic causes, English stated, "When I was there [in his

134   THE 50 GREATEST PLAYERS IN DETROIT LIONS HISTORY

first five seasons], I played because I always played. I was motivated as much as I could motivate myself, which wasn't bad. . . . When I took that year off and saw the forest for the trees, I changed. And what I learned was that football is not important. I thought it was important, and most people do think it's important. It's what you do with that credibility—with the fame from playing and playing well. You have a tremendous bully pulpit. You now have more power than ever."

CAREER HIGHLIGHTS

Best Season

Although English earned his lone First-Team All-Pro nomination in 1982, he performed better in both 1979 and 1983, garnering team MVP honors on defense in the first of those campaigns by making 122 tackles (90 solo) and recording six and a half sacks. Even more dominant in 1983, English gained Second-Team All-Pro recognition by registering 13 sacks, 62 solo tackles, and two safeties.

Memorable Moments/Greatest Performances

English helped lead the Lions to a 17–14 victory over Denver on Thanksgiving Day 1978 by sacking Broncos quarterback Craig Morton four times.

English helped anchor a defense that allowed just 24 yards of total offense and recorded seven sacks during a 23–7 win over the Bears on November 22, 1981.

English recorded two and a half sacks during a 30–10 win over the Packers on December 12, 1982.

English registered the first points of an 11–0 win over Tampa Bay in the opening game of the 1983 regular season when he sacked quarterback Jerry Golsteyn in the end zone for a safety.

English recorded the last of his four career safeties when he brought down Brian Sipe in the end zone during a 31–26 loss to the Browns on September 11, 1983.

English contributed to a 38–14 victory over the Packers on October 9, 1983, by sacking Lynn Dickey twice.

English recorded two of the seven sacks the Lions registered against quarterback Steve Dils during a 13–2 win over the Vikings on December 5, 1983.

Notable Achievements

- Recorded 122 tackles (90 solo) in 1979.
- Recorded 13 sacks in 1983.
- Led NFL with two safeties in 1983.
- Holds share of NFL record for most career safeties (4).
- Ranks ninth in franchise history with 59 career sacks.
- 1983 division champion.
- Two-time Lions team MVP on defense (1979 and 1983).
- Four-time Pro Bowl selection (1978, 1981, 1982, and 1983).
- 1982 First-Team All-Pro selection.
- Three-time Second-Team All-Pro selection (1981, 1983, and 1984).
- 1981 First-Team All-NFC selection.
- 1978 Second-Team All-NFC selection.
- Named to Lions 75th Anniversary All-Time Team in 2008.
- Named to Lions All-Time Team in 2019.

21

ROBERT PORCHER

An elite edge-rusher who also excelled against the run, Robert Porcher spent his entire 12-year NFL career in Detroit, recording the second-most sacks and the fourth-most tackles of any player in franchise history. Porcher, who also ranks first in team annals in forced fumbles, compiled double-digit sack totals five times, leading the Lions in that category on eight separate occasions. A major contributor to teams that made five playoff appearances and won one division title, Porcher gained Pro Bowl and First-Team All-NFC recognition three times each, before being further honored by being named to the Lions All-Time Team in 2019.

Born in Wando, South Carolina, on July 30, 1969, Robert Porcher III grew up in a distinctly rural part of the large suburban town located in Charleston County. Often called "country boy" by his middle school classmates who lived in nearby Mount Pleasant, Porcher looked back fondly on the place of his upbringing, saying, "It was a wonderful place to grow up. I just loved everything about it."

Getting his start in organized sports at a rather late age, Porcher did not begin playing football until his senior year at Huger Cainhoy High School. Following his graduation, Porcher enrolled at Tennessee State University in Nashville, where, after redshirting as a freshman, he started at defensive end his sophomore year. Choosing to transfer to South Carolina State University prior to the start of his junior year, Porcher spent the next two seasons playing for legendary head coach Willie Jeffries, under whom he recorded 15 sacks and 88 tackles as a senior in 1991, earning in the process Mid-Eastern Athletic Conference Defensive Player of the Year and NCAA Division I-AA Defensive Player of the Year honors.

Subsequently selected by the Lions in the first round of the 1992 NFL Draft with the 26th overall pick, Porcher spent his first two years in the league assuming a part-time role in Detroit's 3-4 defense, recording a total of nine and a half sacks. A full-time starter in 1994, Porcher registered three

Robert Porcher recorded the most forced fumbles and the second-most sacks of any player in team annals.

sacks and 69 tackles, with the last figure representing the second-highest mark of his career.

Despite his solid play, Porcher remained extremely dissatisfied with the system the Lions employed on defense, later saying, "To be honest with you, I hated it. I hated playing in our system because I was not a 3–4 defensive end. I wasn't. I just didn't like it. I did good on rushing the passer, but I just didn't do good overall. . . . Then we got a new coordinator and they moved to a 4–3. I was able to get back out at end after my second year in the system, and the rest is history. I was just able to do what I always knew I could do."

138   THE 50 GREATEST PLAYERS IN DETROIT LIONS HISTORY

Agreeing to move to defensive tackle in 1995 for the good of the team, Porcher performed well in Detroit's new 4–3 defense, recording five sacks and 51 tackles. But Porcher did not reach his full potential until the following year, when, after being moved back outside to his more natural position of end and adopting a more grueling workout regimen, he emerged as a true force on the defensive side of the ball.

Porcher's renaissance actually began in 1995, when teammate Barry Sanders inspired him to work harder. Recalling the seminal moment of his career, Porcher stated, "I was a starter, my job was pretty secure, but I wasn't really pleased with my development. I knew I could be better. I wanted to be more than I was. I remember watching Barry running these sprints during one of the defensive periods when the offense is supposed to be on the sidelines resting and wondering why the best running back in the NFL was doing all this extra work. . . . I thought I was doing enough, but I realized I wasn't."

Taking it on himself to increase his workload, Porcher subsequently began running on his own and doing individual drills to improve his footwork and hand placement, remembering, "I went from gassers to eventually running 100-yard sprints. . . . My routine was pretty particular. My drills on the [blocking] bag were moves I knew I would always use. I never got enough work on those things. . . . As soon as I committed myself, my career took off."

Although the nearly 6'4" Porcher reported to training camp in 1996 weighing his normal 285 pounds, he had reduced his body fat, later claiming that he entered the season in the "best shape of his career." And with his increased stamina and improved technique, Porcher thrived as never before. Shifted full-time to left defensive end, Porcher began an exceptional six-year run during which he recorded 68 sacks, which represented the second-highest total in the NFL over that span of time. Particularly outstanding in 1997, 1999, and 2001, Porcher earned Pro Bowl and First-Team All-NFC honors in each of those campaigns by registering 12½, 15, and 11 sacks, respectively, while also leading all Lions defensive linemen in tackles in two of those three seasons.

Extremely strong, Porcher had the ability to overpower his blocker, often using the "bull rush" to apply pressure to opposing quarterbacks. But he also moved well in short spaces and possessed good quickness and an excellent first step, allowing him to frequently outmaneuver his man as well.

After earning the last of his three Pro Bowl nominations the previous year by recording 11 sacks and 52 tackles, the 33-year-old Porcher began to show signs of aging in 2002, registering only five and a half sacks, although he still managed to recover three fumbles and score the only touchdown of his career. Porcher followed that up by recording just four and a half sacks in 2003, before officially announcing his retirement on November 2, 2004, after being deactivated for the first seven games of the season.

Making his decision known to the public during an emotional press conference, Porcher told the assembled media, "I've thought about this day for a lot of the last three years. We all think we can play forever, and I was no different, but now the time has come to step aside. These last seven weeks have been tough. I had always been proud of being part of the solution, not part of the problem. . . . To be able to say you played with the team that drafted you and still have a chance to say goodbye when your career clock expires, I cannot say enough about that."

In his 12 seasons with the Lions, Porcher recorded 95½ sacks and 602 tackles, including 429 of the solo variety. He also forced 18 fumbles and recovered seven others, intercepted one pass, and scored one touchdown.

In addition to his contributions on the playing field, Porcher became heavily involved with countless charitable causes during his time in Detroit, including establishing with his wife, Kimberly, the Robert and Kimberly Porcher Cancer Research and Relief Fund, which has raised thousands of dollars for the University of Michigan Comprehensive Cancer Center. Porcher also served as a longtime spokesman for Michigan's "Fatherhood Is Forever" statewide campaign and founded with his wife the Robert Porcher and Friends Charities, which, among other activities, donates free Thanksgiving food to needy residents each year. For his philanthropic work, the Lions have honored Porcher by naming their annual award for player community involvement after him.

Since retiring from football, Porcher has continued to give back to the community both in Michigan and in his home state of South Carolina. He also has some business interests in Metro Detroit and keeps close tabs on the Lions, saying, "I still do things in Detroit. I'm passionate about our team. I still am. I wanted to be part of trying to get us back on the right track. I have no regrets. The only thing is, at least once I wanted to get us back to the NFC Championship Game."

As for himself, Porcher has just one regret, which he revealed when he stated, "I shake my head sometimes when I look back at my numbers my first five years in the NFL compared to the second half of my career and what could have been if I had been in a 4–3 [defense] the whole time."

THE 50 GREATEST PLAYERS IN DETROIT LIONS HISTORY

CAREER HIGHLIGHTS

Best Season

Porcher performed extremely well for the Lions in 1999, when he finished third in the NFL with a career-high 15 sacks, recorded 47 tackles, and forced three fumbles. But Porcher had his finest all-around season in 1997, when, in addition to ranking among the league leaders with 12½ sacks, he registered a career-best 72 tackles, forced two fumbles, and intercepted a pass.

Memorable Moments/Greatest Performances

Porcher recorded two sacks in one game for the first time in his career during a 21–14 win over the Phoenix Cardinals on December 12, 1993.

Porcher helped lead the Lions to a 21–16 victory over the Bears on October 23, 1994, by registering two sacks and six tackles.

Porcher contributed to a 26–15 win over the Packers on September 28, 1997, by recording an interception and a sack.

Porcher recorded a career-high three and a half sacks during a 32–10 win over the Indianapolis Colts on November 23, 1997.

Porcher earned NFC Defensive Player of the Week honors by registering three sacks and three tackles for loss during a 28–20 win over the Seattle Seahawks in the 1999 regular-season opener.

Porcher gained recognition as NFL Defensive Player of the Week by recording three sacks, recovering a fumble, and registering five solo tackles and three tackles for loss during a 31–21 win over the Giants on November 19, 2000.

Porcher scored the only points of his career when he recovered a fumble in the end zone for a touchdown during a 38–36 loss to the Vikings in the final game of the 2002 regular season.

Notable Achievements

- Scored one defensive touchdown.
- Finished in double digits in sacks five times.
- Finished third in NFL with 15.0 sacks in 1999.
- Finished fourth in NFL with 17 tackles for loss in 2001.
- Led Lions in sacks eight times.
- Led Lions defensive linemen in tackles four times.

ROBERT PORCHER **141**

- Ranks first in franchise history with 18 forced fumbles.
- Ranks among Lions career leaders with 95½ sacks (2nd), 603 tackles (4th), and 187 games played (6th).
- 1993 division champion.
- 1999 Week 1 NFC Defensive Player of the Week.
- 2000 Week 12 NFL Defensive Player of the Week.
- Three-time Pro Bowl selection (1997, 1999, and 2001).
- Three-time First-Team All-NFC selection (1997, 1999, and 2001).
- Named to Lions 75th Anniversary All-Time Team in 2008.
- Named to Lions All-Time Team in 2019.

22

DICK "NIGHT TRAIN" LANE

In discussing Dick "Night Train" Lane, former San Francisco 49ers head coach Red Hickey said, "Train was the greatest defensive back that ever played the game. Period."

A tremendous cover corner who became known for his superior ball-hawking skills and ability to deliver devastating hits to the opposition, Lane proved to be a bane in the existence of quarterbacks and receivers throughout the NFL for 14 seasons, the last six of which he spent in Detroit. Although Lane had many of his finest seasons for the Los Angeles Rams and Chicago Cardinals, earning four Pro Bowl selections and three All-Pro nominations while playing for those two teams, he still had a lot left by the time he arrived in Detroit in 1960, gaining Pro Bowl and All-Pro recognition three times each during his time in the Motor City. One of pro football's career leaders in both interceptions and interception-return yards, Lane, who the NFL named as its greatest all-time cornerback during its 50th anniversary celebration in 1969, received the additional honors of gaining induction into the Pro Football Hall of Fame, being included on both the *Sporting News*' 1999 list and the NFL Network's 2010 list of the 100 Greatest Players in NFL History, and being named to the NFL 100 All-Time Team in 2019.

Born in Austin, Texas, on April 16, 1928, Richard Lane suffered the indignity of being abandoned as an infant by his biological parents, a prostitute and a pimp, who left him in a dumpster, covered in newspapers. Detailing the events that transpired at that early stage of his life, Lane recounted, "My father was called Texas Slim. I never saw him—I don't know if he's the one that told my mother to throw me away. A pimp told my mother I had to go. They put me in a trash can and took off. Some people heard me crying. They thought it was a cat."

Adopted and raised by Ella Lane, a woman with four other children who ran a laundry business out of her home, Lane grew up poor, helping the family make ends meet by busing tables at local hotels and shining shoes. After getting his start in sports by competing against other children

Dick "Night Train" Lane ranks among the greatest defensive backs in NFL history.

in his neighborhood, Lane began to display his athletic skills at L. C. Anderson High School, an all-black school in Austin, where he excelled in football, baseball, and basketball.

Following his graduation from Anderson High, Lane moved to Nebraska to live with his birth mother, Etta Mae King, with whom he had reconciled during his youth. Lane subsequently spent one year attending Scottsbluff Junior College, starring for the school's football, baseball, and basketball teams, before enlisting in the U.S. Army in 1948. Lane ended up serving in the military for four years, during which time he rose to the rank of lieutenant colonel. Stationed much of the time at Fort Ord in Monterey Bay, California, Lane continued to compete on the gridiron, garnering Second-Team All-Army honors in 1949, before gaining First-Team All-Army recognition two years later by catching 18 touchdown passes.

Discharged from the army in 1952, Lane took a job working in an aircraft plant in Los Angeles, where he made his living lifting heavy sheets of

144   THE 50 GREATEST PLAYERS IN DETROIT LIONS HISTORY

metal out of a bin and placing them onto a press. Seeking something more rewarding, Lane showed up one day at the offices of the Los Angeles Rams, bringing with him a scrapbook that contained clippings from his high school, junior college, and military days. Granted a tryout by the Rams, the 24-year-old Lane, who had previously played almost exclusively on offense, ended up earning the starting right cornerback job on defense.

Performing magnificently as a rookie, Lane set an NFL single-season record that still stands by recording 14 interceptions, which he returned for 298 yards and two touchdowns. Meanwhile, Lane acquired his famous nickname his first year in the league from his association with Rams Hall of Fame receiver Tom Fears, who often played Jimmy Forrest's hit song "Night Train" when the two men met to go over plays, pass patterns, and defensive moves.

Lane spent one more year in Los Angeles, picking off another three passes in 1953, before being inexplicably traded to the Chicago Cardinals following the conclusion of the campaign. Continuing to perform at an elite level during his time in the Windy City, Lane recorded a total of 30 interceptions, amassed 628 interception-return yards, and scored two more times on defense over the course of the next six seasons, earning in the process four trips to the Pro Bowl, three All-Pro selections, and two First-Team All-Eastern Conference nominations. Particularly outstanding in 1954 and 1956, Lane led the NFL with 10 interceptions and 181 interception-return yards in the first of those campaigns, before gaining official First-Team All-Pro recognition for the first time in his career two years later by ranking among the league leaders with seven picks and 206 interception-return yards.

Blessed with outstanding speed, superior reflexes, and excellent instincts, Lane had the ability to cover any receiver in the league one-on-one. Often engaging his man at the line of scrimmage, Lane typically pestered him all over the field, with former Rams head coach Sid Gillman saying, "Night Train was the first corner man that I ever saw in the National Football League that could play the bump-and-run."

A thinking man's player, Lane frequently baited opposing quarterbacks to throw the ball in his direction by making it appear as if his man were open, before swooping in for the interception.

More than anything, though, Lane became known for his tremendous physicality. Extremely strong, the 6'1", 194-pound Lane developed a reputation as one of the league's hardest hitters and most ferocious tacklers, often sending opposing players to the sidelines with his aggressive style of play, which led to several changes in the rules. After Lane's face-mask tackle of Jon Arnett in 1961 left the Rams running back lying motionless on the field for several minutes, the NFL adopted a new rule the following year that prohibited the grasping of an opponent's head gear. The league also banned Lane's practice of driving opponents to the turf with a carefully delivered forearm blow to the chin and his favorite maneuver of tackling them around the head and neck, which, after initially being called a "Night Train Necktie," later became known as a clothesline.

In explaining the rationale behind using such brutal tactics, Lane offered, "My object is to stop the guy with the ball before he gains another inch. I'm usually dealing with ends who are trying to catch passes, and if I hit them in the legs, they may fall forward for a first down. There is nothing I hate worse than a first down."

Despite everything Lane brought to the Cardinals, he found himself headed elsewhere once again when they dealt him to the Lions for lineman Gerry Perry on August 22, 1960, in what Joe Schmidt later called "one of the greatest trades that will ever be made in any sport."

Joining a talented defensive secondary that included right cornerback Dick LeBeau and safeties Gary Lowe and Yale Lary, the 31-year-old Lane picked up right where he left off, gaining Pro Bowl, First-Team All-Western Conference, and unofficial First-Team All-Pro recognition from the Newspaper Enterprise Association his first year in Detroit by recording five interceptions, one of which he returned 80 yards for a touchdown. Continuing to perform at an elite level on the left side of the Lions' defense from 1961 to 1963, Lane picked off a total of 15 passes, earning in the process All-Pro honors each season.

Although Lane no longer possessed the blazing speed that he had earlier in his career by the time he arrived in the Motor City, he remained one of the NFL's finest cover corners. Still capable of staying with virtually any receiver in the league, Lane also used his experience and knowledge of his opponent's tendencies to his advantage. Meanwhile, Lane continued to display the same tenacity and aggressiveness on which he built his reputation, with former Colts running back Alex Hawkins, who competed against him during his time in Detroit, remembering, "He was one of the few players that hurt you every time he tackled you, [Dick] Butkus being the other one."

Lions assistant coach Aldo Forte recalled a hit that Lane placed on New York Giants quarterback Y. A. Tittle during the early stages of a 1962 contest that literally "knocked the plays out of his head," rendering the quarterback unable to remember any of the team's plays until after halftime.

Hampered by injuries in both 1964 and 1965, Lane appeared in a total of just 14 games, starting only seven of those, before being released by the

146 THE 50 GREATEST PLAYERS IN DETROIT LIONS HISTORY

Lions and subsequently announcing his retirement. Over the course of 14 NFL seasons, Lane recorded 68 interceptions, which he returned for 1,207 yards and five touchdowns. Lane also recovered 11 fumbles and scored three other TDs. As a member of the Lions, Lane recorded 21 interceptions, amassed 272 interception-return yards, recovered four fumbles, and scored one touchdown.

Following his playing days, Lane remained with the Lions as a special assistant for six years, before spending two seasons serving as an assistant coach at the collegiate level. Lane also briefly worked as road manager for comedian Redd Foxx and spent 17 years serving as director of the Police Athletic League for underprivileged children in Detroit. Retiring to private life in 1992, Lane returned to his hometown of Austin, Texas, where he lived until January 29, 2002, when he died from a heart attack at the age of 73 after spending his final years suffering from diabetes and CTE.

Continuing to be ranked among the all-time greats long after his playing days ended, Lane received high praise from Pat Summerall, who stated, "I played with him and against him. He was the best I've ever seen."

Meanwhile, former Lions teammate Wayne Walker suggested, "Probably, if he was playing today, Night Train Lane would be as good as any cornerback in football. I mean, he had to be the prototype for what an NFL cornerback should be."

LIONS CAREER HIGHLIGHTS

Best Season

Although Lane performed better for the Rams and Cardinals in three or four other years, he had his finest season as a member of the Lions in 1961, when he gained First-Team All-Pro recognition from both the AP and the Newspaper Enterprise Association by recording six interceptions, which he returned a total of 73 yards.

Memorable Moments/Greatest Performances

Lane clinched a 30–17 victory over the Colts on October 23, 1960, when he returned his fourth-quarter interception of a Johnny Unitas pass 80 yards for a touchdown.

Lane contributed to a 24–0 shutout of the 49ers on November 6, 1960, by picking off John Brodie twice.

Lane recorded another pair of interceptions during a 17–13 win over the Packers in the opening game of the 1961 regular season.

Lane helped lead the Lions to a 13–7 win over the Vikings on December 10, 1961, by picking off a pair of Fran Tarkenton passes.

Notable Achievements

- Scored one defensive touchdown.
- Recorded at least five interceptions three times.
- Amassed more than 100 interception-return yards once.
- Led Lions in interceptions three times.
- Ranks among NFL career leaders with 68 interceptions (4th) and 1,207 interception-return yards (6th).
- Three-time Pro Bowl selection (1960, 1961, and 1962).
- Two-time First-Team All-Pro selection (1961 and 1962).
- 1963 Second-Team All-Pro selection.
- 1960 Newspaper Enterprise Association First-Team All-Pro selection.
- Four-time First-Team All-Western Conference selection (1960, 1961, 1962, and 1963).
- Named to NFL 50th Anniversary All-Time Team in 1969.
- Named to NFL 75th Anniversary All-Time Team in 1994.
- Named to NFL 100 All-Time Team in 2019.
- Number 19 on the *Sporting News'* 1999 list of the 100 Greatest Players in NFL History.
- Number 30 on the NFL Network's 2010 list of the NFL's 100 Greatest Players.
- Named to Lions 75th Anniversary All-Time Team in 2008.
- Named to Lions All-Time Team in 2019.
- Inducted into Lions Ring of Honor in 2009.
- Inducted into Pro Football Hall of Fame in 1974.

23

ROGER BROWN

The most physically imposing member of a Lions defensive line that became known as the "Fearsome Foursome," Roger Brown spent seven seasons in Detroit dominating the opposition from his right tackle position. A massive man who excelled as both a run-stuffer and a pass-rusher, Brown brought down opposing quarterbacks behind the line of scrimmage more than 10 times in a season on four separate occasions, en route to recording the fourth-most sacks in franchise history. A five-time Pro Bowler who also earned three All-Pro nominations during his time in the Motor City, Brown later received the additional honors of gaining induction into the Lions Ring of Honor and being named to both the Lions 75th Anniversary Team in 2008 and their All-Time Team in 2019.

Born in Surrey County, Virginia, on May 1, 1937, Roger Lee Brown, who lost his biological mother at the age of four, moved with his father, stepmom, and two siblings at an early age to Nyack, New York, where he attended Nyack High School. Although Brown did not compete in organized sports until the ninth grade, he quickly developed into a star on the gridiron in high school, earning the starting fullback job on the varsity squad by the end of his freshman year.

After manning that post for the Redhawks for three seasons, Brown enrolled at the University of Maryland Eastern Shore, a small all-black school that competed in the National Association of Intercollegiate Athletics (NAIA). Recalling how he ended up at that institution, Brown said, "I was supposed to go to Michigan State, and I was supposed to go to Syracuse. But my grades out of high school weren't that strong. So, they said if I went to a junior college and obtained a C average, they would accept me as a transfer."

Choosing to remain at Maryland Eastern Shore even after he attained a 3.0 grade-point average, Brown spent four seasons playing for head coach Vernon "Skip" McCain, who shifted him from fullback to defensive tackle prior to the start of his sophomore year. Adapting extremely well to his new position, Brown helped lead the Hawks to the Central Intercollegiate

Roger Brown recorded more than 10 sacks in four of his seven seasons with the Lions.

Athletic Association title in 1957, before earning NAIA and *Pittsburgh Courier* Black All-America honors in each of the next two seasons.

In discussing the impact that Brown made during his college career, National Football Foundation chairman Archie Manning stated, "Roger Brown was an absolute force on the defensive line at Maryland Eastern Shore. He was a huge part of HBCU football history and helped usher in the era of massive linemen to the game."

Despite his small college background, Brown became a much-sought-after commodity following his graduation, with the Lions selecting him

150 THE 50 GREATEST PLAYERS IN DETROIT LIONS HISTORY

in the fourth round of the 1960 NFL Draft with the 42nd overall pick, the New York Titans claiming him in that year's AFL Draft, and the Saskatchewan Rough Riders of the Canadian Football League recruiting him to play north of the border. Recalling his selection by the Lions, Brown stated, "I was drafted in 1960 number four, which at the time was the highest draft of any black athlete at an all-Black college or university. Some writeups say that I came from Pittsburgh to the Detroit Lions. What happened was that the Lions got an extra fourth-round pick from the Steelers when they traded Bobby Layne to Pittsburgh. So, they used that extra draft choice to draft me."

Ultimately choosing to sign with the Lions for $8,000 even though he received a better offer from Saskatchewan, Brown made an extremely favorable impression on Detroit defensive line coach Les Bingaman at his first pro training camp, with the former lineman telling reporters following the first day of practice, "Brown has everything needed to be great in this league: size, speed, quickness, and real desire; and if he works hard at improving himself, he can become a great tackle."

Anointed the Lions' starting right tackle prior to the start of the regular season, Brown spent his rookie campaign starting alongside Alex Karras, with whom he combined the next several years to form the league's most dominant pair of interior defensive linemen. Developing into nearly the equal of his Hall of Fame linemate by his second NFL season, Brown gained unofficial Second-Team All-Pro recognition from both UPI and the Newspaper Enterprise Association by recording a team-high 12 sacks and recovering three fumbles. Even better in 1962, Brown helped the Lions compile a regular-season record of 11–3 by finishing third in the league with 14 sacks, recovering another three fumbles, and registering two safeties, earning in the process Pro Bowl and First-Team All-Pro honors for the first time.

Blessed with great size and tremendous strength, Brown, who stood 6'5" and spent most of his career playing at a weight somewhere between 300 and 320 pounds, proved to be the largest player in the game during the early 1960s. Yet, despite his size, Brown possessed exceptional quickness, once being clocked at 5.4 seconds for 50 yards while also posting a personal-best time of 10 seconds flat in the 100-yard dash.

In addressing his foot speed during a 2018 interview with MLive.com, Brown said, "For a big 320-pound guy, not too many people could run faster than me. I caught a lot of halfbacks, a lot of quarterbacks, got past a lot of people."

Claiming that his former teammate's rare combination of size, speed, and strength made him one of the league's most dominant players, Mike

Lucci stated, "Roger was probably 10 or 15 pounds north of 300. When he wanted to play, they couldn't block him."

Known for the head slap that he first began using in college, Brown often employed that maneuver against opposing offensive linemen, making him even more difficult for them to block. Also noted for his consistency and strong work ethic, Brown received high praise during the early stages of the 1963 campaign from Les Bingaman, who stated, "Roger had one of the greatest days any tackle ever had against the Packers last year, but while he is not always that spectacular, he has turned in consistently outstanding games for us since 1960. . . . He never stops trying to improve himself."

Bingaman then added, "We've got the two best tackles anywhere, maybe at any time."

While Brown and Karras combined to give the Lions a tremendous pairing on the interior of their defensive line, they received a considerable amount of assistance on the outside from ends Darris McCord and Sam Williams, who helped form a four-man front that became known as the "Fearsome Foursome." Wreaking havoc on opposing offenses their four years together, the quartet helped the Lions record a total of 189 sacks from 1962 to 1965, with Brown registering 45½ of those.

Although Brown registered just five and a half sacks in 1963, he earned his second All-Pro nomination and the second of his six straight Pro Bowl selections, before gaining First-Team All-Western Conference recognition in each of the next two seasons by recording a total of 26 sacks. Despite being plagued by bone chips in his left knee for much of the 1966 campaign, Brown appeared in every game the Lions played for the seventh straight season, bringing his string of consecutive starts to a total of 96.

But after Brown underwent surgery to repair his injured knee the following offseason and reported to training camp still complaining of soreness, former teammate and new Lions head coach Joe Schmidt decided to trade him to the Los Angeles Rams for three high draft picks, saying at the time, "Roger has been a standout for us for many years. But we are looking to the future and feel our younger players are adequate."

Although initially despondent on learning of the deal, Brown eventually came to embrace his new home, remembering, "I mean, I was floored. I couldn't believe it. I had just gotten married and just bought a house, and I wanted to think about it. . . . It turned out to be a better deal for me. I got more money and more notoriety. I went out there to play with a group of guys who were on the verge of winning a championship."

Brown, who left Detroit with career totals of 63½ sacks, 11 fumble recoveries, three safeties, and two interceptions, ended up spending three seasons playing alongside Deacon Jones, Merlin Olsen, and Lamar Lundy on another outstanding defensive line that borrowed the nickname "Fearsome Foursome" from his former team. Choosing to announce his retirement after losing his starting job to Coy Bacon in 1969, Brown ended his career with 79 sacks, 15 fumble recoveries, and the same three safeties and two interceptions he recorded as a member of the Lions.

Looking back on his 10-year NFL career years later, Brown said, "To play on two of the greatest defensive lines in the history of pro football, that was the biggest highlight. To play for Detroit and then to play for George Allen and the Rams, that was another highlight."

Further expounding on his time in Detroit, Brown recalled, "The things I remember most about Lion highlights is that we had a great defensive team. We had the 'Four L's' in the backfield and the best front four in football at that time. The four L's were Dick LeBeau, Yale Lary, Dick 'Night Train' Lane, and Gary Lowe."

Extremely proud of his ability to take the field each week, Brown, who appeared in a total of 140 games, including the postseason, added, "In my 10 years with the Lions and the Rams, I never missed a game. I had broken hands and broken bones. But probably not as many as I caused. I had 12 operations."

After retiring from football, Brown, who owned a recording business in Detroit during his playing days, became a restaurateur,, first opening a chain of fried chicken restaurants in Chicago, before eventually relocating to the Hampton Roads area of Virginia, where he ran a restaurant that he named after himself. In between, Brown worked for McDonald's, initially as an operations manager trainee, before becoming the human resources manager for California and the West.

Brown, who developed an eating problem during the latter stages of his playing career that caused him to eventually balloon up to 450 pounds, altered his lifestyle after experiencing a health scare in retirement. After having his stomach stapled, Brown implemented a diet that enabled him to maintain a weight of 225 pounds for the rest of his life. Brown lived until September 17, 2021, when he died at the age of 84 from an undisclosed illness.

Following his passing, Lions owner Sheila Ford Hamp issued a statement that read, "Roger Brown will always hold a special place in our team's history. Roger's career accomplishments solidify his legacy alongside some of the all-time greats of our game. I am happy we were able to induct Roger into the Pride of the Lions in 2018 to ensure that his contributions to the Lions will never be forgotten."

LIONS CAREER HIGHLIGHTS

Best Season

Brown ranked second in the NFL in 1964 with an unofficial total of 14½ sacks, which represented the highest single-season mark of his career. Yet, even though Brown is listed as having recorded 11½ sacks the following year, he claimed that he registered several more, once stating, "I know in 1965, in total, I had 19 sacks just that season because the defensive coaches used to keep track of how many times you got to the quarterback." Nevertheless, the 1962 campaign would have to be considered the finest of Brown's career. While pro football researchers later credited Brown with an unofficial total of 14 sacks, Lions team stats indicate that he registered 19 on the season. Furthermore, Brown recovered three fumbles and set an NFL record by scoring twice on safeties, with his dominant play earning him the first of his two First-Team All-Pro nominations, a fourth-place finish in the league MVP voting, and recognition from the *Los Angeles Times* as both the NFL Lineman of the Year and the NFL Defensive Player of the Year.

Memorable Moments/Greatest Performances

In addition to intercepting a pass during a 45–14 rout of the St. Louis Cardinals on November 12, 1961, Brown helped anchor a defense that created four turnovers and registered eight sacks.

Brown recorded the first of his three career safeties when he sacked Johnny Unitas in the end zone during a 29–20 win over the Colts on September 30, 1962.

Brown turned in the most dominant performance of his career during a 26–14 victory over the eventual NFL champion Green Bay Packers on Thanksgiving Day 1962. In addition to recording seven of the 11 sacks the Lions registered against Bart Starr, Brown caused a fumble that teammate Sam Williams returned for a touchdown, tackled Starr in the end zone for a safety, and blocked a Jerry Kramer field goal attempt.

Brown again proved to be too much for the Packers to handle during a 12–7 Lions win on November 7, 1965, earning NFL Defensive Player of the Week honors by recording a safety and anchoring a defense that allowed just 68 yards of total offense and sacked Bart Starr 11 times.

Notable Achievements

- Finished in double digits in sacks four times.
- Recorded seven sacks vs. Green Bay Packers on Thanksgiving Day 1962.
- Led NFL with two safeties in 1962.
- Finished second in NFL with 14½ sacks in 1964.
- Finished third in NFL with 14.0 sacks in 1962.
- Led Lions in sacks three times.
- Ranks among Lions career leaders with 63½ sacks (4th) and 11 fumble recoveries (tied for 8th).
- 1965 Week 8 NFL Defensive Player of the Week.
- *Los Angeles Times* 1962 NFL Lineman of the Year.
- *Los Angeles Times* 1962 NFL Defensive Player of the Year.
- Finished fourth in 1962 NFL MVP voting.
- Five-time Pro Bowl selection (1962, 1963, 1964, 1965, and 1966).
- Two-time First-Team All-Pro selection (1962 and 1963).
- 1965 Second-Team All-Pro selection.
- Two-time Newspaper Enterprise Association Second-Team All-Pro selection (1961 and 1964).
- Three-time First-Team All-Western Conference selection (1964, 1965, and 1966).
- Pro Football Reference All-1960s Second Team.
- Named to Lions 75th Anniversary All-Time Team in 2008.
- Named to Lions All-Time Team in 2019.
- Inducted into Lions Ring of Honor in 2018.

24

DOAK WALKER

lready a legend by the time he arrived in Detroit in 1950, Doak Walker previously spent three seasons starring on the gridiron at Southern Methodist University (SMU), where he established himself as the greatest college football player in the nation with his superior all-around play. A three-time First-Team All-American who won the Heisman Trophy his junior year, Walker continued to perform at an elite level during his six seasons in the Motor City, helping the Lions win three division titles and two NFL championships by amassing more than 1,000 all-purpose yards three times and leading the league in scoring twice. An extraordinarily versatile player who did a little bit of everything for the Lions, Walker earned five Pro Bowl selections and four First-Team All-Pro nominations, before being further honored by having his No. 37 retired by the organization, being named to the Lions All-Time Team in 2019, and gaining induction into the Pro Football Hall of Fame.

Born in Dallas, Texas, on January 1, 1927, Ewell Doak Walker II acquired his love for football at an early age from his father, a teacher and coach at North Dallas High School who earlier competed in multiple sports while attending Texas Christian University in nearby Fort Worth. The younger Walker, who began playing organized football in grade school, became so obsessed with the sport by his early teenage years that he often snuck into the closet in his father's classroom, grabbed one of the footballs, and imagined himself scoring touchdowns without anyone being able to catch him.

Eventually emerging as a standout athlete at Highland Park High School, Walker starred in football, baseball, basketball, swimming, and track. Particularly outstanding on the gridiron, Walker excelled as a running back on offense and a cornerback on defense while playing alongside future Lions teammate Bobby Layne.

After briefly serving in the Merchant Marine following his graduation, Walker spent one year in the U.S. Army, before enrolling at SMU following

155

Doak Walker led the NFL in scoring twice.

his discharge early in 1947. Performing brilliantly for the Mustangs the next three seasons, Walker gained consensus All-America recognition each year by excelling in virtually every aspect of the game. In addition to running well with the football, Walker caught passes, played defensive back, punted, and returned punts and kickoffs. Named the winner of the Heisman Trophy following the conclusion of the 1948 campaign, Walker later received high praise from fellow SMU alum Jim Sid Wright, who said, "I don't think he had any peers. He was the last of the great single-wing tailbacks. He was the best all-around tailback that I ever saw."

Former SMU tight end Raleigh Blakely, a teammate of Walker's for two seasons, marveled, "You just had to see him to believe what he could do."

Francis Pulattie also spoke highly of his former Mustang teammate, saying, "Having Doak on our team was like having loaded dice or marked cards.

We just felt like we had to do our part and Doak would do the rest. The most amazing thing is that he did it all so effortlessly. He made it look so simple. . . . No one ever questioned his leadership. He'd kneel down and say, 'Okay, we've got to do this,' and everybody would just bust their butt for him."

An exceptional all-around athlete, Walker also played outfield for SMU's baseball team and served as a backup on the school's basketball squad, once saying, "Other than golf, I never really tried a sport that, inside of 30 minutes, I couldn't play pretty well."

Selected by the New York Bulldogs with the third overall pick of the 1949 NFL Draft, Walker appeared headed for Detroit when the Lions acquired him from the Bulldogs for back John Rauch. But with the Cleveland Browns also selecting Walker in the ninth round of that year's AAFC Draft with the 69th overall pick, they had a claim to his services as well following the merger of the two leagues. Forced by NFL commissioner Bert Bell to resolve the dispute, the two sides completed a trade in which the Lions sent a second-round pick in the 1950 NFL Draft to the Browns for the exclusive rights to Walker.

Arriving in Detroit prior to the start of the 1950 campaign, Walker, who stood just 5'10" and weighed only 173 pounds, later recalled how he felt around his new teammates during the early stages of his pro career, saying, "Everybody looked so big. I felt smaller than I was."

Nevertheless, Walker quickly established himself as one of the league's finest all-around players, earning Pro Bowl and First-Team All-Pro honors as a rookie by amassing 920 yards from scrimmage, ranking among the league leaders with 1,262 all-purpose yards and 11 touchdowns, and topping the circuit with 128 points scored while seeing action as both a running back and a wide receiver on offense, a cornerback on defense, and a punter, kicker, and return man on special teams. Walker followed that up with another strong season, gaining Pro Bowl and First-Team All-Pro recognition again in 1951 by accumulating 777 yards from scrimmage, scoring six touchdowns, and placing near the top of the league rankings with 1,270 all-purpose yards and 97 points scored.

Plagued by a torn leg muscle in 1952 that limited him to just seven games, Walker gained only 196 yards from scrimmage and scored just 15 points. But he returned to top form the following year, helping the Lions capture their second straight NFL championship by amassing 839 yards from scrimmage and 978 all-purpose yards, finishing third in the league with 93 points scored, and placing second in the circuit with a career-high 12 field goals, earning in the process Pro Bowl and First-Team All-Pro honors for the third time.

158   THE 50 GREATEST PLAYERS IN DETROIT LIONS HISTORY

Excelling at the professional level despite his smallish frame, Walker overcame anything he lacked in size with his superior athletic ability, fleetness afoot, outstanding instincts, and indomitable spirit, once saying, "If you're scared, you have no business in the game. It has to be rough, and that's the way we want it. . . . I don't ever think of survival. When you are on the field, you are just too busy for that. Slowing up can be fatal, but speed isn't the answer. I'd like to think the good Lord is taking care of me."

Described in a 1955 article that appeared in *Sports Illustrated* as "a marvelous, natural running back who has been just about the most effective operator in the NFL the past five years," Walker, who spent most of his time in Detroit sharing the offensive backfield with quarterback Bobby Layne and two other running backs as part of the then-popular "T" formation the team employed, proved to be much more than just an outstanding runner. An excellent pass-catcher, Walker amassed more than 500 receiving yards three times. Assuming many other roles as well, Walker often lined up on defense as a member of the Lions' secondary, occasionally returned punts and kickoffs, and spent most of his career serving as the team's primary placekicker. In fact, Walker led the league in extra points made, finished second in the circuit in field goals made, and successfully converted more than 60 percent of his field goal attempts twice each.

Walker remained with the Lions for two more years, earning another two Pro Bowl selections and his final All-Pro nomination, before announcing his retirement following the conclusion of the 1955 campaign with career totals of 1,520 rushing yards, 152 receptions, 2,539 receiving yards, 4,059 yards from scrimmage, 5,371 all-purpose yards, 34 touchdowns, 534 points scored, and two interceptions along with a rushing average of 4.9 yards per carry and a punting average of 39.1 yards per kick.

In explaining his decision to leave the game while still in his prime, Walker told Jerry Green of the *Detroit News* in 1986, "I'd been on three division champions and two world champions. I'd been to five Pro Bowls and made All-Pro four times. What else was there to do?"

Further expounding on his reasons for retiring when he did in his 1997 autobiography, *Doak Walker: More Than a Hero*, Walker told writer Whit Canning, "I didn't retire in 1955 because I lost the desire. I had achieved just about everything that I felt I could. I always knew it was something you couldn't do forever, and I didn't want to be one of those guys who stayed a year too long. I didn't want to leave burned out or crippled. . . . No, I don't have any regrets about quitting football when I did. I'm not sorry because I've got all my teeth, both knees—and most of my faculties."

DOAK WALKER **159**

Following his playing days, Walker took a job working in public relations for an electrical construction company and married former Olympic skier Skeeter Werner, with whom he moved to Colorado after the business transferred him there. Eventually, Walker went into business for himself as the head of Walker Chemicals.

Walker lived until September 27, 1998, when he died at Routt Hospital in Steamboat Springs, Colorado, at the age of 71 after being paralyzed in a skiing accident eight months earlier. Barely able to speak and unable to use his arms and legs following the accident, Walker received thousands of letters from well-wishers and fans worldwide that helped lift his spirits prior to his passing, with family spokesman Rod Hanna saying, "His eyes would come alive, his expression was wonderful, he was able to talk in short phrases."

Recalling his former teammate some years later, Joe Schmidt stated, "When I look back, I think of Doak's honesty and sincerity. He was the All-American boy who was handsome, not big or the fastest guy, but a clutch player who could just do everything very, very well. Everyone was disappointed when he quit because he was so important to our team. He was so young and vibrant and could have played several more years."

CAREER HIGHLIGHTS

Best Season

Although Walker also performed brilliantly in 1951 and 1954, scoring 97 points and amassing a career-high 1,270 all-purpose yards in the first of those campaigns, before tallying 106 points and accumulating 1,093 all-purpose yards in the second, he had his finest all-around season as a rookie in 1950. In addition to scoring 128 points, which represented the second-highest single-season total in NFL history at the time, Walker finished second in the league with 11 TDs and ranked among the circuit leaders with 920 yards from scrimmage, 1,262 all-purpose yards, and eight field goals made.

Memorable Moments/Greatest Performances

In addition to rushing for 87 yards and gaining another 30 yards on three pass receptions during a 10–7 win over the Pittsburgh Steelers on

160 THE 50 GREATEST PLAYERS IN DETROIT LIONS HISTORY

September 24, 1950, Walker tallied all the points the Lions scored on an 11-yard touchdown reception and a 20-yard field goal.

Walker starred in defeat on October 22, 1950, scoring a touchdown on a 30-yard pass from Bobby Layne and amassing 204 all-purpose yards during a 28–27 loss to the 49ers, gaining 52 yards on seven carries, 73 yards on three pass receptions, and another 79 yards on special teams.

Walker led the Lions to a 24–21 win over the Packers on November 19, 1950, by rushing for 47 yards, gaining another 67 yards on four pass receptions, and scoring all 24 of his team's points on a 35-yard field goal and three touchdown catches, the longest of which covered 33 yards.

Walker proved to be the difference in a 24–22 victory over the Los Angeles Rams on December 9, 1951, running for one touchdown and throwing a game-winning 22-yard TD pass to Leon Hart late in the fourth quarter.

Walker helped lead the Lions to a 17–7 win over the Browns in the 1952 NFL Championship Game by rushing for 97 yards and one touchdown, which came on a 67-yard run in the third quarter.

Walker collaborated with Bobby Layne on a career-long 83-yard touchdown reception during a 14–7 win over the Packers on November 15, 1953.

Walker displayed his tremendous versatility during a 48–23 victory over the Bears in the 1954 regular-season opener, making three receptions for 79 yards, carrying the ball five times for 37 yards and one touchdown, and scoring again on a 70-yard punt return.

Notable Achievements

- Amassed more than 1,000 all-purpose yards three times.
- Averaged more than five yards per carry twice.
- Scored more than 100 points twice.
- Returned one punt for a touchdown.
- Scored 11 touchdowns in 1950.
- Led NFL in points scored twice.
- Finished second in NFL in points scored once, touchdowns once, field goals made twice, and field goal percentage once.
- Led Lions in receptions and receiving yards once each.
- Ranks among Lions career leaders with 534 points scored (6th) and 34 touchdowns (tied for 11th).
- Three-time division champion (1952, 1953, and 1954).
- Two-time NFL champion (1952 and 1953).

- Five-time Pro Bowl selection (1950, 1951, 1953, 1954, and 1955).
- Four-time First-Team All-Pro selection (1950, 1951, 1953, and 1954).
- 1955 Newspaper Enterprise Association Second-Team All-Pro selection.
- Number 37 retired by Lions.
- Named to Lions 75th Anniversary All-Time Team in 2008.
- Named to Lions All-Time Team in 2019.
- Inducted into Lions Ring of Honor in 2009.
- Inducted into Pro Football Hall of Fame in 1986.

25

JASON HANSON

The longest-tenured player in franchise history, Jason Hanson spent 21 seasons in Detroit, scoring more points, kicking more field goals, converting more extra points, and appearing in more games than anyone else in team annals. A member of the Lions from 1992 to 2012, Hanson, who also holds NFL records for most years played with one team and most field goals made of at least 40 yards (189), tallied more than 100 points in a season on 12 separate occasions despite playing for teams that often struggled to score. One of the NFL's most accurate kickers for much of his career, Hanson successfully converted more than 95 percent of his field goal attempts twice, with his consistently excellent kicking earning him two Pro Bowl selections, one All-Pro nomination, and a spot on the Lions All-Time Team.

Born in Spokane, Washington, on June 17, 1970, Jason Douglas Hanson spent much of his leisure time as a youth playing soccer, before gradually transitioning to other sports as he grew older. Lettering in football, basketball, and soccer at Mead High School, Hanson began his career on the gridiron as a quarterback/wide receiver/kicker on the junior varsity squad. However, after realizing that his kicking ability far exceeded his passing and pass-catching skills, Hanson elected to focus exclusively on further developing that part of his game. Proving that he made the right choice, Hanson gained All-Greater Spokane League recognition as both a kicker and a punter his senior year while also earning First-Team All-State honors from the Washington Sportswriters Association. An excellent student as well, Hanson, who, before deciding to pursue a career in football, planned to become a doctor, maintained a perfect 4.0 grade-point average.

Following his graduation, Hanson enrolled at Washington State University, where he went on to establish himself as the finest kicker in the nation over the course of the next four seasons. A two-time First-Team All-American who also earned First-Team All-Pac-10 honors three times, Hanson set several NCAA records, including kicking the most field goals from 50 yards or more (20) and compiling the highest field goal percentage

Jason Hanson scored more points, kicked more field goals, and appeared in more games than anyone else in franchise history.

on kicks of at least 50 yards (57.1). Meanwhile, Hanson set school records for most points scored (328), field goals made (63), and point-after attempts converted (139). An outstanding punter as well, Hanson led the NCAA with a punting average of 45.5 yards per kick his junior year. Also continuing his excellent work in the classroom, Hanson gained Academic All-America recognition three times.

Impressed with Hanson's exceptional play at the collegiate level, the Lions selected him in the second round of the 1992 NFL Draft with the 56th overall pick. With Detroit subsequently waiving fan favorite Eddie Murray, who had spent the previous 10 years serving as the team's place-kicker, Hanson knew that he had big shoes to fill. But as he did throughout his career, Hanson never let the pressure get to him, earning NFL Offensive

164 THE 50 GREATEST PLAYERS IN DETROIT LIONS HISTORY

Rookie of the Year honors from the Pro Football Writers Association by successfully converting 21 of his 26 field goal attempts (80.8 percent). Outstanding again in 1993, Hanson gained unofficial First-Team All-Pro recognition from the *Sporting News* by finishing second in the league with 34 field goals and 130 points scored, hitting on 34 of his 43 field goal attempts (79.1 percent).

Somewhat less successful in 1994, Hanson converted just 66.7 percent of his field goal attempts (18 of 27), scoring in the process only 93 points. Nevertheless, Hanson gained the confidence of his teammates when he gave the Lions a 20–17 overtime win over the Dallas Cowboys in week 3 by splitting the uprights from 44 yards out, with Lomas Brown recalling, "That was the game where we really said, 'Hey, this guy's more than a kicker.' When we needed him in the clutch, then you could just tell he would be a special player."

Performing well under pressure throughout his career, Hanson kicked 17 game-winning field goals during his time in Detroit, with a record nine of those coming in overtime. Blessed with an extremely strong leg, the 6', 190-pound Hanson also holds NFL records for the most 40-plus- and 50-plus-yard field goals made.

Despite the success he experienced, Hanson acknowledged that place-kicking proved to be a nerve-racking way to make a living, saying, "Pressure-wise, it's as scary as anything in sports. There's no forgiveness if you miss. And it's a lot of money at stake and a lot of jobs."

Gradually establishing himself as one of the NFL's finest kickers during the 1990s, Hanson consistently ranked among the league leaders in field goals made and field goal percentage, earning in the process one All-Pro selection and two First-Team All-NFC nominations. Particularly outstanding in 1995 and 1997, Hanson finished third in the league with 132 points scored in the first of those campaigns, before tallying 117 points and successfully converting 89.7 percent of his field goal attempts in the second.

Maintaining his status as one of the league's elite kickers during his second decade in Detroit, Hanson had two of his finest seasons, successfully converting 22 of his 23 field goal attempts (95.7 percent) in 2003, before hitting on 21 of his 22 attempts (95.5 percent) in 2008, including all eight of his efforts from beyond the 50-yard line.

A fixture in the Detroit lineup each week, Hanson appeared in all but one game the Lions played his first 18 years in the league, before sustaining an injury to his right knee in 2010 that forced him to miss eight contests. Returning for his 20th season in 2011, Hanson received words of praise during the early stages of the campaign from tight end Tony Scheffler, who grew up rooting for the Lions in Chelsea, Michigan, a farming community located some 60 miles west of the Motor City. In discussing what his teammate meant to him and the entire region, Scheffler said, "Aside from Barry Sanders, he's been the steadiest, most go-to player this organization has had in a while, and his name rings throughout the state. . . . I can remember watching him as a kid. I'm 28 now, and it's still pretty cool to see him. It's a pretty surreal experience. I find myself just staring at the guy once in a while."

When asked to explain his incredible longevity, Hanson stated, "I think in the process of becoming a pro, you realize that there are some disciplines that you have to maintain. A routine is very important to maintaining success. That's part of what becoming a pro is; making your sport not just a hobby, but a profession, and learning how to take care of your body, to have a routine every day of warming up, preparing and practicing, and not compromising on anything or slacking off."

With Hanson electing to return for one more year in 2012, Peter King of *Sports Illustrated* said, "These guys [the Lions] are not married to Jason Hanson. They're married to the guy who's going to help them win games. And year after year, training camp after training camp, he beats out the best and brightest from the guys in college football. And that's why it's so admirable a story to me."

Meanwhile, Lions long snapper Don Muhlbach, who spent much of his career hiking the ball for Hanson to kick, commented, "Kickers are kickers, and specialists are specialists, in a locker room full of big guys and tough football players everywhere. But he has a lot of respect. Twenty-one years in—that earns enough respect from everybody in here."

Finally choosing to call it quits after successfully converting 32 of his 36 field goal attempts (88.9 percent) and scoring a career-high 134 points in 2012, Hanson made his decision known to the public on April 4, 2013, when he told the assembled media, "It's time. I gave serious thought and consideration to playing in 2013. While the determination and willpower are still there, the wear and tear on my body, especially the issues I had and still have with my heel, have convinced me that it's time to retire."

Expressing his appreciation to Hanson for his many contributions to the organization, Lions president Tom Lewand stated, "Jason Hanson is the gold standard. He had an exemplary, Hall-of-Fame worthy career on the field, and for those of us fortunate to know him well, he is an even better person, teammate, friend, husband, and father."

Hanson, who successfully converted just over 82 percent of his field goal attempts during his 21 seasons in Detroit, ended his career with 495 field goals, 665 extra points, and 2,150 points scored, all of which continue

166   THE 50 GREATEST PLAYERS IN DETROIT LIONS HISTORY

to place him among the NFL's all-time leaders. Having occasionally filled in at punter as well, Hanson amassed a total of 534 yards on his 15 kicks, giving him an average of 35.6 yards per punt.

Since retiring from football, Hanson, a devout Christian who pointed to the sky with both arms to give thanks to the heavens after every successful field goal conversion, has remained with his wife and three children in the metro Detroit area, where he gives private lessons to kickers, does motivational speaking, and supports several charities and faith-based events. Extremely active in his church, Hanson credits much of his faith to his career in football, saying, "You can have all the fame, glory, and success, and you kind of end up like, 'Really, is this it?' It can easily be taken away. It doesn't satisfy. . . . My faith grew because of success in sports."

Claiming that his beliefs helped him endure the many losing seasons he experienced in Detroit, Hanson says, "We had some really miserable years. When you are losing, even as the kicker, it's hard to show up. The season is half over, and you are missing the playoffs. Faith was part of that. It was hard, but I felt God was at work."

As for why he chose to remain in the Motor City for his entire career, Hanson says, "I never really pursued playing for another team, as they [the Lions] were willing to re-sign me, and I was willing to stay. I liked not having to move my family, and throughout my career I thought, 'Why not try to win and be successful here?' as opposed to trying to find the highest bidder in the free agent market. The team success never happened, but I don't regret playing only for the Lions."

CAREER HIGHLIGHTS

Best Season

Although Hanson scored more points in a few other seasons and posted a higher field goal percentage two other times, he turned in his finest all-around performance in 1997, when he earned Pro Bowl honors and his lone All-Pro nomination by ranking among the league leaders with 117 points scored and an 89.7 field goal percentage, successfully converting all but three of his 29 field goal attempts.

Memorable Moments/Greatest Performances

Hanson earned NFC Special Teams Player of the Week honors for the first of 12 times by successfully converting field goal attempts of 44, 37, and 37 yards during a 30–13 win over the Atlanta Falcons in the opening game of the 1993 regular season.

Hanson followed that up in week 2 by giving the Lions a 19–16 win over the Patriots when he kicked a 38-yard field goal in overtime.

Hanson came up big in the clutch again in the 1994 regular-season opener, when his 37-yard field goal less than five minutes into the overtime session gave the Lions a 31–28 win over Atlanta.

Hanson provided further heroics two weeks later, when his 44-yard field goal in overtime gave the Lions a 20–17 victory over the Dallas Cowboys.

Hanson gained NFC Special Teams Player of the Week recognition by kicking four field goals during a 27–24 win over the 49ers on September 25, 1995, with his 32-yarder with just a little over one minute left in regulation providing the margin of victory.

Hanson earned that honor again by converting all four of his field goal attempts during a 26–15 win over the Packers on September 28, 1997, with the longest of his kicks coming from 53 yards out.

Hanson contributed to a 32–10 victory over the Indianapolis Colts on November 23, 1997, by kicking field goals of 38, 52, and 55 yards, earning in the process NFC Special Teams Player of the Week honors.

After successfully converting field goal attempts of 45, 52, and 35 yards during regulation, Hanson gave the Lions a 19–16 win over the Pittsburgh Steelers on November 26, 1998, by driving the ball through the uprights from 42 yards out a little over two minutes into overtime.

Hanson earned NFL Special Teams Player of the Week honors for the first of six times by kicking a career-high six field goals during a 25–23 win over the Vikings on October 17, 1999, with his 48-yarder with just seven seconds left in regulation providing the margin of victory.

Hanson earned that honor again by kicking five field goals during a 15–10 win over Washington on September 10, 2000, with the longest of his kicks traveling 54 yards.

Hanson again tallied every point the Lions scored when he kicked three field goals during a 9–7 win over Dallas on November 3, 2002, with his 43-yarder with just 48 seconds left in regulation providing the margin of victory.

Hanson's four field goals enabled the Lions to defeat the Bears, 12–10, on November 9, 2003, with his 48-yarder with just 39 seconds left in the final period providing the winning margin.

Hanson gave the Lions a 13–12 victory over the Saints on December 24, 2005, when he kicked a 39-yard field goal as time expired in regulation.

THE 50 GREATEST PLAYERS IN DETROIT LIONS HISTORY

Hanson's four field goals proved to be the difference in a 26–23 overtime win over the Eagles on October 14, 2012, with his 45-yarder four minutes into overtime providing the margin of victory.

Notable Achievements

- Scored more than 100 points 12 times, topping 120 points on five occasions.
- Converted more than 95 percent of field goal attempts twice.
- Finished second in NFL in points scored once, field goals made once, and field goal percentage twice.
- Holds NFL records for most 40-plus-yard field goals (189) and seasons played with one team (21).
- Ranks among NFL career leaders in points scored (4th), field goals made (4th), extra points made (9th), and games played (7th).
- Holds Lions career records for most points scored (2,150), field goals made (495), extra points made (665), seasons played (21), and games played (327).
- Holds Lions single-season record for most field goals made (34 in 1993).
- 1993 division champion.
- Member of 1992 NFL All-Rookie Team.
- 1992 Pro Football Writers Association NFL Offensive Rookie of the Year.
- 12-time NFC Special Teams Player of the Week.
- Six-time NFL Special Teams Player of the Week.
- Five-time NFC Special Teams Player of the Month.
- Two-time Pro Bowl selection (1997 and 1999).
- 1997 Second-Team All-Pro selection.
- Two-time First-Team All-NFC selection (1997 and 1999).
- Named to Lions 75th Anniversary All-Time Team in 2008.
- Named to Lions All-Time Team in 2019.
- Inducted into Lions Ring of Honor in 2013.

26

JIM DAVID

Nicknamed the "Hatchet" for his propensity to deliver big hits to the opposition, Jim David spent his entire eight-year NFL career in Detroit, serving as an integral member of Lions teams that won four division titles and three league championships. An outstanding defensive back who excelled as both a tackler and a pass-defender, David recorded 36 interceptions during his eight-year stint in the Motor City, which represents the fifth-highest total in franchise history. A durable player who appeared in every game the Lions played from 1952 to 1959, David earned six Pro Bowl selections and two Second-Team All-Pro nominations, before being further honored by being named to the Pro Football Reference All-1950s Second Team and the Lions All-Time Team.

Born in Florence, South Carolina, on December 2, 1927, James Theodore David spent most of his formative years living some 100 miles south, in the city of North Charleston, where he starred in football and baseball at Chicora High School. Choosing to enlist in the U.S. Army following his graduation, David served as a staff sergeant in the infantry for three years, during which time he did a tour of duty in Europe. Enrolling at Colorado A&M (now known as Colorado State University) on an athletic scholarship following his discharge, David earned letters in his top two sports, proving to be especially proficient on the gridiron, where, as a receiver on offense and halfback on defense, he finished second in the nation in receptions his senior year.

Turning pro at the rather advanced age of 24 after being selected by the Lions in the 22nd round of the 1952 NFL Draft with the 261st overall pick, David laid claim to the starting left cornerback job immediately on his arrival in Detroit, joining in the process an extremely talented secondary that also included future Hall of Famers Jack Christiansen and Yale Lary. Performing exceptionally well as a rookie, David helped the Lions capture the first of their back-to-back NFL championships by finishing second on the team with seven interceptions. Outstanding in each of the next two

Jim David appeared in every game the Lions played during his eight seasons in Detroit.

seasons as well, David intercepted a total of 11 passes, with his seven picks in 1954 earning him Second-Team All-Pro honors and the first of his six consecutive Pro Bowl nominations.

An excellent ball-hawk, David possessed good speed, superior instincts, and an uncanny ability to read the minds of opposing quarterbacks, who frequently avoided throwing to his side of the field. Perhaps even more effective as a tackler, David proved to be one of the league's hardest hitters despite his smallish 5'11", 178-pound frame. Showing little regard for his body, David played with reckless abandon, delivering hits that left opposing players thinking that they had been struck by a much larger man. Making the two most notable tackles of his career in consecutive weeks in 1953, David became known as the "Hatchet" after he delivered devastating blows to San Francisco 49ers quarterback Y. A. Tittle and Los Angeles Rams wide receiver Tom Fears that knocked both future Hall of Famers out of their respective games with the Lions.

Continuing to perform well for the Lions at left cornerback the rest of the decade, David picked off another 18 passes from 1955 to 1959, earning in the process Pro Bowl honors each year and his second All-Pro nomination. Announcing his retirement following the conclusion of the 1959 campaign, David ended his career with five fumble recoveries and 36 interceptions, which he returned a total of 259 yards. An outstanding big-game player, David also recorded an interception in three of the four championship games in which he appeared.

After retiring as an active player, David spent four years serving as defensive backs coach of the Los Angeles Rams, before joining former Lions teammate Jack Christiansen's coaching staff in San Francisco. Following a three-year stint with the 49ers, David returned to Detroit, where he spent the next six seasons serving as defensive coordinator of the Lions under head coach and former teammate Joe Schmidt. Choosing to enter the business world after being relieved of his duties following the conclusion of the 1972 campaign, David became owner of Jim David and Associates, a manufacturer's representative firm located in metro Detroit. Eventually retiring to private life, David returned to his hometown of Florence, South Carolina, where he died at the age of 79 on July 29, 2007, following a long illness.

On learning of David's passing, Lions owner and chairman William Clay Ford issued a statement that read, "When you talk about great players from that era, you always talk about Jimmy. He was the epitome of a team player. Jimmy would do anything for his teammates and anything to help the Lions win."

Meanwhile, Hall of Fame cornerback Lem Barney, who spent his first several years in Detroit playing under David, said of his former defensive coordinator, "I had a love for him like a father. I respected and adored him, not only as a coach, but as a great defensive back. The things I learned were because of the instructions and all the information Jimmy gave me about playing cornerback in the NFL. I loved him. He was a headsy guy, very intelligent. He came up with great defensive schemes. One of the things he tried to stress was, you've got to study the game to play the game. Just a phenomenal guy."

172   THE 50 GREATEST PLAYERS IN DETROIT LIONS HISTORY

CAREER HIGHLIGHTS

Best Season

David earned Second-Team All-Pro honors in both 1954 and 1956, recording seven interceptions in each of those campaigns. With the Lions advancing to the NFL Championship Game and David also gaining First-Team All-Pro recognition from UPI and the *New York Daily News* in 1954, we'll identify that as the finest season of his career.

Memorable Moments/Greatest Performances

David contributed to a 52–17 thrashing of the Packers on October 26, 1952, by picking off two passes in one game for the first time in his career.

David recorded another two interceptions during a 41–6 rout of the Dallas Texans in the final game of the 1952 regular season.

David made a key interception during the Lions' 17–16 victory over the Browns in the 1953 NFL Championship Game, which he subsequently returned 36 yards.

David helped lead the Lions to a 21–17 win over the Packers on November 21, 1954, by recording a pair of interceptions, which he returned a total of 48 yards.

David recorded a career-high three interceptions during a 31–14 win over the Baltimore Colts on October 6, 1956.

Notable Achievements

- Never missed a game in eight seasons, appearing in 96 consecutive contests.
- Recorded seven interceptions three times.
- Led Lions in interceptions once.
- Ranks fifth in franchise history with 36 career interceptions.
- Four-time division champion (1952, 1953, 1954, and 1957).
- Three-time NFL champion (1952, 1953, and 1957).
- Six-time Pro Bowl selection (1954, 1955, 1956, 1957, 1958, and 1959).
- Two-time Second-Team All-Pro selection (1954 and 1956).
- Four-time Newspaper Enterprise Association Second-Team All-Pro selection (1955, 1957, 1958, and 1959).
- Pro Football Reference All-1950s Second Team.
- Named to Lions 75th Anniversary All-Time Team in 2008.
- Named to Lions All-Time Team in 2019.

27
MIKE LUCCI

The Lions' spiritual and emotional leader on defense for nearly a decade, Mike Lucci spent nine seasons in Detroit, starting at middle linebacker in eight of those. Providing the Lions with consistently excellent play at that post, Lucci led the team in tackles seven times, earning in the process team MVP honors on defense on three separate occasions. A one-time Pro Bowler, Lucci also earned one All-Pro selection and two All-NFC nominations, before being further honored by being named to the Lions All-Time Team in 2019.

Born in Ambridge, Pennsylvania, on December 29, 1939, Michael Gene Lucci grew up some 16 miles northwest of Pittsburgh, where he learned the value of hard work from his father, who made his living working in the local steel mills. Part of a first-generation Italian immigrant family, Lucci never played football until his senior year at Ambridge High School, when his gym teacher suggested that he try out for the school team.

Taking to the game immediately, Lucci performed so well that he earned a football scholarship to the University of Pittsburgh. However, after just one year there, Lucci elected to transfer to the University of Tennessee, where he spent two seasons starring for the Vols on both sides of the ball. A single-wing center on offense and a linebacker/end on defense, Lucci earned Third-Team All-SEC honors in 1960, before gaining Second-Team All-SEC and honorable mention All-America recognition the following year.

Selected by the Cleveland Browns in the fifth round of the 1961 NFL Draft with the 69th overall pick, Lucci became a starter his first year in the league, earning All-Rookie honors with his strong play at right-outside linebacker. But after losing his starting job and playing mostly on special teams the next two seasons, Lucci found himself headed to Detroit when the Lions acquired him prior to the start of the 1965 campaign as part of a complicated three-way trade they completed with the Browns and Giants that also sent offensive lineman Darrell Dess and a draft pick to the Motor

Mike Lucci earned team MVP honors on defense three times.

City, Lions quarterback Earl Morrall to New York, and Giants defensive back Erich Barnes to Cleveland.

Looking back on the deal years later, Lucci, who won an NFL championship while serving as a backup linebacker and special teams demon with the Browns in 1964, told the *Cleveland Plain Dealer* in 2014, "I was dejected following the trade, but, as the years went by, it obviously was good for everybody. . . . That was the only championship for me. We made the playoffs only once in my career with the Lions."

With Hall of Fame middle linebacker Joe Schmidt in the final season of his illustrious career in 1965, Lucci spent his first year in Detroit

MIKE LUCCI **175**

playing mostly on special teams, seeing a limited amount of duty on defense while backing up Schmidt and outside backers Wayne Walker and Ernie Clark. But following the retirement of Schmidt at the end of the year, Lucci laid claim to the starting middle linebacker job, which he retained for the next eight seasons.

Performing extremely well throughout the period, Lucci proved to be a stout run-defender who also excelled in pass coverage. Blessed with superior instincts, great intelligence, and the ability to shed blockers well, the 6'2", 230-pound Lucci led the Lions in tackles seven straight times. Known even more for his cover skills, Lucci did an outstanding job of guarding tight ends and running backs coming out of the backfield, recording a total of 21 interceptions, four of which he returned for touchdowns. Extremely durable as well, Lucci missed a total of just six games, at one point starting 56 consecutive contests.

The cornerstone of one of the league's better defensive units, Lucci, who spent his final six seasons in Detroit serving as team captain, helped the Lions remain competitive even though they often failed to perform as well on the other side of the ball. Respected for his outstanding play and strong leadership ability, Lucci earned team MVP honors on defense three straight times from 1969 to 1971, with Lions head coach Joe Schmidt calling him "the best linebacker in the NFL this year" at one point during the first of those campaigns. Although often overlooked in favor of Chicago Bears great Dick Butkus, who played in the same division, Lucci also earned the respect of players and coaches throughout the league, gaining Pro Bowl, All-Pro, and All-NFC recognition at different times while also garnering NFL MVP consideration in 1970 with his exceptional play for the 10–4 Lions.

Lucci continued to excel for the Lions at middle linebacker until 1973, when he announced his retirement at the end of the year after sustaining an injury that forced him to miss three contests. Lucci, who, in addition to picking off 21 passes, amassed 308 interception-return yards, recorded 12 sacks, recovered eight fumbles, scored four touchdowns, and made an unknown number of tackles on defense, briefly served as an analyst for Lions games on WJR Radio following his playing days, before beginning a successful career as a business executive and entrepreneur in the metro Detroit area that included a lengthy stint as president of Bally's Total Fitness and co-ownership of 19 Burger Kings in Michigan and Illinois. A noted philanthropist, Lucci also became heavily involved in several charitable causes. In addition to establishing an education endowment fund and raising more than $2 million for local children through a charity golf tournament he ran for 30 years, Lucci hosted an annual golf tournament in

176 THE 50 GREATEST PLAYERS IN DETROIT LIONS HISTORY

Florida that raised more than $650,000 for Gridiron Greats, an organization led by his longtime friend Mike Ditka that assists former NFL players who have fallen on hard times. Lucci continued to give of himself to others until October 26, 2021, when he died at the age of 81 in Boca Raton, Florida, after an extended illness.

Following his passing, Lions owner Sheila Ford Hamp released a statement that read, "We are deeply saddened to learn of the passing of Mike Lucci, whose passion for life was felt by all who knew him. Many will remember Mike for his toughness as a player during his nine seasons with the Lions. . . . His positive presence as a leader within our Lions Legends community made him a familiar face to all, and his willingness to give back will always be part of his great legacy. We extend our heartfelt sympathies to his wife, Patricia, and the entire Lucci family."

LIONS CAREER HIGHLIGHTS

Best Season

Lucci had an outstanding season in 1971, earning First-Team All-NFC honors and his lone Pro Bowl selection by recording five interceptions, which he returned for a total of 74 yards and two touchdowns. Lucci also performed extremely well the previous year, when his two picks, three fumble recoveries, and superior leadership for a Lions team that advanced to the playoffs as a wild card earned him Second-Team All-NFC honors and a fifth-place finish in the NFL MVP voting. But Lucci gained All-Pro recognition for the only time in his career in 1969, when both the AP and UPI accorded him Second-Team honors after he helped the Lions finish second in the league in total defense.

Memorable Moments/Greatest Performances

Although the Lions lost to the 49ers, 27–24, on October 23, 1966, Lucci recorded the first two interceptions of his career, which he returned a total of 36 yards.

Lucci earned NFL Defensive Player of the Week honors by picking off three Fran Tarkenton passes during a 32–31 win over the Vikings on November 13, 1966, returning one of his interceptions 63 yards for a touchdown.

Lucci contributed to a 45–3 rout of the 49ers on October 29, 1967, by returning his interception of a John Brodie pass 31 yards for a touchdown.

Lucci lit the scoreboard again on September 26, 1971, when he returned his interception of a Jim Plunkett pass 26 yards for a touchdown during a 34–7 victory over the New England Patriots.

Lucci gained recognition as NFL Defensive Player of the Week by recording three interceptions during a 28–3 win over the Bears on November 21, 1971, returning one of his picks 27 yards for a touchdown.

Lucci contributed to a 30–7 victory over the Bears on November 18, 1973, by recording a pair of interceptions, which he returned a total of 25 yards.

Notable Achievements

- Scored four defensive touchdowns.
- Recorded five interceptions and amassed 118 interception-return yards in 1966.
- Led Lions in tackles seven times.
- Ranks among Lions career leaders with 308 interception-return yards (10th) and four touchdown interceptions (2nd).
- Two-time NFL Defensive Player of the Week.
- Three-time Lions team MVP on defense (1969, 1970, and 1971).
- Finished tied for fifth in 1970 NFL MVP voting.
- 1971 Pro Bowl selection.
- 1969 Second-Team All-Pro selection.
- 1971 First-Team All-NFC selection.
- 1970 Second-Team All-NFC selection.
- Named to Lions All-Time Team in 2019.

28

NDAMUKONG SUH

A dominant interior defensive lineman who excelled as both a pass-rusher and a run-stopper, Ndamukong Suh spent five tumultuous years in Detroit, gaining general recognition as one of the NFL's finest players at his position while also garnering a considerable amount of criticism for his overly aggressive play. Starting at both tackle spots at different times for the Lions, Suh proved to be a huge contributor to teams that made two playoff appearances, often displaying the ability to take over a game all by himself. A four-time Pro Bowler who also earned four All-Pro nominations, Suh later received the additional honor of being named to the NFL 2010s All-Decade Team. Nevertheless, when Lions fans recall Suh's days in the Motor City, they are likely to be reminded of the reprehensible conduct he exhibited on the playing field at times that prompted his peers to once identify him as the "dirtiest player" in the NFL.

Born in Portland, Oregon, on January 6, 1987, Ndamukong Suh grew up with his four sisters in a loving and learning environment with each of his parents, who divorced shortly after he turned two years of age. Although Suh also formed an extremely close bond with his mother, an elementary school teacher who emigrated to the United States from Spanish Town, Jamaica, he identified his African-born father, a mechanical engineer and former semipro soccer player who runs his own heating and cooling company in Portland, as his greatest childhood influence, once saying, "My dad probably doesn't know it, but he was my idol."

Often accompanying his dad on house calls as a youngster, Suh recalled, "I was a weird kid. I didn't want to go to the park. I wanted to go to work with him." But while Suh secretly hoped to follow in his 5'8" father's footsteps, he outgrew him early in life, acquiring his height gene from his 7'3" great-grandfather.

Eventually emerging as a standout athlete at Grant High School, Suh lettered in football, basketball, soccer, and track and field, excelling in the latter in the shot put, where he won the Oregon School Activities

Ndamukong Suh gained Pro Bowl and All-Pro recognition four times each during his time in Detroit.
Courtesy of Mike Morbeck

Association Class 4A title in 2005 with a school-record throw of 61'4". Starring on the gridiron as well as a two-way lineman, Suh gained First-Team All-Portland Interscholastic League recognition on both offense and defense as a junior, before earning *Parade* magazine high school All-America honors his senior year by making 65 tackles, recording 10 sacks, and recovering four fumbles.

Rated as a four-star recruit by Rivals.com, Suh received several scholarship offers as graduation neared, with Nebraska, Mississippi State, Oregon State, Miami (FL), and California proving to be his most ardent suitors. Ultimately choosing to enroll at the University of Nebraska, Suh spent five seasons playing for the Cornhuskers, seeing a limited amount of duty

180   THE 50 GREATEST PLAYERS IN DETROIT LIONS HISTORY

as a redshirt freshman and true freshman, before establishing himself as a full-time starter his sophomore year. Performing exceptionally well over the course of the next three seasons, Suh gained First-Team All-Big 12 and honorable mention All-America recognition as a junior, before earning Big-12 Defensive Player of the Year, College Football Player of the Year, and unanimous First-Team All-America honors his senior year by recording 12 sacks, 85 tackles, 20½ tackles for loss, 28 quarterback hurries, and three blocked kicks. Also named the winner of the Bronko Nagurski Trophy, the Chuck Bednarik Award, the Outland Trophy, and the Lombardi Award, the 6'4", 313-pound Suh received high praise heading into the 2010 NFL Draft from ESPN analyst Mel Kiper Jr., who, impressed by his rare combination of size, strength, speed, and agility, described him as "maybe the most dominating defensive tackle I've seen in 32 years."

Projected to go No. 1 overall by Kiper, Suh ended up being selected by the Lions with the second overall pick, just behind Oklahoma quarterback Sam Bradford. Laying claim to the starting left tackle job immediately on his arrival in Detroit, Suh made an enormous impact his first year in the league, earning Pro Bowl, First-Team All-Pro, and NFL Defensive Rookie of the Year honors by recording 10 sacks, 66 tackles, one forced fumble, one fumble recovery, and one defensive touchdown. Continuing to perform at an extremely high level the next two seasons, Suh helped the Lions advance to the playoffs as a wild card in 2011 by registering four sacks and 36 tackles, before gaining Pro Bowl and Second-Team All-Pro recognition the following year by recording eight sacks and 34 tackles.

Yet, even as Suh rose to prominence in the NFL, he developed a reputation as someone who sought to gain an edge over his opponent by showing little regard for the rules that govern the game. After being fined $7,500 by the league office for twisting the face mask of Cleveland Browns quarterback Jake Delhomme during a preseason contest his rookie year, Suh incurred additional fines of $5,000 in week 9 for using an opponent as leverage while trying to block a field goal and $15,000 in week 13 for unnecessary roughness against Chicago Bears signal-caller Jay Cutler.

Continuing to display a lack of sportsmanship in 2011, Suh received a $20,000 fine for a late hit on Cincinnati quarterback Andy Dalton during the preseason, before drawing a two-game suspension for his horrific actions during a Thanksgiving Day game with Green Bay, when, after pushing the head of Packers offensive lineman Evan Dietrich-Smith into the ground three times, he stomped on his arm. While Suh initially denied the claims made against him, saying that he merely attempted to gain his balance, he later wrote on his Facebook page that he had "made a mistake" from which he hoped to learn. Meanwhile, the Lions issued a statement that called Suh's actions "unacceptable." Exactly one year later, on Thanksgiving Day 2012, Suh again went beyond the bounds of decency when he kicked Houston Texans quarterback Matt Schaub in the groin, drawing in the process a $30,000 fine.

Voted the "dirtiest player" in the NFL by his fellow players in a poll conducted by the *Sporting News* and named the NFL's "least-liked player" in a *Forbes*-publicized Nielsen report in October 2012, Suh attempted to defend himself by saying, "A dirty player is somebody who ultimately is trying to hurt somebody. There's a huge difference. There's no gray in that. Like, you have no conscience, no nothing, no guilt. I don't have that mean streak in me. I don't play angry. It's not anger. . . . If you find my aggressive and dominating play dirty, then that's your opinion. But I would assume most people want someone who is going to do anything and everything within the lines to win for their team, because I know I would."

Suh continued, "A lot of players have told me they see me as a protector of my teammates, that, side by side, I'm there when something goes down, and I step up beside them and for them when things get nasty. I play the game hard, and I play it physical. . . . I never want to intimidate a player. I just want to impose my will on a player and have them respect me. I don't want anybody ever to fear me, but to respect me."

Seeking to create a softer image of himself on another occasion, Suh stated, "I guess I'm a fun-loving teddy bear. I've got two sides to me. Obviously, there's the football side that a lot of people see—the mean, ferocious, coming-after-the-quarterback guy. But off the field, I'm a calm, cool, collected guy."

Claiming that Suh proved to be a victim of his time, NFL analyst and Hall of Fame defensive end Howie Long commented, "He was born in 1987. The problem with Ndamukong Suh is he was born 27 years too late. Anyone who played when we played has to feel a little bit hypocritical being critical of this guy. But the reality of the situation is, it's not 1984, and that being said, it's unfortunate that he put himself in this position, because now the narrative is all about Ndamukong Suh the dirty player, and not about what a great player Ndamukong Suh really is."

Despite Suh's many transgressions, his teammates named him a team captain prior to the start of the 2013 campaign, with former Bears defensive end Israel Idonije saying of his new linemate, "The guy works just as hard as anyone I have ever seen. He is one of the first people here in the morning, working his craft. The truth is, when I first got in the league in 2003, those hits and those plays [where Suh had been fined] and the effort, not a single flag would have been thrown in '03. But the game has evolved. He just wants to win. It's always interesting what the perception is and the reality."

182 THE 50 GREATEST PLAYERS IN DETROIT LIONS HISTORY

Excelling in each of the next two seasons, Suh earned consecutive Pro Bowl and First-Team All-Pro selections by recording a total of 14 sacks and 102 tackles. But Suh failed to mend his ways, incurring a $100,000 fine for a low block he threw on Minnesota Vikings center John Sullivan that nullified an apparent DeAndre Levy pick-six in the 2013 regular-season opener and drawing a one-game suspension for intentionally stepping on quarterback Aaron Rodgers's leg during a 30–20 loss to the Packers in the final game of the 2014 regular season.

With Suh subsequently becoming a free agent at the end of the year, the Lions allowed him to hit the open market, prompting former Tampa Bay Buccaneers general manager and director of pro scouting Mark Dominik to proclaim, "Ndamukong Suh is the best player in this generation to hit free agency since Reggie White." Ultimately signed to a six-year, $114 million contract by the Miami Dolphins, Suh became the highest-paid defensive player in NFL history at the time.

Suh, who, in his five seasons with the Lions, recorded 36 sacks, 98 hits on opposing quarterbacks, 238 tackles, 66 tackles for loss, two forced fumbles, one fumble recovery, one interception, one safety, and one touchdown, ended up spending three years in Miami, earning Pro Bowl and All-Pro honors once each, before being released following the conclusion of the 2017 campaign to create space under the salary cap. Suh subsequently signed with the Buccaneers, with whom he won a Super Bowl in his second season. After one more year in Tampa Bay, Suh joined the Philadelphia Eagles, with whom he spent the 2022 season assuming a backup role. Waived by the Eagles at the end of the year, Suh failed to draw serious interest from any other team, forcing him to sit out the next two seasons. Although Suh has yet to officially announce his retirement as of this writing, it appears likely that he has played his last game of professional football. If so, he will end his career with 71½ sacks, 600 tackles, five forced fumbles, nine fumble recoveries, one interception, one safety, and three touchdowns.

LIONS CAREER HIGHLIGHTS

Best Season

It could be argued that Suh played his best ball for the Lions in 2014, when he helped them compile a record of 11–5, finish third in the league in points allowed, and become just the ninth team in NFL history to yield

NDAMUKONG SUH **183**

fewer than 70 rushing yards per game by registering eight and a half sacks and 53 tackles. But Suh posted better overall numbers as a rookie in 2010, when he gained consensus First-Team All-Pro recognition by recording a career-high 10 sacks while also registering 66 tackles (49 solo), 13 tackles for loss, and 17 hits on opposing quarterbacks, with his 10 sacks placing him first among all NFL rookies and defensive tackles.

Memorable Moments/Greatest Performances

Suh recorded the only interception of his career during a 44–6 rout of the Rams on October 10, 2010, subsequently returning the ball 20 yards to the St. Louis 30-yard line.

In addition to recording two sacks during a 37–25 victory over Washington on October 31, 2010, Suh scored his first touchdown as a pro when he rumbled 17 yards after recovering a Rex Grossman fumble.

Suh contributed to a 40–32 win over the Bears on September 29, 2013, by registering two sacks, forcing a fumble, and making four solo tackles, two of which resulted in a loss.

Suh helped lead the Lions to a 17–3 win over the Vikings on October 12, 2014, by recording two sacks, four solo tackles, and three tackles for loss.

Notable Achievements

- Scored one defensive touchdown.
- Recorded 10 sacks in 2010.
- Finished third in NFL with 21 tackles for loss in 2014.
- Led Lions in sacks twice.
- Led Lions defensive linemen in tackles three times.
- 2010 NFL Defensive Rookie of the Year.
- 2010 *Sporting News* NFL Rookie of the Year.
- Four-time Pro Bowl selection (2010, 2012, 2013, and 2014).
- Three-time First-Team All-Pro selection (2010, 2013, and 2014).
- 2012 Second-Team All-Pro selection.
- Three-time First-Team All-NFC selection (2010, 2013, and 2014).
- Pro Football Hall of Fame All-2010s Team.
- Pro Football Reference All-2010s First Team.

29

OX EMERSON

An exceptional two-way lineman who attained the honor of being named to the NFL 1930s All-Decade Team, Ox Emerson proved to be a tremendous force on both sides of the ball over the course of his eight-year professional career that included time with both the Lions and their forefathers, the Portsmouth Spartans. A guard on offense, Emerson served as the top blocker on a 1936 Lions team that set an NFL record for a 12-game season by gaining a total of 2,885 yards on the ground. A standout defensive lineman as well, Emerson helped the Lions post seven shutouts and limit the opposition to just 59 points in 1934, with his dominant play up front earning him five First-Team All-Pro nominations and a place on the Lions All-Time Team.

Born in the small East Texas town of Douglass on December 18, 1907, Grover Conner Emerson acquired his famous nickname while playing football for Orange High School, when, after failing to make the correct read on a play, his quarterback told him, "Emerson, you are a big dumb ox."

Offered an athletic scholarship to the University of Texas following his graduation from Orange High, Emerson spent two seasons starting at left guard for the Longhorns, gaining All-SWC recognition in 1930, before being declared ineligible for his senior year because he participated in two plays against Baylor as a freshman in 1928. After initially appealing the decision, Emerson dropped the court action and signed with the Portsmouth Spartans, who had entered the NFL one year earlier.

Named a starter immediately on his arrival in Portsmouth, Emerson helped the Spartans compile a record of 11–3, outscore their opponents 175–77, and post six shutouts during his rookie year of 1931. Emerson continued to perform well for the Spartans on both sides of the ball the next two seasons, earning First-Team All-Pro honors in both 1932 and 1933, before traveling with his teammates some 300 miles north when the franchise relocated to Detroit and changed its name to the Lions in 1934.

Ox Emerson earned a spot on the NFL 1930s All-Decade Team with his exceptional two-way play.

Continuing his string of five straight First-Team All-Pro nominations his first year in the Motor City, Emerson helped the Lions compile a record of 10–3 and outscore their opponents, 238–59, during the regular season, with the 59 points they surrendered representing the third-lowest total in NFL history. Emerson subsequently missed the first five games of the 1935 campaign with a broken vertebra in his back, causing the Lions to struggle to an early season record of just 2–2–1. But following his return to action, the Lions posted a mark of 5–1–1 the rest of the year, enabling them to win the Western Division title. They subsequently laid claim to their first league championship by defeating the Giants, 26–7, in

186 THE 50 GREATEST PLAYERS IN DETROIT LIONS HISTORY

the NFL title game, with Emerson's strong play down the stretch prompting Detroit head coach Potsy Clark to proclaim following the conclusion of the contest, "I regard Emerson as one of the greatest linemen I have ever seen perform on a football field."

Standing just 5'11" and weighing barely 200 pounds, Emerson typically gave away a considerable amount of size to the man who lined up across from him at the point of attack. Nevertheless, Emerson's speed, quickness, and tremendous desire enabled him to more than hold his own against virtually anyone in the league.

Playing mostly right guard on offense, Emerson excelled as both an in-line and a downfield blocker, proving to be particularly effective at leading the interference on off-tackle plays and end sweeps by the wingback, with UPI writing in 1935, "Emerson plays guard like an end; big, fast, and smart."

Emerson, who Chicago Bears Hall of Fame fullback Bronko Nagurski named one of the guards on his all-time NFL team after he retired, also performed brilliantly on defense as part of a six-man front the Lions typically employed. A sure tackler who did an outstanding job of evading would-be blockers, Emerson drew praise for his superior defensive play from the immortal Red Grange, who wrote in 1934, "Emerson, the Detroit guard, according to [Hall of Fame offensive tackle] Link Lyman of our Bears, is the fastest 'slicing' forward and the hardest to block he has ever met in football."

Bears tackle George Musso expressed similar sentiments when he stated, "He was an Ox. He was hard to handle. Ox was just a good guard, hard to block."

Praising Emerson for his savvy, Giants Hall of Fame center Mel Hein said, "I tried for a long while to figure out how to handle him, but he always fooled me."

Meanwhile, former Lions teammate Glenn Presnell stated, "Ox wasn't very big for a professional guard—he weighed about 195 pounds. But he was so quick and agile that he made a lot of tackles and was hard to block. So, he was in the opponent's backfield an awful lot. He was very exceptional."

Emerson earned the last of his five consecutive First-Team All-Pro nominations in 1936 by helping the Lions rush for 2,885 yards, a mark that remained an NFL record until 1972, when the undefeated Miami Dolphins gained 2,960 yards on the ground in 14 games. Emerson remained in Detroit for one more year, moving to left guard after spending the previous six seasons playing on the right side of the Lions' offensive line. Offered the position of line coach for the Brooklyn Dodgers football team at the end of the year, Emerson announced his retirement, although new Brooklyn

OX EMERSON   **187**

head coach Potsy Clark eventually convinced him to spend the 1938 campaign serving the team as a player-coach. Retiring for good at season's end, Emerson returned to Detroit, where he took a job working in the Personnel Department of the Ford Motor Company and remained close to the game by coaching at Wayne State University.

Emerson later enlisted in the U.S. Navy during World War II, eventually rising to the rank of lieutenant commander. Experiencing a harrowing ordeal while serving aboard the aircraft carrier USS *Block Island,* which a German U-boat sunk in the Atlantic, Emerson found himself stranded on a life raft in the middle of the ocean for several hours with several other members of the crew, before finally being rescued by a destroyer. Emerson subsequently transferred stateside, where he spent his remaining time in the military coaching the Corpus Christi Naval Air Station football team. Following his discharge, Emerson continued to coach football at the high school, junior college, and college levels for the next 40 years, before finally retiring to private life in 1985 after spending the previous 10 years coaching and teaching American history at St. Louis Catholic School. Emerson lived until November 26, 1998, when he died of pneumonia in Austin, Texas, three weeks shy of his 91st birthday.

SPARTANS/LIONS CAREER HIGHLIGHTS

Best Season

Emerson performed magnificently in 1936, when his superior blocking helped the Lions gain 2,885 yards on the ground and set a still-existing single-season NFL record by averaging 240.4 rushing yards per game. However, injuries forced him to miss two contests. On the other hand, Emerson started all 13 games the Lions played in 1934, when their defense registered seven shutouts and surrendered just 59 points to the opposition the entire year, making that the most impactful season of his career.

Memorable Moments/Greatest Performances

Emerson made a huge impact in his very first game as a pro, blocking a punt that a teammate recovered for a touchdown during a 14–0 victory over the Brooklyn Dodgers in the 1931 regular-season opener.

Emerson helped the Lions gain 373 yards on the ground during a 38–0 thrashing of the Cincinnati Reds on October 28, 1934.

188   THE 50 GREATEST PLAYERS IN DETROIT LIONS HISTORY

Emerson and his linemates turned in another dominant performance the following week, with the Lions rushing for an NFL-record 426 yards during a 40–7 manhandling of the Pittsburgh Pirates on November 4, 1934.

Emerson's outstanding blocking at the line of scrimmage helped the Lions rush for 370 yards and four touchdowns during a 35–0 win over the Philadelphia Eagles in the opening game of the 1935 regular season.

Emerson performed brilliantly on both sides of the ball for the Lions during their 26–7 victory over the Giants in the 1935 NFL Championship Game, providing superior blocking for an offense that gained 246 yards on the ground and rushed for four touchdowns while helping to limit New York to just one TD.

Emerson helped the Lions gain a season-high 393 yards on the ground during a 13–7 victory over the Bears on November 26, 1936.

Notable Achievements

- 1935 division champion.
- 1935 NFL champion.
- Five-time First-Team All-Pro selection (1932, 1933, 1934, 1935, and 1936).
- Pro Football Hall of Fame All-1930s Team.
- Named to Lions All-Time Team in 2019.

30
HARLEY SEWELL

One of the finest pulling guards in the NFL for nearly a decade, Harley Sewell proved to be a huge contributor to Lions teams that won three division titles and two league championships during the 1950s. Known for his hustle, determination, durability, and superior conditioning, Sewell, who started at left guard for the Lions from 1953 to 1962, performed equally well as a run-blocker and pass-protector, with his outstanding all-around play earning him four Pro Bowl selections and four All-Pro nominations. Later named to the Lions All-Time Team in 2019, Sewell missed just four games during his 10 seasons in Detroit, before ending his career as a backup with the Los Angeles Rams in 1963.

Born in Jefferson County, Oklahoma, on April 18, 1931, Harley Edward Sewell moved with his family at a young age to the tiny Texas town of St. Jo, where he starred in football while attending St. Jo High School. A standout two-way lineman for the Panthers, Sewell drew the attention of college scouts despite his small–high school background, with University of Texas alum Phil Bolin, then serving as a bird-dog scout for his alma mater, driving some 275 miles north to offer him a scholarship. Discovering Sewell atop a telephone pole working a summer job as a lineman, Bolin shouted to the youngster, "How would you like to play football for the University of Texas?"

Sewell answered, "Be fine," beginning in the process his ascent to a career in the pros.

A true country boy, Sewell arrived in Austin a few weeks later with just a pair of faded blue jeans, a couple of T-shirts, and one slightly scuffed pair of work boots. Growing homesick before long, Sewell seriously considered returning to St. Jo, before Longhorns assistant coach J. T. King convinced him to stay the course.

Eventually emerging as one of the finest two-way players in the nation, Sewell spent three seasons starring for the Longhorns as a guard on offense and a linebacker on defense, earning All-SWC honors twice

Harley Sewell spent 10 seasons starting at left guard for the Lions.

and gaining First-Team All-America recognition as a senior in 1952, when he helped lead Texas to a record of 9–2 and a 16–0 victory over Tennessee in the 1953 Cotton Bowl. Impressed with Sewell's outstanding play at the collegiate level, the Lions selected him in the first round of the 1953 NFL Draft with the 13th overall pick, after which they decided to use him on offense exclusively.

Displacing Jim Martin as the starter at left guard during the early stages of his rookie campaign, Sewell performed well at that post for a Lions team that captured its second straight NFL championship. Although the Lions failed to repeat as league champions in any of the next three seasons, Sewell became known as one of the NFL's finest players at his position despite often being overshadowed by future Hall of Famer Lou Creekmur, who lined up immediately next to him at left tackle. After being accorded unofficial Second-Team All-Pro honors by the Newspaper Enterprise Association in both 1955 and 1956, Sewell gained Pro Bowl and official Second-Team

All-Pro recognition from the AP for the first time in 1957, when he helped the Lions win their third NFL title in six seasons.

Although slightly undersized at 6'1", 230 pounds, Sewell proved to be extremely effective as both a run-blocker and a pass-protector, excelling in particular at leading Detroit running backs on end sweeps, inside traps, and counter plays. Extremely quick and agile, Sewell often cleared out larger defenders before they had time to counter his attack. Noted for always putting forth 100 percent effort, Sewell received praise from Lions line coach Aldo Forte, who stated, "Harley has hustled for us every minute since he joined the Lions."

Also known for his tremendous conditioning, Sewell was a tireless worker who never took anything for granted, once saying, "I never feel like I have a job cinched."

In addition to his superior blocking on offense, Sewell excelled on special teams as well. A regular member of the punting and kickoff units, Sewell received credit one year for making 85 percent of the team's tackles on kickoffs.

Continuing to perform at an elite level from 1958 to 1962, Sewell earned three more Pro Bowl selections and one more All-Pro nomination while combining with John Gordy to give the Lions arguably the finest pair of guards in the league. However, after Sewell sustained an injury during the latter stages of the 1963 campaign that forced him to miss just the fourth game of his career, the Lions released him at the end of the year. Sewell subsequently signed with the Los Angeles Rams, with whom he appeared in only two contests in 1963, before announcing his retirement.

Sewell, who, over the course of 11 NFL seasons, appeared in a total of 122 games, 114 of which he started, embarked on a lengthy career in scouting following his playing days. Remaining with the Rams for the next 37 years, Sewell continued to serve the organization as a scout until 2000, when he retired to private life and returned to his home state of Texas. Sewell lived until December 17, 2011, when he died at the age of 80 following an extended illness.

LIONS CAREER HIGHLIGHTS

Best Season

Sewell had his finest season for the Lions in 1957, when, in addition to earning his first Pro Bowl nomination, he gained official All-Pro recognition

192 THE 50 GREATEST PLAYERS IN DETROIT LIONS HISTORY

from the AP for the only time by helping Detroit running backs gain 1,811 yards on the ground and average 4.4 yards per carry.

Memorable Moments/Greatest Performances

Sewell recorded the only interception of his career during a 31–19 loss to the Los Angeles Rams on October 18, 1953.

Sewell scored his only touchdown as a pro when he recovered a fumble in the end zone during a 27–3 win over the Baltimore Colts on November 6, 1954.

Sewell helped the Lions amass 468 yards of total offense during a lopsided 42–10 victory over the Bears on December 2, 1956, with 214 of those yards coming on the ground and the other 254 through the air.

Sewell and his linemates dominated the 49ers at the point of attack on November 17, 1957, with the Lions gaining 370 yards through the air and amassing 515 yards of total offense during a 31–10 win over their Western Division rivals.

Notable Achievements

- Missed just four games in 10 seasons, appearing in 120 of 124 contests.
- Three-time division champion (1953, 1954, and 1957).
- Two-time NFL champion (1953 and 1957).
- Four-time Pro Bowl selection (1957, 1958, 1959, and 1962).
- 1957 Second-Team All-Pro selection.
- Three-time Newspaper Enterprise Association Second-Team All-Pro selection (1955, 1956, and 1962).
- Two-time First-Team All-Western Conference selection (1957 and 1960).
- Named to Lions 75th Anniversary All-Time Team in 2008.
- Named to Lions All-Time Team in 2019.

31
AL "BUBBA" BAKER

The most feared member of the Lions' famed "Silver Rush" defensive line that terrorized opposing quarterbacks from 1978 to 1982, Al "Bubba" Baker proved to be one of the NFL's premier pass-rushers during his relatively brief stay in the Motor City. The holder of the top three single-season sack marks in franchise history, Baker continues to rank third in team annals in that category more than four decades after he played his last game for the Lions. A three-time Pro Bowler and one-time All-Pro who left Detroit following the conclusion of the 1982 campaign due to differences with team management, Baker later received the additional honor of being named to the Lions All-Time Team in 2019.

Born in Jacksonville, Florida, on December 9, 1956, James Albert London Baker grew up in Newark, New Jersey, where he first developed the pass-rush moves for which he later became so well known at a nearby cemetery, remembering, "The only place where there was dirt and a little bit of grass was the graveyard. I learned to do the arm over from when I watched a football game on Sunday. I never knocked over any of the headstones. . . . If you think about it, it's kind of taken out of an Our Gang movie. It was in the fifth and sixth grade. By the seventh grade, we were playing organized sports. We called that 'Where the big kids played after school.'"

The son of a special services trainer at Fort Dix, New Jersey, and a businesswoman, Baker, who spent his vacations and summer breaks living with his uncle in Jacksonville, became known to his friends as "Bubba" due to his great size. An outstanding all-around athlete, Baker starred in baseball, basketball, football, and track and field (shot put) at Newark's Weequahic High School, excelling in particular on the gridiron as an offensive lineman.

Offered an athletic scholarship to Colorado State University, Baker underwent a major transformation in college, recalling, "I was 6'6" and 300 pounds—this mush of a kid. I didn't have a tough bone in my body. I was used to playing basketball. . . . I look back at that, and I say, 'Thank you.'

Al "Bubba" Baker holds the top three single-season sack marks in franchise history.

That gave me something to shoot for. That gave me determination. That gave me drive to shoot for. I saw guys go to the weight room."

Moved to the defensive side of the ball shortly after he arrived at Colorado State, Baker eventually established himself as one of the nation's top edge-rushers, gaining All-Western Athletic Conference recognition as a senior in 1977, when he combined with All-American Mike Bell to give the 9–2–1 Rams the most formidable pair of defensive ends in the conference.

Selected by the Lions in the second round of the 1978 NFL Draft with the 40th overall pick, Baker quickly learned at his first pro training camp that his status as an early round draft pick meant nothing to defensive line coach Floyd Peters, recalling, "Floyd started out by telling me how nobody else wanted me. I looked at the other kids being hugged by the commissioner [at the draft] and said to myself, 'I get it.' In hindsight, that was the best thing that happened to me."

Although Baker ended up developing a strong bond with Peters, who he later credited with much of his success, he admitted that he never seemed to do enough to satisfy him, saying, "I'd get three sacks, seven hits in a game with an interception. On Monday, he'd say, 'Take a look at this play. Is that the best you've got?'"

With Peters's demands having their desired effect on him, Baker performed extraordinarily well his first year in the league after being inserted at right end, earning Pro Bowl, First-Team All-Pro, NFL Defensive Rookie of the Year, and NFL Rookie of the Year honors from both UPI and the *Sporting News* by recording an unofficial total of 23 sacks, the highest single-season mark in NFL history. Baker followed that up with two more excellent seasons, gaining Pro Bowl recognition in both 1979 and 1980 by finishing second in the league with 16 sacks in the first of those campaigns, before topping the circuit with 17½ sacks in the second.

Part of an outstanding Detroit defensive line that also included right tackle Doug English, left tackle William Gay, and left end Dave Pureifory, Baker helped the Lions bring down opposing quarterbacks behind the line of scrimmage a total of 144 times his first three years in the league, with their 55 sacks in 1978 setting a single-season franchise record that still stands.

The most dominant pass-rusher of the four, the 6'6", 265-pound Baker combined exceptional quickness with great strength to overwhelm his opponent at the point of attack. Blessed with extremely long arms that enabled him to distance himself from his blocker, Baker possessed a wide variety of moves, although he relied most heavily on a grab-and-throw maneuver and an inside spin that he learned from his basketball days. And once he reached his destination, Baker did so with bad intentions, saying, "If you had a chance to hit the quarterback after all those chop blocks . . . when you arrived at the quarterback, you wanted to arrive in a bad mood. I think I embodied that."

Yet Baker proved to be a paradox of sorts, stating, "I'm a big baby. If I tear my finger up, I go crying to the trainer and he'll pat me on the back and tell me it's OK. The problem is, I'm a three-year-old kid inside a 26-year-old body. I can't sit still for two hours. I like to crack jokes."

Although Baker failed to gain Pro Bowl recognition in either of the next two seasons, he continued to perform well for the Lions, collecting nine sacks in 1981, before recording eight and a half sacks in just nine games during the strike-shortened 1982 campaign.

Nevertheless, Baker's relationship with the Lions grew increasingly contentious over time. After sitting out the opening game of the 1980 regular season over a dispute for more money, Baker engaged in a shouting match with head coach Monte Clark on an airplane the following year. Baker again drew the ire of team brass in 1982 when he missed a playoff game due to a foot injury that management did not consider serious enough to sideline him for a contest of that magnitude.

THE 50 GREATEST PLAYERS IN DETROIT LIONS HISTORY

Finally choosing to part ways with Baker, the Lions traded him to the St. Louis Cardinals for defensive end Mike Dawson and a third-round draft pick prior to the start of the 1983 campaign. Expressing his happiness to be leaving Detroit shortly after he arrived in St. Louis, Baker, who recorded 74 sacks, recovered four fumbles, and intercepted two passes as a member of the Lions, said, "I had requested a trade three years ago. I was willing to leave that place to go to Baltimore. This is the best I've felt since I was drafted."

Reunited in St. Louis with defensive line coach Floyd Peters, a reenergized Baker stated during the early stages of the campaign, "In Detroit, we all had our separate lives and had nothing in common. Here, it's like an old high school team again. . . . I wondered what happened to the old college attitude when you practiced and then all went out and had a beer together. On the field, it's going to make a difference. I wouldn't be afraid to say good things are going to happen to this team."

Baker added, "I don't have the additional pressure of people screaming at me, 'Go get a sack, Bubba.' If I get one sack, Floyd Peters is going to pat me on the back and be happy."

Playing well for mostly mediocre Cardinals teams the next four seasons, Baker registered a total of 37½ sacks, before splitting his final four years in the league between the Cleveland Browns and Minnesota Vikings. Announcing his retirement following the conclusion of the 1990 campaign, Baker ended his career with an unofficial total of 131 sacks, placing him 21st in NFL history as of this writing. Baker also recovered eight fumbles and intercepted four passes.

Following his playing days, Baker settled with his family in the Cleveland suburb of Avon, where he opened Bubba Q's Restaurant and Catering, a restaurant and catering business that won several "Best in Cleveland" awards for its superior southern-style barbecue cuisine. Although Bubba Q's eventually closed in 2019, the now 69-year-old Baker continues to oversee on a somewhat limited basis sales of a series of signature sauces and dry rubs he launched several years ago.

LIONS CAREER HIGHLIGHTS

Best Season

Was there ever any doubt? Although Baker also performed exceptionally well in each of the next two seasons, he reached the apex of his career as a rookie in 1978, when, in addition to making 71 tackles and forcing two fumbles, he registered an unofficial total of 23 sacks, which remained the unrecognized single-season NFL record until 2021, when Pro Football Reference added to its catalog previously unrecorded sack statistics from 1960 to 1981.

Memorable Moments/Greatest Performances

Baker made an enormous impact in just his second game as a pro, recording five sacks during a 15–7 win over Tampa Bay on September 9, 1978.

Baker recorded the first of his four career interceptions when he picked off a Danny White pass during a 27–24 win over the Dallas Cowboys on November 15, 1981.

Baker recorded two of the five sacks the Lions registered during a 17–10 win over the Bears in the opening game of the 1982 regular season.

Baker contributed to a 30–10 victory over the Packers on December 12, 1982, by recording two and a half sacks.

Notable Achievements

- Finished in double digits in sacks three times.
- Holds unofficial NFL single-season record for most sacks (23 in 1978).
- Recorded five sacks in one game vs. Tampa Bay Buccaneers on September 9, 1978.
- Led NFL in sacks twice.
- Finished second in NFL in sacks once.
- Led Lions in sacks five times.
- Ranks third in franchise history with 74 career sacks.
- Member of 1978 NFL All-Rookie Team.
- 1978 AP NFL Defensive Rookie of the Year.
- 1978 UPI and *Sporting News* NFL Rookie of the Year.
- 1978 NFLPA NFC Defensive Lineman of the Year.
- Three-time Pro Bowl selection (1978, 1979, and 1980).
- 1978 First-Team All-Pro selection.
- 1979 Newspaper Enterprise Association Second-Team All-Pro selection.
- 1978 First-Team All-NFC selection.
- Named to Lions 75th Anniversary All-Time Team in 2008.
- Named to Lions All-Time Team in 2019.

32
JOHN GORDY

A fixture on the interior of the Lions' offensive line for a decade, John Gordy spent his entire 10-year NFL career in Detroit starting at right guard. One of the league's most durable players, Gordy never missed a game during his 10 seasons in the Motor City, starting all but six contests in which he appeared. A key member of the Lions' 1957 NFL championship ball club, Gordy provided the team with consistently excellent play up front, earning three Pro Bowl selections and three All-Pro nominations, before being further honored by being named to the Lions 75th Anniversary All-Time Team in 2008. And following the conclusion of his playing career, Gordy helped improve conditions for players throughout the league while serving as head of the NFLPA.

Born in Nashville, Tennessee, on July 17, 1935, John Thomas Gordy grew up in the city's Inglewood section, where, as the son of "Poppa" John Gordy, a popular Dixieland jazz bandleader who recorded with Chet Atkins and briefly toured with Elvis Presley, he developed a fondness for country-and-western music at an early age. Equally passionate about football, Gordy starred on the gridiron at Isaac Litton High School, where he earned Second-Team All-Nashville Interscholastic League honors as a two-way lineman his senior year.

Enrolling at the University of Tennessee following his graduation, Gordy spent two seasons starting at guard for the Volunteers, who he helped lead to a perfect 10–0 regular-season record, the SEC championship, and a No. 2 ranking in the final AP poll as a senior in 1956, garnering in the process All-SEC honors.

Selected by the Lions in the second round of the 1957 NFL Draft with the 24th overall pick, Gordy laid claim to the starting right guard job immediately on his arrival in Detroit, after which he spent his rookie season playing on an excellent line that also included veteran center Frank Gatski, right tackle Charlie Ane, left guard Harley Sewell, and future Hall of Fame left tackle Lou Creekmur. Gordy subsequently left the game for one year to

John Gordy never missed a game during his 10 seasons in Detroit.

pursue a coaching position at the University of Nebraska, before rejoining the Lions in 1959.

Beginning a string of nine straight seasons in which he appeared in every game the Lions played, Gordy returned to his familiar position of right guard, where he remained for the rest of his career. Gradually establishing himself as one of the league's finest interior offensive linemen, Gordy performed consistently well from 1959 to 1962, before finally gaining Pro Bowl recognition for the first of three straight times in 1963. Also accorded First-Team All-Western Conference and Second-Team All-Pro honors three times between 1963 and 1967, Gordy proved to be one of the few bright spots on mostly mediocre Lions teams.

A superior run blocker who also did an outstanding job in pass-protection, the 6'3", 248-pound Gordy excelled as both an in-line and a downfield blocker. Particularly effective at pulling out from his guard position and leading Lions running backs beyond the line of scrimmage, Gordy possessed quick feet and excellent mobility.

THE 50 GREATEST PLAYERS IN DETROIT LIONS HISTORY

Perhaps more than anything, though, Gordy became known for his intelligence, leadership ability, and strong moral fiber, which he exhibited with the pivotal role he played in the civil rights movement during the 1960s. Along with teammate Gail Cogdill, Gordy publicly defended the rights of African American players in the NFL, going so far as to boycott the league's annual All-Star Game in 1964 as a way of protesting its policies regarding segregation. Meanwhile, Gordy displayed the intellectual side of his persona by collaborating with teammate Mike Lucci on a book titled *The Rookie*, which offered a candid and insightful look into the world of professional football from the perspective of a first-year player.

Continuing to perform at an extremely high level his entire time in Detroit, Gordy earned the last of his All-Pro nominations in 1967, before a knee injury prompted him to announce his retirement following the conclusion of the campaign. Over the course of 10 NFL seasons, Gordy appeared in a total of 134 games, 128 of which he started.

Following his playing days, Gordy, who helped found the NFLPA early in his career, assumed the title of president of the organization. Exhibiting his skills as a tactician and labor negotiator while serving in that capacity, Gordy led the players to a strike in 1968 that resulted in the first collective bargaining agreement in major professional sports.

Eventually retiring to San Clemente, California, Gordy became very active in the Fellowship of Christian Athletes (FCA), helping to raise funds that led to the formation of an FCA Board of Directors in Southern California, sending hundreds of student athletes to various FCA camps in the area, and establishing and leading FCA Huddle groups in the middle of gang-infested areas such as South Central (Los Angeles) and Santa Anita. Gordy also briefly served as president of Visual Sounds, Inc., the audio-visual subsidiary of A & R Recording in Manhattan. Gordy lived until January 30, 2009, when he died at the age of 73 following a lengthy battle with pancreatic cancer.

CAREER HIGHLIGHTS

Best Season

Gordy had his finest season for the Lions in 1964, when he earned All-Pro honors for the first time, with Pro Football Reference assigning him an "Approximate Value" of 11, which represented the highest mark of his career.

Memorable Moments/Greatest Performances

Gordy helped the Lions rush for a season-high 200 yards during a 13–10 win over the Los Angeles Rams on October 14, 1962.

Gordy's strong blocking helped the Lions amass 509 yards of total offense during a 45–7 rout of the 49ers on November 3, 1963, with 308 of those yards coming through the air and the other 201 on the ground.

Gordy and his linemates enabled the Lions to gain 238 yards on the ground and amass 461 yards of total offense during a 31–14 win over the Browns on September 24, 1967.

Notable Achievements

- Never missed a game, appearing in 134 consecutive contests, 128 of which he started.
- 1957 division champion.
- 1957 NFL champion.
- Three-time Pro Bowl selection (1963, 1964, and 1965).
- Three-time Second-Team All-Pro selection (1964, 1966, and 1967).
- Three-time First-Team All-Western Conference selection (1963, 1964, and 1966).
- Named to Lions 75th Anniversary All-Time Team in 2008.

33

GAIL COGDILL

Known for his ability to make spectacular catches, Gail Cogdill spent parts of nine seasons in Detroit, establishing himself as one of the NFL's foremost receivers. The Lions' top wideout most of his time in the Motor City, Cogdill led the team in receptions twice and receiving yards three times, amassing more than 900 yards through the air on three separate occasions. A three-time Pro Bowler and three-time Second-Team All-Pro selection, Cogdill, who left Detroit as the franchise's career leader in receptions and receiving yards, later received the additional honor of being named to the Lions All-Time Team in 2019, accomplishing all he did even though he never had the good fortune of playing with an elite quarterback.

Born in Worland, Wyoming, on April 7, 1937, Gail Ross Cogdill moved with his family at the age of 14 to Spokane, Washington, where he starred in multiple sports while attending Lewis and Clark High School. Attaining All-State honors in football, basketball, and track his senior year, Cogdill performed especially well on the gridiron, with his outstanding play at receiver and defensive back helping the Tigers win the state championship.

Offered a football scholarship to Washington State University, Cogdill spent three seasons excelling for the Cougars on both sides of the ball, making a total of 64 receptions for 1,256 yards and 13 touchdowns, en route to earning All-America honors twice. Competing in track as well, Cogdill won a Pacific Coast Conference hurdles championship.

Selected by the Lions in the sixth round of the 1960 NFL Draft with the 63rd overall pick, Cogdill received high praise shortly thereafter from Detroit head coach George Wilson, who touted him as "one of the top receivers to come into professional football in a long time."

Living up to Wilson's expectations his first year in the league, Cogdill earned Pro Bowl honors and gained recognition from both UPI and the *Sporting News* as NFL Rookie of the Year by making 43 receptions for 642 yards and one touchdown. Recalling the immediate impact that Cogdill made on his arrival in the Motor City, former Lions tight end Jim Gibbons

Gail Cogdill led the Lions in receptions twice and receiving yards three times.

stated, "Gail came to Detroit with enthusiasm, ability, and cockiness. His ability demanded that he be a starter, and he started."

Although Cogdill failed to gain Pro Bowl recognition in 1961, he posted even better numbers, making 45 receptions, amassing 956 receiving yards, scoring six TDs, and posting an average of 21.2 yards per reception, which represented the second-highest mark in the league. Cogdill followed that up with the two most productive seasons of his career, earning Pro Bowl, Second-Team All-Pro, and First-Team All-Western Conference honors in both 1962 and 1963 by making 53 receptions for 991 yards and seven touchdowns in the first of those campaigns, before catching 48 passes, amassing 945 receiving yards, and scoring 10 TDs in the second.

Blessed with soft hands, outstanding speed, and precise route-running ability, Cogdill did an excellent job of separating himself from his defender, beating his man deep, and catching virtually anything within his reach. Extremely acrobatic, the 6'3", 200-pound Cogdill developed a reputation for making circus catches, with sportswriter George Puscas recalling, "He was the only football player I've ever seen who caused teammates to interrupt their own work to watch him do his."

Despite his superior ability as a pass-catcher, Cogdill often found himself being miscast on running plays as a second tight end who had the responsibility of blocking men much larger than himself. Claiming that the Lions' coaching staff did not take full advantage of Cogdill's unique skill set, former teammate Pat Studstill said, "Gail was big, strong, and fast, and he had the best hands on the team. He could block, and he was quick. Gail was not used properly. They never threw to him enough. It's too bad because he could have been greater than he turned out—which was great anyway."

Further hampered by a lack of consistent quarterback play, Cogdill remembered, "Jim Ninowski [Detroit's starting quarterback his first two years in the league] used to throw to me quite a bit. Then he was traded back to Cleveland, and we had Milt Plum and Earl Morrall. A few years later, they got rid of Morrall and obtained Karl Sweetan, backed up by Plum. So, I never really had a 'true one quarterback' in my years with Detroit. George Wilson told me a couple of times, 'Gail, it's a shame you're playing here, because you will never break any records.' That was true. The Lions didn't throw the ball that much."

Cogdill also recalled the difficulties he and the other receivers of his time faced, saying, "We also had bump-and-run all the way down the field, which the receivers don't have today. . . . I had quick moves, and I could get away from the defender. Today, you can't touch the receiver. Back then, they could beat the holy stuffing out of you before you got off the line. You'd line up, and a linebacker would be in front of you, and you knew what was going to happen. He'd pound on you for two or three yards, and the defensive halfback was gonna get you and release you to the safety, and he was gonna pound you! For a long time in the 1960s, we weren't scoring very many points. The passing game just wasn't that good. Most of the receivers had a tough time getting open. Now, the offensive linemen can reach up and grab the defender, so the quarterback may have 5, 6, 7 seconds to release the ball. I watch these games today and I see receivers dropping the ball. Man, I think back, and I don't remember dropping more than five or six balls in my whole career."

Despite missing the final three games of the 1964 campaign with a dislocated shoulder he sustained during a 23–23 tie with the Minnesota Vikings in week 11, Cogdill had another solid season, earning his third straight Second-Team All-Pro nomination by making 45 receptions for

665 yards and two touchdowns. But after fracturing his right kneecap in the final preseason game the following year, Cogdill made a huge mistake that led to his ultimate downfall. Choosing to try to play through his injury, Cogdill appeared in the first three games of the regular season, remained on the sidelines for the next five weeks, and then started the final six contests. Failing to take the time off that he needed to fully recover, Cogdill subsequently suffered a series of related injuries that caused him to experience a precipitous fall from grace.

Recalling his error in judgment years later, Cogdill, who finished the 1965 season with just 20 receptions, 247 receiving yards, and no touchdowns, stated, "I played nine games on a broken kneecap. The leg gave out on me, so I had part of the kneecap taken out after the season. In 1966, I was really having trouble because I tore a quad. I was working the weights to come back from the knee injury, and I tore a quad up here, by my hip. But nobody knew about it. They kept saying, 'You're getting slower, you're getting slower.' Hell, I was dragging my leg is what I was doing. My leg was taped all the time, from my hip to my knee. So, it was pretty hard to drag it around."

Cogdill added, "Today I've got sciatic nerve problems really bad on that right side. I've also got arthritis in my right foot because of that. I should have never played until the leg was completely healed. But what are you going to do? You know, when you're a young guy, you always think you're tough, don't you?"

Despite being unable to run or cut properly, Cogdill finished third on the team with 47 receptions. But with his speed compromised greatly, he averaged just 8.7 yards per catch, giving him a total of only 411 receiving yards. Reduced to a part-time role in 1967, Cogdill made just 21 receptions for 322 yards and one touchdown, before being released by the Lions during the early stages of the ensuing campaign.

Cogdill, who, during his time in Detroit, made 325 receptions, amassed 5,221 receiving yards and 5,234 all-purpose yards, caught 28 touchdown passes, scored 30 total TDs, and averaged 16.1 yards per reception, subsequently signed with the Baltimore Colts, with whom he spent the remainder of the year assuming a backup role. Announcing his retirement after the Colts lost to the Jets in Super Bowl III, Cogdill decided to return to action when Baltimore traded him to the Atlanta Falcons. He spent the next two seasons in Atlanta, making a total of 31 catches for 475 yards and six touchdowns, before retiring for good at the end of 1970 with career totals of 356 receptions, 5,696 receiving yards, 34 touchdown catches, and 36 touchdowns.

Although Cogdill spent the better part of three seasons playing for other teams, he always held his years with the Lions closest to his heart, once saying, "I played with and against the very best players in the NFL. With [Jim] Gibbons, [Pat] Studstill, and [Terry] Barr, Detroit had great receivers. If the ball had been thrown then like it is today, what careers we would have had! But having teammates like Roger Brown, Alex Karras, Wayne Walker, and the rest of the Lions, I enjoyed playing with the very best."

Following his playing days, Cogdill, who owned a ranch in Oregon, spent five years mining for gold, before beginning a lengthy career in sales. He also dabbled in sports consulting. Eventually moving to Washington, Cogdill began experiencing heart problems during the 1990s that forced him to undergo bypass surgery in 2002. After surviving that ordeal, Cogdill lived until October 20, 2016, when he died at the age of 79 of complications from heart failure, kidney failure, and dementia.

On learning of his passing, former Lions teammate and head coach Joe Schmidt stated, "Gail was simply a great football player, an outstanding receiver and teammate. Frankly, we didn't take advantage of his ability."

Former Lions receiver and punter Pat Studstill added, "It was an honor to have played with Gail, and I learned a lot from him. I used to watch him like a hawk, how he came off the line of scrimmage, the way he ran his out patterns, everything. He had such great hands and was strong as an ox, and I don't believe there was a better athlete on the team. He was so good that he often was double covered, and I was the beneficiary of that."

Meanwhile, Roger Brown spoke of his former teammate and longtime friend's strong sense of justice when he related a story about their time together, saying, "Gail and I became close friends when we arrived together in Detroit as rookies. We wanted to become roommates on the road, but back then they wouldn't allow a black person and white person to room together, so I ended up with Night Train Lane."

Brown continued, "One time when we played in Miami for the Runner Up Bowl, Night Train, Danny Lewis, Willie McLung, and I had to stay in a black hotel in the black section of Miami. When the team bus came to pick us up, Gail and Nick Pietrosante asked, 'What are you guys doing out here?' Gail said, 'We came as a team, we play as a team, and we'll leave as a team.' That night, we all stayed together in the same hotel. . . . Gail was a helluva receiver and just a beautiful person. He was such a good friend, and I am lost by his passing."

GAIL COGDILL **207**

LIONS CAREER HIGHLIGHTS

Best Season

Although Cogdill caught three more touchdown passes the following year, he had his finest all-around season in 1962, when he helped lead the Lions to a record of 11–3 and a close second-place finish to the Packers in the NFL West by making seven TD receptions and establishing career-high marks with 53 receptions and 991 receiving yards, earning in the process team MVP honors and the first of his three straight Second-Team All-Pro nominations.

Memorable Moments/Greatest Performances

Cogdill scored the first touchdown of his career when he caught a seven-yard pass from Earl Morrall during a 23–14 win over the expansion Dallas Cowboys on December 11, 1960.

Cogdill starred in defeat in the 1961 regular-season finale, making seven receptions for 171 yards and one touchdown during a 27–24 loss to the Eagles, with his TD coming on a career-long 84-yard connection with Jim Ninowski.

Cogdill contributed to a 45–24 victory over the 49ers on September 23, 1962, by making four receptions for 147 yards and one touchdown, which came on a 25-yard pass from Milt Plum.

Cogdill helped lead the Lions to a 21–14 win over the Colts on December 2, 1962, by making six receptions for 137 yards.

Cogdill proved to be one of the few bright spots on offense during a 17–14 loss to the Cowboys on October 13, 1963, catching four passes, amassing 150 receiving yards, and scoring both Lions touchdowns on connections of 30 and 70 yards with Earl Morrall.

Cogdill riddled the Los Angeles defensive secondary on November 1, 1964, making seven receptions for 165 yards during a 37–17 win over the Rams.

Notable Achievements

- Surpassed 50 receptions once.
- Surpassed 900 receiving yards three times.
- Amassed more than 1,000 all-purpose yards once.

208 THE 50 GREATEST PLAYERS IN DETROIT LIONS HISTORY

- Scored 10 touchdowns in 1963.
- Finished second in NFL with an average of 21.2 yards per reception in 1961.
- Led Lions in receptions twice and receiving yards three times.
- Ranks among Lions career leaders with 325 receptions (9th) and 5,221 receiving yards (5th).
- 1960 NFL Rookie of the Year.
- 1962 Lions team MVP.
- Three-time Pro Bowl selection (1960, 1962, and 1963).
- Three-time Second-Team All-Pro selection (1962, 1963, and 1964).
- Two-time First-Team All-Western Conference selection (1962 and 1963).
- Named to Lions 75th Anniversary All-Time Team in 2008.
- Named to Lions All-Time Team in 2019.

34

LARRY HAND

A staple of the Lions' defense for 13 seasons, Larry Hand spent his entire NFL career in Detroit, serving as a key member of a unit that often ranked among the league's best. Manning multiple positions along the Lions' defensive front, Hand did an excellent job as both a run-stuffer and a pass-rusher, recording the fifth-most sacks of any player in franchise history. The Lions' 1972 team MVP on defense, Hand also earned All-Pro and All-NFC honors once each at right defensive end, before moving inside to tackle during the latter stages of his career.

Born in Paterson, New Jersey, on July 10, 1940, Lawrence Thomas Hand grew up with his six siblings in the nearby town of Butler, where he failed to make much of a name for himself on the gridiron while attending Butler High School. A late bloomer size-wise, Hand stood just 5'6" and weighed only 135 pounds when he enrolled at Butler High in 1955, preventing him from making the varsity football team until his senior year, when he spent most of his time sitting on the bench after playing for the junior varsity squad the previous two seasons.

Ignored by college scouts, Hand stayed in shape following his graduation by working as a mason in his hometown while also playing sandlot ball. Finally receiving an opportunity to attend college when Jim Duncan, the head football coach at Appalachian State University in Boone, North Carolina, offered him an athletic scholarship in 1960, Hand spent three years starting for the Mountaineers on both sides of the ball, excelling as a tackle on offense and an interior lineman on defense. Standing 6'4" and weighing 220 pounds by the time he arrived in Boone, Hand, who later bulked up to 250 pounds, earned First-Team All-Carolinas Conference honors as a junior in 1963, before being named the most valuable player in the conference the following year. Also named to the NAIA All-America team, Hand played his senior year knowing that a pro career awaited him, with the Lions having selected him as a "future selection" in the 10th round of the 1964 NFL Draft with the 132nd overall pick and the New York Jets

Larry Hand spent his entire 13-year NFL career in Detroit.

having chosen him in the 21st round (163rd overall) of that year's AFL Draft. (Hand remained eligible to compete at the collegiate level because his class had long since graduated.)

Choosing to sign with the Lions, Hand arrived in Detroit at the rather advanced age of 25, after which he spent his first NFL season playing mostly on special teams while also backing up starting defensive ends Sam Williams and Darris McCord. Replacing Williams at right end in 1966, Hand joined an outstanding unit that also included McCord and perennial Pro Bowlers Alex Karras and Roger Brown. Performing well in his first year as a full-time starter, Hand finished second on the team with six sacks, before recording another seven sacks and scoring twice on defense the following season.

Subsequently sidelined for virtually the entire 1968 campaign after injuring his knee in the regular-season opener, Hand appeared in just one game before undergoing season-ending surgery. However, he started every game the Lions played in each of the next five seasons, playing the best ball of his career from 1969 to 1973. Particularly outstanding in 1970, 1972, and 1973, Hand earned Second-Team All-NFC honors in the first of those campaigns by registering six sacks and scoring his third touchdown on defense, with his strong play helping the Lions compile a regular-season record of 10–4, earning them their first playoff berth since 1957. Two years later, Hand gained unofficial Second-Team All-Pro recognition from the Newspaper Enterprise Association by recording a team-high nine sacks. He followed that up with another excellent season, registering a career-high nine and a half sacks in 1973.

Serving as the focal point of the Lions' defensive front for most of that five-year period after spending his first few seasons in Detroit playing in the shadow of Alex Karras, Hand often drew multiple blockers from opposing teams, who respected his ability to rush the passer and defend against the run. Extremely effective at both, Hand used his strength and quickness to apply pressure off the edge and his power, footwork, and excellent technique to shed opposing blockers at the line of scrimmage. Gradually emerging as one of the Lions' leaders on defense, Hand became the most respected member of the team's defensive line after Karras retired at the end of 1970.

Hand's streak of consecutive starts ended in 1974, when he sustained another knee injury that forced him to miss one game and see limited duty in five others. Shifted inside to right tackle the following year, Hand started every game at that post, recording eight sacks and the fourth of his five career interceptions, before missing the final four games of the ensuing campaign with a knee injury he suffered during a 17–16 loss to the New Orleans Saints in week 10. Hand subsequently spent the 1977 season assuming a backup role, before being waived by the Lions at the end of the year. Choosing to announce his retirement, Hand ended his career with 62½ sacks, eight fumble recoveries, and five interceptions, which he returned for a total of 110 yards and three touchdowns. Having appeared in a total of 164 contests, Hand ranked fourth in franchise history in games played at the time of his retirement, behind only Wayne Walker, Dick Le-Beau, and Darris McCord.

Following his playing days, Hand moved with his wife, Darlene, to her hometown of Winston-Salem, North Carolina, where he worked for many years as a stockbroker for E. F. Hutton and Co., Inc., before retiring to private life. Now in his mid-80s, Hand still lives in Winston-Salem, some 80 miles east of where he played his college football.

CAREER HIGHLIGHTS

Best Season

Although Hand earned his lone All-NFC nomination two years earlier, he had his finest all-around season in 1972, when, in addition to gaining Second-Team All-Pro recognition from the Newspaper Enterprise Association, he earned team MVP honors on defense by recovering two fumbles and leading the Lions with nine sacks.

Memorable Moments/Greatest Performances

Hand scored the first points of his career when he returned his interception of a Jim Hart pass two yards for a touchdown during a 38–28 loss to the St. Louis Cardinals on October 1, 1967.

Hand lit the scoreboard again the following week when he ran four yards to paydirt after intercepting a pass during a 27–17 loss to the Packers, making him the first defensive lineman in NFL history to record pick-sixes in consecutive games.

Hand crossed the opponent's goal line for the third and final time when he returned his interception of a Bill Nelsen pass 62 yards for a touchdown during a 41–24 win over the Browns on October 18, 1970.

Notable Achievements

- Scored three defensive touchdowns.
- Led Lions in sacks four times.
- Ranks among Lions career leaders with 62½ sacks (tied for 5th) and three touchdown interceptions (tied for 3rd).
- Lions 1972 team MVP on defense.
- 1972 Newspaper Enterprise Association Second-Team All-Pro selection.
- 1970 Second-Team All-NFC selection.

35

JARED GOFF

Acquired from the Rams in the trade that sent Matthew Stafford to Los Angeles, Jared Goff arrived in Detroit with a reputation as somewhat of an underachiever. Although Goff earned Pro Bowl honors twice during his time in Los Angeles by leading the Rams to two division titles and one NFC championship, he failed to fully live up to the high expectations the organization had for him when it made him the first overall pick of the 2016 NFL Draft, causing him to eventually fall out of favor with head coach Sean McVay. However, since joining the Lions in 2021, Goff has proven to be one of the NFL's most effective signal-callers, guiding them to a pair of NFC North Division titles with his consistently excellent play behind center. A two-time Pro Bowler as a member of the Lions, Goff has thrown for more than 4,400 yards three times and 30 touchdowns twice while also posting the highest career and single-season passer rating and pass-completion percentage of any quarterback in franchise history.

Born in San Rafael, California, on October 14, 1994, Jared Thomas Goff grew up in nearby Novato, where he spent his youth rooting for the San Francisco 49ers. The son of former Major League Baseball player Jerry Goff, who split his six-year big-league career between the Montreal Expos, Pittsburgh Pirates, and Houston Astros, Jared began to display his own athletic ability at Marin Catholic High School, which he led to an overall record of 39–4, three North Coast Section (NCS) playoff appearances, and one NCS championship by throwing for 7,687 yards and 93 touchdowns in his three seasons as starting quarterback of the varsity squad.

Recruited by several college programs as graduation neared, Goff received scholarship offers from Boise State, Fresno State, and Washington State, before choosing to attend the University of California, Berkeley. A three-year starter for the Golden Bears, Goff ended up setting numerous school records, including most career passing yards (12,200) and touchdown passes (96). Especially outstanding his junior year, Goff earned

Jared Goff has led the Lions to two division titles.
Courtesy of All-Pro Reels Photography

First-Team All-Pac-12 honors by leading the conference with 4,719 passing yards and 43 TD passes.

Feeling that he had nothing left to prove at the collegiate level, Goff decided to skip his final year at Cal Berkeley and enter the 2016 NFL Draft, where the Rams selected him with the first overall pick. Joining a Los Angeles team that had not posted a winning record since 2003, Goff spent much of his rookie campaign sitting behind veteran signal-caller Case Keenum, before finally laying claim to the starting job in week 11. Experiencing the usual problems encountered by most first-year quarterbacks, Goff struggled behind center, passing for 1,089 yards and five touchdowns, tossing seven interceptions, and completing just 54.6 percent of his passes in his seven starts, all of which resulted in a loss.

Far more comfortable in his second NFL season, Goff led the Rams to an 11–5 record and the Western Division title by passing for 3,804 yards and 28 touchdowns, tossing only seven interceptions, completing 62.1 percent of his passes, and ranking among the league leaders with a passer rating of 100.5, earning in the process Pro Bowl honors and recognition from the Pro Football Writers Association as the NFL's Most Improved Player. A Pro Bowler again in 2018, Goff helped the Rams advance to the Super Bowl by passing for 4,688 yards and 32 touchdowns, completing 64.9 percent of his passes, and posting a passer rating of 101.1. However, Goff struggled against New England in Super Bowl LIII, completing just 50 percent of his passes and throwing a costly interception late in the fourth quarter of a 13–3 loss.

Although Goff subsequently passed for 4,638 yards and 22 touchdowns in 2019, he also threw 16 interceptions for a Rams team that finished third in the NFC West with a record of just 9–7. Posting similar numbers the following year, Goff passed for 3,952 yards, threw 20 TD passes, and tossed 13 interceptions, before failing to distinguish himself during a 30–20 win over Seattle and a 32–18 loss to Green Bay in the playoffs.

With neither Goff nor the Rams performing at the same level they did during his first two full seasons as the team's starting quarterback, head coach Sean McVay grew increasingly impatient with the former No. 1 overall draft pick, with ESPN's Lindsey Thiry reporting at one point during the 2020 campaign, "In the span of two seasons, routine coach and quarterback sideline squabbles turned into one-sided shouting matches, with McVay no longer holding back. On the sideline, McVay would routinely yell at his quarterback, but some noticed there came a point when McVay wouldn't circle back to apologize. Some chalked it up to the competitive environment, others to McVay's inability to hide his frustration with Goff."

With the relationship between the two men finally reaching a boiling point, the Rams completed a trade with the Lions on March 18, 2021, that sent Goff, a pair of first-round draft picks, and a third-round pick to Detroit for fellow quarterback Matthew Stafford.

Joining a team that had won only five games the previous season, Goff failed to make much of an impact his first year in the Motor City, leading the Lions to a record of just 3–13–1 in 2021. Nevertheless, Goff posted respectable numbers, concluding the campaign with 3,245 passing yards, 19 touchdown passes, eight interceptions, a pass-completion percentage of 67.2, and a passer rating of 91.5 despite missing three games due to injury. Returning to his earlier form the following year, Goff led the Lions to a record of 9–8 and a second-place finish in the NFC North by passing for 4,438 yards and 29 touchdowns, throwing just seven picks, completing

216   THE 50 GREATEST PLAYERS IN DETROIT LIONS HISTORY

65.1 percent of his passes, and posting a passer rating of 99.3, earning in the process Pro Bowl honors and a sixth-place finish in the NFL Comeback Player of the Year voting.

Commenting on his improved play at the end of the year, Goff said, "Being shipped off and sent to a place to die, essentially, is what a lot of people think it [his trade to the Lions] was. And I was never going to allow that to happen. I'm fortunate enough to be around a lot of good coaches and players in Detroit who support me and help me reach my potential."

Lions head coach Dan Campbell displayed some of that support prior to the start of the ensuing campaign when he said of Goff, "He's a better quarterback than he was there [in Los Angeles], in my opinion. Because he can do more things. He's mentally on it. We've come light years ahead of where he was two years ago."

Campbell continued, "We ask him to do a lot more, in my opinion, than what they were actually doing out there. They had a lot of pretty good pieces out there, as well, as we know. Damn good defense, all those things. I just feel like I know from speaking with him and watching him over the last two years, I just feel like we put a lot of things on him where I'm not so sure that's ultimately what they were doing."

Informed of Campbell's comments, Goff responded, "I think as you get older and get more mature in the league that happens, and I'd certainly say so. I think I said that a handful of times last year that I thought I was playing the best football of my career, and I plan on continuing to do that."

Continuing his resurgence in 2023, Goff led the Lions to a regular-season record of 12–5, their first division title in 30 years, and a berth in the NFC Championship Game by ranking among the league leaders with 4,575 passing yards and 30 touchdown passes, completing 67.3 percent of his passes, and posting a passer rating of 97.9.

While much of the success Goff has experienced in Detroit could certainly be attributed to the fact that he plays behind arguably the NFL's best offensive line, he deserves much of the credit himself. Although not blessed with the league's strongest throwing arm, the 6'4", 220-pound Goff throws the deep ball well, is accurate with his short and intermediate passes, and is an excellent game-manager. And even though Goff possesses somewhat limited mobility, he moves well in the pocket and does a good job of avoiding the pass rush. Extremely intelligent, Goff also collaborates well with Lions offensive coordinator Ben Johnson in running the team's offense, stating, "I think he [Johnson] allows for me personally to kind of be creative, and I get a lot of decision-making capabilities at the line of scrimmage. He puts a lot in my hands, a lot on my plate, and allows me to play quarterback and really direct the offense."

After signing a four-year, $212 million contract extension with the Lions on May 16, 2024, Goff rewarded the organization for the faith it placed in him by having the finest season of his career. En route to leading the Lions to a record of 15–2 and their second straight division title, Goff threw for 4,629 yards and 37 touchdowns, completed 72.4 percent of his passes, and posted a passer rating of 111.8, earning in the process his second Pro Bowl nomination as a member of the team.

Unfortunately, Goff subsequently faltered against Washington in the playoffs, throwing three interceptions and losing one fumble during a 45–31 loss to the Commanders in the divisional round of the postseason tournament. But at only 30 years of age, there is still time for Goff to redeem himself in the eyes of Lions fans.

Heading into the 2025 campaign, Goff boasts career totals of 35,058 passing yards and 222 touchdown passes, a pass-completion percentage of 65.6, and a passer rating of 95.7. Since joining the Lions, Goff has thrown for 16,887 yards and 115 touchdowns, tossed 39 interceptions, completed 67.9 percent of his passes, and posted a passer rating of 100.2.

LIONS CAREER HIGHLIGHTS

Best Season

Although Goff has performed extremely well for the Lions in each of the past three seasons, the 2024 campaign would have to be considered his finest as a member of the team. In addition to throwing for 4,629 yards and a career-high 37 touchdowns, Goff set single-season franchise records for highest pass-completion percentage (72.4) and passer rating (111.8).

Memorable Moments/Greatest Performances

Goff earned NFC Offensive Player of the Week honors by throwing for 296 yards and three touchdowns during a 29–27 victory over the Vikings on December 5, 2021, with his 11-yard TD toss to Amon-Ra St. Brown on the game's final play giving the Lions their first win of the season.

Goff led the Lions to a 36–27 victory over Washington on September 18, 2022, by passing for 256 yards and four touchdowns, connecting twice with Amon-Ra St. Brown and once each with Josh Reynolds and D'Andre Swift.

Goff helped lead the Lions to a 40–14 win over Jacksonville on December 4, 2022, by completing 31 of 41 passes for 340 yards and two touchdowns.

218   THE 50 GREATEST PLAYERS IN DETROIT LIONS HISTORY

Goff gained recognition as NFC Offensive Player of the Week by throwing for 353 yards and two touchdowns during a 20–6 win over Tampa Bay on October 15, 2023.

Goff led the Lions to a lopsided 42–17 victory over the Denver Broncos on December 16, 2023, by passing for 278 yards and five touchdowns.

En route to earning NFC Offensive Player of the Week honors for the third time as a member of the Lions, Goff made history during a 42–29 win over the Seattle Seahawks on September 30, 2024, when, in addition to being on the receiving end of a seven-yard TD pass from Aman-Ra St. Brown, he completed all 18 of his pass attempts for 292 yards and two touchdowns, becoming in the process the first quarterback ever to achieve a 100 percent completion rate with at least 11 pass attempts.

Goff led the Lions to a 52–6 pasting of the Jacksonville Jaguars on November 17, 2024, by throwing for 412 yards and four touchdowns, the longest of which came on a 64-yard connection with Jameson Williams.

Although the Lions lost a 48–42 shootout with the Buffalo Bills on December 15, 2024, Goff performed magnificently, throwing for five touchdowns and a franchise-record 494 yards.

Notable Achievements

- Has passed for more than 4,000 yards three times.
- Has thrown at least 30 touchdown passes twice
- Has completed more than 65 percent of passes four times, topping 70 percent once.
- Has posted passer rating above 90.0 four times, finishing with mark above 100.0 once.
- Has posted touchdown-to-interception ratio of better than 2–1 four times.
- Has finished second in NFL in pass completions once, passing yards twice, and passer rating once.
- Holds franchise single-season records for highest completion percentage (72.4 in 2024) and highest passer rating (111.8 in 2024).
- Holds franchise records for highest completion percentage (67.9) and passer rating (100.2).
- Ranks among Lions career leaders with 2,225 pass attempts (3rd), 1,511 pass completions (2nd), 16,887 passing yards (2nd), and 115 touchdown passes (3rd).
- Two-time division champion (2023 and 2024).
- Three-time NFC Offensive Player of the Week.
- October 2024 NFC Offensive Player of the Month.
- Two-time Pro Bowl selection (2022 and 2024).

36

ED FLANAGAN

One of the NFL's finest centers for much of his career, Ed Flanagan spent 10 seasons anchoring the middle of the Lions' offensive line, gaining notoriety for his consistently excellent play, tremendous durability, and superior leadership skills. Starting all but one game the Lions played from 1965 to 1974, Flanagan used his strength, quickness, intelligence, and outstanding technique to impose his will against his opponent, earning in the process four Pro Bowl selections and two First-Team All-NFC nominations. A team captain his last five seasons in Detroit, Flanagan later received the additional honor of being named to the Lions All-Time Team in 2019.

Born in San Bernardino, California, on February 23, 1944, Edward Joseph Flanagan grew up in a middle-class Irish American family that moved to Altoona, Pennsylvania, during his youth. The son of a former member of the Pittsburgh Steelers taxi squad who served as a sergeant in the U.S. Army during World War II, Flanagan began playing organized football in the fifth grade, before earning the starting fullback job at Keith Junior High School. Following his graduation, Flanagan enrolled at Altoona High School, where he failed to distinguish himself on the gridiron until his senior year, when, after assuming the role of a backup running back and long-snapper his first two seasons, he earned honorable mention All-State honors as an offensive lineman.

Recalling his days at Altoona High, Flanagan, who also wrestled in high school, said, "My dad was our high school's center before me. He was a single-wing center, and he taught me how to snap the ball. I won my letter in my junior year by snapping for all the punts and extra points."

Offered an athletic scholarship to Purdue University, Flanagan sat out his freshman year, before earning a spot on the varsity squad as a long-snapper the following season after experiencing a 40-pound growth spurt that increased his weight from 190 to 230 pounds. Remembering how his physical transformation took his coach by surprise the first time he walked onto the practice field as a sophomore, Flanagan stated, "Coach

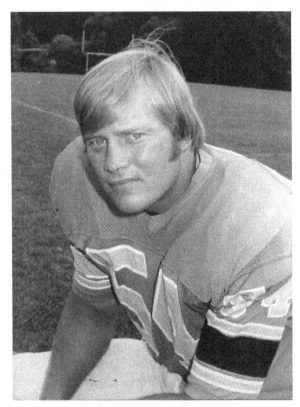

Ed Flanagan spent 10 seasons anchoring the Lions' offensive line from his center position.

had to ask my name. Someone said, 'That's Flanagan.' I got pretty big in college, but we didn't use steroids. It was all natural growth. I never lifted a weight in my life!"

Finally named a starter his senior year, Flanagan emerged as a standout performer on both sides of the ball, gaining Second-Team All-Big Ten and honorable mention All-America recognition by helping the Boilermakers compile a record of 6–3 that earned them a third-place finish in the conference. Looking back on his final season of college ball, Flanagan said, "Back then, you played both ways. If you played center at Purdue, you automatically played linebacker. In 1964, my senior year, the Big Ten switched to two-platoon football, where you could have an offensive team and a defensive team. We had a line coach, Ernie Zawhlan, who had faith in me, and I ended up starting. I also became co-captain along with Jim Garcia, a defensive end."

Selected by the Lions in the fifth round of the 1965 NFL Draft with the 64th overall pick, Flanagan experienced his "welcome to the NFL moment" shortly after he arrived at his first pro training camp, remembering, "The Lions used to have what they called a 'rookie camp.' They brought in all the rookies and a couple of veterans that were sort of subpar guys. We actually had two teams. . . . Fortunately, I was the only center. I had to run with both teams, and they ran my butt off the first week! The veterans came the following week. I played well against the rookies, but this was different. I had to face Roger Brown on one side, and he weighed about 320 pounds. Alex Karras was on the other side. And the middle linebacker was Joe Schmidt. You talk about a beating! It seemed like every time they knocked me down, Nick Pietrosante, the fullback from Notre Dame who weighed about 230, would make it a point to run over me. So, I had cleat marks up my front, my back, and everywhere. I remember calling my father and saying, 'Dad, I don't think I'm going to make it. These guys are pretty tough. I'll be lucky if I make the taxi squad.'"

Despite his early doubts, Flanagan ended up displacing veteran center Bob Whitlow as the starter at that post, beginning in the process a string of nine straight seasons in which he started every game the Lions played. Performing consistently well throughout the period, Flanagan gained general recognition as one of the finest players at his position, earning Pro Bowl honors four times between 1969 and 1973.

Although the 6'3", 250-pound Flanagan possessed average size for an offensive lineman of his day, his strength, determination, and superior technique gave him the ability to play like a much larger man, with former Lions guard Bob Kowalkowski, who called Flanagan the finest center of his era, recalling, "Ed had great blocking technique. Usually, when he hit somebody, they went down."

Former Lions offensive line coach Chuck Knox also spoke highly of his one-time protégé, saying during a 2015 interview, "He called all the blocking adjustments. He was a Pro Bowl center and was a member of what was regarded as the best offensive line in the NFL at the time. He was an outstanding center. He had been a wrestler in high school and college and had good balance. Plus, he was tough and smart."

Flanagan also made an extremely favorable impression on former Cincinnati Bengals defensive tackle Mike Reid, who recalled, "There were three guys I played against that were centers that were easily marked as the best I played against. Jeff Van Note of the Falcons was a technical wizard. Jim Langer of the Dolphins was all power and strength, and the third guy was Eddie Flanagan. Eddie was a good-sized center—bigger than Jeff or

Jim—and a fantastic technician, but, man, was he ever smart. . . . I'd be in the gap between the center and the guard, and he had hand movement on the ball that would always draw me offsides. My experience with Eddie is that he could beat you physically, and he could outsmart you."

Meanwhile, Larry Hand observed, "As long as Ed Flanagan stayed healthy, nobody could challenge him. With Ed at center, we developed one of the best offensive lines in the NFL for years."

Admired by his teammates for his tremendous resolve and ability to block out pain, Flanagan spent the entire 1971 season playing with a ruptured disk in his back, remembering, "There were times I lay on the ground and didn't think I could make it back to the huddle. But then tackles Rockne Freitas and Jim Yarbrough would lower their shoulders and lift me to my feet. I was team captain. I could not let my teammates down."

Although he acquired the nickname "Easy Ed" for his relatively calm demeanor and easygoing personality, Flanagan found it difficult to tolerate the behavior of Chicago's Dick Butkus, with whom he engaged in a famous feud that lasted his entire career. Often accusing the Hall of Fame middle linebacker of using dirty tactics, Flanagan once said, "He'd kick, spit, grab my facemask, anything to get to the ball-carrier. He bit me once in a pileup. In the leg. Butkus was just nasty."

On another occasion, Flanagan called his frequent foe "a wild man on defense . . . one of the most foul-mouthed guys in the league . . . he insults you, your mother, and the team."

After gaining Pro Bowl recognition for the fourth time in five seasons in 1973, Flanagan signed with the Honolulu Hawaiians of the World Football League at the end of the year. When the Lions subsequently refused to match the offer, Flanagan played out his option in 1974, starting all but one game the Lions played at his familiar position of center. But with the WFL in financial trouble by 1975, Honolulu expressed an interest in restructuring Flanagan's contract, causing him to approach the Lions once again. Recalling the response of head coach Rick Forzano, Flanagan said, "Forzano basically told me he didn't want me back because the previous year we had a mini-strike, and he didn't like the fact that I was the team's player rep."

Rebuffed by the Lions, Flanagan signed with the San Diego Chargers, with whom he spent the next two seasons starting at center, before announcing his retirement following the conclusion of the 1976 campaign. Over the course of 12 NFL seasons, Flanagan appeared in 165 out of 168 games, starting all but one of those.

Looking back on his playing career years later, Flanagan said, "You know, in pro ball you have to be in the right spot at the right time. Later, I had guys come up who tried to take my position, and some were better athletes than I was. But I was the center, and I was entrenched, and I did a pretty good job for the Lions. Pro football is a thinking man's game. The only position where you can get away without thinking and just having raw talent is on the defense. They just point those guys and tell them to get the quarterback or the running back. But when you play offense, you've got to be pretty sharp. You have to know the plays and know the blocking patterns."

Flanagan continued, "There's not much glory in being an O-lineman, but I wouldn't trade my experiences. In fact, I played the 1971 season with a ruptured fourth lumbar. I didn't practice for the second half of the season. When I couldn't play the Pro Bowl, I got an examination, and the trainer said you have a ruptured disc. I had surgery after the season. But I was lucky to avoid serious injury. At times I had both knees taped, my knuckles were messed up most of the time, my shoulders were beaten up. I was always beat up, but I only missed one game with the Lions. I started 139 out of 140 games."

Following his playing days, Flanagan remained in the San Diego area, where he went into the printing business, before trying his hand at coaching. After serving as offensive line coach of the Oakland Invaders of the USFL for three seasons, Flanagan spent several years coaching in the Arena Football League. Choosing to return to Altoona, Pennsylvania, in 2011, Flanagan remained there until May 10, 2023, when he died from heart failure at the age 79.

LIONS CAREER HIGHLIGHTS

Best Season

Although Flanagan also performed exceptionally well in 1969 and 1971, he had the finest season of his career in 1970, when he gained consensus First-Team All-NFC recognition and earned unofficial Second-Team All-Pro honors from the Pro Football Writers by anchoring an offensive line that helped the Lions finish second in the NFL in points scored (347) and yards rushing (2,127).

Memorable Moments/Greatest Performances

Flanagan helped the Lions amass 468 yards of total offense during a 42–0 rout of the Bears on September 22, 1968.

Flanagan's superior blocking at the line of scrimmage helped the Lions gain a season-high 266 yards on the ground during a 40–0 pasting of the Packers in the 1970 regular-season opener.

Flanagan and his linemates again dominated the Packers at the point of attack on October 10, 1971, with the Lions rushing for 178 yards and amassing 465 yards of total offense during a 31–28 win.

Notable Achievements

- Missed just one game in 10 seasons, starting 139 out of 140 contests.
- Four-time Pro Bowl selection (1969, 1970, 1971, and 1973).
- 1969 Newspaper Enterprise Association Second-Team All-Pro selection.
- Two-time First-Team All-NFC selection (1970 and 1971).
- Named to Lions 75th Anniversary All-Time Team in 2008.
- Named to Lions All-Time Team in 2019.

37

BENNIE BLADES

Described by former Lions teammate Lomas Brown as "the hardest-hitting, no-holds barred safety I've ever been around," Bennie Blades spent nine seasons in Detroit, making significant contributions to teams that won two division titles and appeared in one NFC Championship Game. Combining the speed of a cornerback with the size and hitting power of a linebacker, Blades excelled as both a pass-defender and a tackler, recording the second-most stops of any player in franchise history. A one-time Pro Bowler, Blades also earned three unofficial All-Pro nominations from the Newspaper Enterprise Association, before being further honored by being named to the Lions All-Time Team in 2019.

Born in Fort Lauderdale, Florida, on September 3, 1966, Horatio Benedict Blades grew up surrounded by sports. The son of a professional boxer who often sparred with Muhammad Ali, and the nephew of a standout baseball player, Blades received his introduction to organized sports at the age of seven, when, due to his unusually large size, the other neighborhood parents insisted that he compete with and against children a year or two older than himself when he joined a local football league. After further honing his skills by playing in pickup games with his older brother, Brian, and future NFL stars Michael Irvin and Lorenzo White, Blades emerged as a two-way standout on the gridiron at Piper High School in nearby Sunrise, Florida. Excelling at both running back and defensive back, Blades proved to be particularly outstanding on defense, where he displayed a gift for finding the football and intercepting passes while also punishing receivers and talking trash. Even more dominant in track, Blades won the state championship in the 200- and 400-meter dashes twice each, earning in the process an invitation to compete at the 1984 U.S. Olympic Trials.

Recruited by several major colleges as graduation neared, Blades ultimately decided to enroll at the University of Miami, where he spent four years playing under head coach Jimmy Johnson. A starter at free safety in each of his final three seasons, Blades set school records for most career

Bennie Blades ranks second in franchise history in tackles.

interceptions (19), interception-return yards (305), and total tackles by a safety (286), with his tremendous all-around play gaining him consensus First-Team All-America recognition twice. Also named the winner of the Jim Thorpe Award as the nation's outstanding defensive back his senior year, Blades later received high praise from Johnson, who identified him as "the best player at his position that I ever coached."

Impressed with Blades's exceptional play at the collegiate level, the Lions selected him with the third overall pick of the 1988 NFL Draft, making him the first safety in 25 years to be selected that high (Jerry Stovall went second overall to the St. Louis Cardinals in 1963). Immediately assigned starting strong safety duties on his arrival in Detroit, Blades earned a spot on the NFL All-Rookie Team and the first of his three Second-Team All-Pro nominations from the Newspaper Enterprise Association by intercepting two passes, forcing three fumbles and recovering four others, and recording 102 tackles. Blades followed that up with another strong season, forcing two fumbles and finishing second on the team to Chris Spielman with 100 combined tackles in 1989. Continuing to perform at an elite level the next three seasons, Blades intercepted six passes and averaged 90 tackles a year from 1990 to 1992, earning in the process a pair of Second-Team All-Pro selections from the Newspaper Enterprise Association and his lone Pro Bowl nomination.

Despite his superior play, Blades never developed into quite the turnover machine he was in college, recording only 12 interceptions during his nine years in Detroit. In explaining his relatively low number of picks, Blades said, "When I was at Miami, I was a free safety that was a ball hawk. That's all they needed me to do. I hit people now and then when need be. We had linebackers that would make tackles all over the field. When I got to Detroit, they needed me in other ways. They needed me as a strong safety, as an outside linebacker, as a free safety. I had to play different roles. I knew that ball hawk safety was a role that they didn't need. If I can't be that, then let me be the most physical safety the league has ever known. Ronnie Lott was a corner that moved to safety. Dave Duerson was the guy I patterned my game after. Dave Duerson, Kenny Easley, and Jack Tatum, those were the guys I wanted to be. That's why I called myself 'The Punisher.'"

Living up to his self-proclaimed moniker, Blades established himself as arguably the hardest-hitting safety of his era. Although officially listed at 221 pounds, Blades carried close to 240 pounds on his 6' frame, making him an imposing figure to any receiver who had the misfortune of lining up across from him. Extremely aggressive, Blades harassed his man all over the field while also intimidating anyone who entered his vicinity in zone coverage. Known for taunting his opponent as well, Blades displayed such physicality that he even played linebacker in certain passing situations toward the end of his career. And despite his added bulk, Blades remained fast enough to cover most receivers deep downfield.

After missing just a handful of games his first five years in the league, Blades sustained an injury to his back in 1993 that limited him to just four contests. Returning to action full-time in 1994, Blades started all but one game the Lions played over the course of the next three seasons, picking off four more passes, recording nearly 300 tackles, and scoring the second of his two career touchdowns, before signing with the Seattle Seahawks as a free agent following the conclusion of the 1996 campaign.

In discussing his departure from the Motor City, Blades recalled, "My last year in Detroit was arguably one of my better years. And they just told me, 'You are getting too old. We are going to replace you with younger guys.' . . . When Seattle gave me an offer, I had my agent call back over to Detroit and say, 'Well, can you match it?' Or 'Can you just give me a little bit less, and I'll come back to Detroit?' They didn't even call him back."

THE 50 GREATEST PLAYERS IN DETROIT LIONS HISTORY

Blades, who, in his nine seasons with the Lions, recorded 790 tackles, intercepted 12 passes, amassed 219 interception-return yards, forced nine fumbles and recovered 11 others, registered four sacks, and scored two touchdowns, ended up spending just one year in Seattle, recording 70 tackles and picking off two passes for the Seahawks in 1997, before problems with his back forced him to announce his retirement.

Following his playing days, Blades returned to his hometown of Fort Lauderdale, where he spent almost two decades working in the city's parks and recreation department. At various times, Blades also served as dean of students at Central Charter School, helped oversee club sports programs at the University of Fort Lauderdale, coached a youth football team, and officiated youth football games in the area. The father of six children from six different women, Blades often found it difficult to make the necessary child support payments, forcing him to file for bankruptcy protection at one point.

Further troubled by poor health in retirement, Blades has four or five herniated discs in his back that he said made his muscles seize up every time he hit someone during the latter stages of his career to the point that "it would leave my right leg pretty much paralyzed." Blades, who sustained eight documented concussions during his NFL career, also suffers from regular migraine headaches and experiences occasional bouts of depression, one of which caused him to remain at home for 20 days.

In discussing his condition, Blades stated in an article that appeared in the *Detroit Free Press* in 2018, "With all the concussions I've had, I'm sure my brain is mush right now. And what scares me, sometimes I wake up, I have twitching of an eye and real bad migraines, and you wonder, 'Okay, look, how long do you have?'"

Nevertheless, Blades added, "I tell people, I wouldn't trade anything that I've done. I've been playing that game since [I was] seven years old. I retired at 31. And the only reason I retired is because they told me I was going to be paralyzed. If it wasn't for that, I probably would have still been playing the game."

LIONS CAREER HIGHLIGHTS

Best Season

Blades performed exceptionally well for the Lions in his first and last seasons in Detroit, recording 102 tackles, two interceptions, three forced fumbles, and four fumble recoveries as a rookie in 1988, before registering

106 tackles and two interceptions, one of which he returned 98 yards for a touchdown, eight years later. But Blades made his greatest overall impact in 1991, when he helped the Lions capture the NFC Central Division title by making 93 tackles, picking off one pass, and forcing two fumbles and recovering three others, earning in the process First-Team All-NFC honors, his lone Pro Bowl selection, and the second of his three Newspaper Enterprise Association Second-Team All-Pro nominations.

Memorable Moments/Greatest Performances

Blades contributed to a 19–9 victory over the Packers on November 20, 1988, by recovering a fumble and recording the first interception of his career.

Blades tallied his first points as a pro when he returned a blocked punt seven yards for a touchdown during a 27–13 loss to the Packers on November 1, 1992.

Blades lit the scoreboard again on September 29, 1996, when he returned his interception of a Trent Dilfer pass 98 yards for a touchdown during a 27–0 shutout of the Tampa Bay Buccaneers.

Notable Achievements

- Scored two touchdowns.
- Amassed more than 100 interception-return yards once.
- Recorded more than 100 tackles three times.
- Led Lions with 106 tackles in 1996.
- Ranks among Lions career leaders with 790 tackles (2nd), nine forced fumbles (tied for 7th), and 11 fumble recoveries (tied for 8th).
- Two-time division champion (1991 and 1993).
- Member of 1988 NFL All-Rookie Team.
- 1992 Lions team MVP on defense.
- 1991 Pro Bowl selection.
- 1991 First-Team All-NFC selection.
- Three-time Newspaper Enterprise Association Second-Team All-Pro selection (1988, 1991, and 1992).
- Named to Lions 75th Anniversary All-Time Team in 2008.
- Named to Lions All-Time Team in 2019.

38

KEVIN GLOVER

The leader of an offensive line that helped Barry Sanders win four rushing titles, Kevin Glover spent 13 of his 15 NFL seasons in Detroit, starting at either center or guard in 11 of those. A starter on the interior of the Lions' offensive front from 1987 to 1997, Glover proved to be a key contributor to teams that made five playoff appearances and won two division titles. An outstanding run-blocker who also provided superior pass-protection, Glover earned three trips to the Pro Bowl, one All-Pro nomination, and four All-NFC selections, before receiving the additional honor of being named to the Lions All-Time Team in 2019.

Born in Washington, D.C., on June 17, 1963, Kevin Bernard Glover attended Largo High School in nearby Prince George's County, Maryland, where he lettered in football, basketball, and track and field. Especially proficient on the gridiron, Glover performed so well that he earned an athletic scholarship to the University of Maryland, where, after moving from offensive tackle to center at the end of his sophomore year, he gained First-Team All-ACC and All-America recognition as a senior in 1984.

Selected by the Lions in the second round of the 1985 NFL Draft with the 34th overall pick, Glover sustained knee injuries in each of his first two seasons that limited him to a total of just 14 games and one start. But even though Glover appeared in only four contests in 1986, he learned a valuable lesson that helped shape the rest of his career. Recalling his exchange with offensive line coach Bill Muir, Glover recounted, "My knee was bothering me, and I told him I thought I needed a day off and a practice off. He told me straight off, 'You can't afford to take a day off.' And he just walked away."

Adopting a new attitude after laying claim to the starting right guard job in 1987, Glover later said, "Not only won't I take a day off, I won't take a play off. That was my goal every year. I was going to play every snap of every season."

Moved to left guard in 1988, Glover began a string of 64 consecutive starts that continued after the coaching staff shifted him to center prior to

Kevin Glover helped Barry Sanders win four rushing titles with his superior blocking up front.

the start of the ensuing campaign. Although a broken leg limited him to just seven games in 1992, Glover began another streak when he returned to action the following year, starting every game the Lions played in each of the next five seasons.

Glover's iron-man status helped him gradually emerge as one of the Lions team leaders. So, too, did his outgoing persona and caring nature. In discussing his role of leadership, Glover stated, "I wanted to be a strong leader. We'd have get-togethers, Halloween parties, Bible study. All the players' wives were close and supported each other. The older ones would look out for the younger ones and their families.... That era was special. We all had great relationships. When you had a teammate, a friend, somebody as talented as Barry [Sanders] is, and as humble as he is—people don't realize how humble he is—it makes it that much more special."

Also developing into one of the NFL's finest centers, the 6'2", 278-pound Glover helped the Lions advance to the playoffs five times from

232 THE 50 GREATEST PLAYERS IN DETROIT LIONS HISTORY

1991 to 1997, with the team placing in the league's top five in total offense on three separate occasions.

Although Glover did an excellent job of protecting the many quarterbacks who lined up behind center for the Lions during his time in Detroit, he proved to be even more effective as a run-blocker, with Barry Sanders saying of his former teammate, "Most of the yards I ran for during my career, I was running behind his blocks. . . . He took great pride in being a centerpiece of that offensive line, as well as the anchor of our team. He knew that many of us were looking to him for leadership, and he never let us down. He was, quite frankly, that guy that you just never wanted to take the field without him."

Named to the Pro Bowl three straight times from 1995 to 1997, Glover also gained First-Team All-NFC recognition in each of those seasons while serving as the Lions' NFLPA representative. But with team management failing to offer him the money he felt he deserved, Glover signed with the Seattle Seahawks as a free agent following the conclusion of the 1997 campaign, ending in the process his lengthy association with the organization.

Glover, who left Detroit having appeared in a total of 177 games, 161 of which he started, ended up spending two injury-marred seasons in Seattle, experiencing back problems in both 1998 and 1999 that limited him to a total of just 14 starts, before announcing his retirement. Following his playing days, Glover worked as a sports agent until 2004, when he returned to the University of Maryland. After spending more than a decade assuming various roles in the school's athletic department, Glover became his alma mater's director of player development in 2017. Glover's job responsibilities include overseeing the involvement in community service efforts of student-athletes, assisting with internship opportunities, and helping to maintain strong connections with Maryland's alumni base. Glover also is an active speaker in local youth and church organizations.

Looking back favorably on the time he spent in the Motor City, Glover vividly recalls the thrill he got every time he entered the Silverdome on game day, saying, "To step up in that dome, on any given Sunday, the intensity and volume were unbelievable. You could stand one foot or maybe 10 inches away from somebody and scream as loud as you could, and they couldn't hear you. . . . The Silverdome floor was cement. You could feel it vibrate. It was a very, very good era. Pontiac, Detroit, and the surrounding areas, they really deserved that for all the years they gave the organization."

Glover also has nothing but fond memories of his playing days, stating, "There are so many things you take away from your time. It starts way back—from getting a phone call, flying to a city you never visited, meeting

KEVIN GLOVER **233**

all these people. . . . It's absolutely worth it, and I'd definitely do it again. I've had about 10 surgeries . . . a couple were after playing ball. I'd absolutely do it again—without any regrets."

LIONS CAREER HIGHLIGHTS

Best Season

Glover earned the last of his three straight Pro Bowl selections in 1997, when he helped Barry Sanders rush for a career-high 2,053 yards. But in addition to gaining Pro Bowl recognition in 1995, Glover garnered his lone All-Pro nomination by anchoring a line that enabled the Lions to finish first in the NFL in total offense.

Memorable Moments/Greatest Performances

Glover helped the Lions gain a season-high 267 yards on the ground during a 34–14 win over the Vikings on November 24, 1991.

Glover did another expert job in the middle of the Lions' offensive line on November 7, 1993, helping them rush for 241 yards during a 23–0 win over Tampa Bay.

Glover and his linemates again dominated the Tampa Bay defensive front on November 13, 1994, with the Lions gaining 243 yards on the ground during a 14–9 victory over the Buccaneers.

Glover's superior blocking at the point of attack helped the Lions rush for 222 yards and amass 496 yards of total offense during a lopsided 55–20 victory over the Bears on November 27, 1997.

Notable Achievements

- Missed just two games from 1988 to 1997, starting 151 out of 153 contests.
- Ranks 9th in franchise history with 177 games played.
- Two-time division champion (1991 and 1993).
- Three-time Pro Bowl selection (1995, 1996, and 1997).
- 1995 Second-Team All-Pro selection.
- Four-time First-Team All-NFC selection (1994, 1995, 1996, and 1997).
- Named to Lions 75th Anniversary All-Time Team in 2008.
- Named to Lions All-Time Team in 2019.

39

PENEI SEWELL

rguably the finest offensive lineman in the game today, Penei Sewell has spent the last four seasons providing the Lions with consistently excellent play from the right tackle position. An outstanding pass-protector and dominant run-blocker who serves as a cornerstone of an offense that ranks among the league's best, Sewell has already earned three Pro Bowl selections and two All-Pro nominations with his exceptional all-around play, which has helped lead the Lions to two division titles.

Born in the village of Malaeimi in American Samoa on October 9, 2000, Penei Sewell grew up with his three brothers near the capital of Pago Pago, where he spent his early years living in simplicity, recalling, "I stayed in the small village of Malaeimi. Man, we all stayed at the shack there, and it's a beach. It's an island surrounded by nothing but water, and probably you can hit the whole island in a 40-minute drive. It was real small, life was real simple."

With their father serving as a football coach on the island, Penei and his three brothers, two of whom also currently play in the NFL, adopted the sport at a young age. Remembering how he received his introduction to football, Sewell said, "I got roughed up until I was bigger. My older brother, Gabe—he was the one that set the tone. Nephi was right above me also until it was my time, when I got about 6'2" in seventh or eighth grade. Then, I hit the weight room and just tried to get better. So, really, those guys got me better, to be honest. And then, I tried to pass it on to my little brother [Noah]."

Seeing the potential in his sons, Sewell's father relocated the family to St. George, Utah, in 2012—a move that proved to be quite beneficial to Penei, who soon developed into a star on the gridiron at Desert Hills High School. Ranked by 247 Sports as the No. 1 prospect in the state of Utah for the 2018 class, Sewell received an athletic scholarship to the University of Oregon, where he spent two seasons excelling at tackle for the Ducks, winning the Outland Trophy as the best interior lineman in college football as a sophomore, before sitting out his junior year due to the coronavirus

Arguably the finest offensive lineman in the game today, Penei Sewell has gained First-Team All-Pro recognition in each of the past two seasons.
Courtesy of All-Pro Reels Photography

pandemic. Choosing to forgo his final year of college, Sewell declared himself eligible for the 2021 NFL Draft, where the Lions selected him in the first round with the seventh overall pick.

Claiming that the Lions entered the draft hoping that Sewell would fall to them at No. 7, Detroit head coach Dan Campbell stated after making the selection, "We knew it right when Miami made their pick, we knew exactly what was going down. We didn't need to worry about anything else. That was our guy. This is a big man who can move. He has great feet, a temperament about him, an attitude and he's a cornerstone player, man. He's somebody you can build a team around, and that's exactly why we got him."

236   THE 50 GREATEST PLAYERS IN DETROIT LIONS HISTORY

Named a starter immediately on his arrival in the Motor City, Sewell performed well his first year in the league while splitting his time between both tackle positions, earning a spot on the NFL All-Rookie Team with his strong play. Inserted at right tackle full-time in 2022, Sewell took his game up a notch, gaining Pro Bowl recognition by serving as the dominant figure on an offensive line that helped the Lions post their first winning record in five seasons.

Blessed with good size, great strength, and tremendous athleticism, the 6'5", 335-pound Sewell possesses all the physical attributes teams look for in an offensive tackle, with Lions quarterback Jared Goff saying of his teammate, "He might be the best athlete in the league. Pound for pound, you find somebody that runs like that, that can move like that, that has a little bit of wiggle like he has. He's as good as I've ever seen."

Lions run game coordinator/defensive line coach Terrell Williams expressed similar sentiments when he stated, "Penei Sewell is the best offensive lineman I've seen, and I've been in this league a long time. Just from a workman's standpoint, I mean he had a play early on in camp where he took off and ran, I don't know, 50 yards. I'm just like, I don't think it's fair that somebody that big can run like that."

Equally effective at protecting his quarterback and blocking for the run, Sewell drew high grades in both areas from SI.com, which quoted one AFC executive as saying, "Sewell is a dominant run blocker and arguably the [league's] best anchor in pass protection. Some OTs are great pass blockers but just average in the run game. He's elite in both phases. Very consistent. Plays with an edge."

As that AFC exec suggested, Sewell also has a mean streak in him that he is not afraid to exhibit, stating on one occasion, "I like to play real physical. I like to use my body type to my advantage and to really get up under people's chins and really showcase my mentality also, to go along with my physicality, that I'm coming off the ball every play with violent intentions, and that nothing less is coming from that."

Praising his team's top lineman prior to the start of the 2023 season, Dan Campbell said, "I can't say enough great things about Sewell. I mean, there's a reason why he was the first pick we had two years ago because we wanted to build around a guy like him. He's our foundation, man."

Campbell continued, "He's one of those pillars that we talk about, but I mean, he's something else. He's a man on a mission. I feel like we're a team on a mission, but he is a man on a mission. And you talk about being wired right, a guy that comes in every day, puts in the work, and he's got so much ability, but he's got the right attitude too, and I think that's what makes him dangerous."

On learning of Campbell's remarks, Sewell responded, "I mean, I think it's exactly what he said, to be honest. I set high goals for me, and I have high expectations for myself, and he knows that, the team knows that, and I just strive to work at that each and every day."

Lions offensive line coach Hank Fraley, who spent three seasons playing alongside Hall of Fame left tackle Joe Thomas in Cleveland, likened Sewell to his former teammate when he stated, "He reminds me a lot of Joe Thomas, just how he prepares, how he takes care of himself, his mental mind makeup and going out there on that daily grind to become a good player or great player like Joe. So, that's what I get to see, that daily competition within himself and with everybody else out here. It doesn't stop."

Continuing to perform at an elite level in 2023 and 2024, Sewell helped the Lions capture consecutive division titles with his superior blocking, earning in the process Pro Bowl and First-Team All-Pro honors each season. With Sewell signing a four-year, $112 million contract extension with the Lions in April 2024 that promises to keep him in Detroit through the 2029 season, he figures to add significantly to his list of accomplishments and greatly improve his place in these rankings in the coming years.

CAREER HIGHLIGHTS

Best Season

As well as Sewell performed in 2023, it could be argued that he made a greater overall impact in 2024, when he helped the Lions set a single-season franchise record by scoring a league-leading 564 points.

Memorable Moments/Greatest Performances

Sewell helped the Lions gain a season-high 229 yards on the ground during a 16–16 tie with the Pittsburgh Steelers on November 14, 2021.

Sewell's superior blocking helped the Lions amass 464 yards of total offense during a 34–23 win over the Vikings on December 11, 2022, with 330 of those yards coming through the air.

Sewell continued his string of three consecutive games in which he did not allow a single pressure of Jared Goff during a 42–24 victory over the Carolina Panthers on October 8, 2023.

Sewell and his linemates dominated the opposition at the point of attack on October 30, 2023, with the Lions amassing 486 yards of total offense and gaining 222 yards on the ground during a 26–14 victory over the Las Vegas Raiders.

Sewell helped the Lions amass a franchise-record 645 yards of total offense during a 52–6 rout of the Jacksonville Jaguars on November 17, 2024, with 449 of those yards coming through the air and the other 196 on the ground.

Notable Achievements

- Two-time division champion (2023 and 2024).
- Member of 2021 NFL All-Rookie Team.
- Three-time Pro Bowl selection (2022, 2023, and 2024).
- Two-time First-Team All-Pro selection (2023 and 2024).
- Two-time First-Team All-NFC selection (2023 and 2024).

40

LES BINGAMAN

One of pro football's first big, quick defenders, Les Bingaman spent seven seasons in Detroit anchoring the Lions' defensive line from his middle guard position. The NFL's heaviest player throughout his career, Bingaman, who frequently tipped the scales at close to 350 pounds, proved to be an immovable object up front, with his girth and ability to shed blockers making him a forerunner of the modern-day nose tackle. A three-time All-Pro and two-time Pro Bowler, Bingaman made huge contributions to Lions teams that won three division titles and two league championships, before announcing his retirement at only 29 years of age because he found it increasingly difficult to maintain his playing weight.

Born in McKenzie, Tennessee, on February 3, 1926, Lester Alonza Bingaman moved with his family at an early age to Gary, Indiana, where he established himself as a standout two-way lineman at Lew Wallace High School. Offered an athletic scholarship to the University of Illinois, Bingaman spent three seasons starring at tackle for the Fighting Illini football team, which he helped lead to the Big Ten Conference championship and a No. 5 ranking in the final AP poll in 1946.

Selected by the Lions in the third round of the 1948 NFL Draft with the 15th overall pick, Bingaman assumed various spots along Detroit's defensive line his first two years in the league, before settling in at middle guard in 1950, when, starting every game at that post, he gained unofficial Second-Team All-Pro recognition from both UPI and the *New York Daily News*. Developing into the league's finest player at his position the following year, Bingaman helped lead the Lions to their first winning record in six seasons with his dominant play up front, which earned him Pro Bowl and First-Team All-Pro honors for the first time. Continuing his strong play in 1952 and 1953, Bingaman garnered First-Team All-Pro honors from at least one major news source both years by serving as the centerpiece of a dominant defense that led the Lions to back-to-back NFL championships.

239

Les Bingaman proved to be a forerunner of the modern-day nose tackle.

A massive man who forced opposing teams to assign him multiple blockers on almost every play, Bingaman proved to be too much for any one man to handle. Although officially listed at 6'3", 272 pounds, Bingaman spent much of his career playing at a weight well in excess of 300, making him extremely effective at clogging up the middle against the run. Meanwhile, Bingaman's surprising quickness and agility enabled him to pursue opposing ball-carriers along the line of scrimmage and apply inside pressure to opposing quarterbacks.

With Bingaman, whom one account published in 1960 called "the biggest man who ever played professional football," weighing as much as he did, his size often became a topic of conversation. Debating the point with assistant coach Buster Ramsey during training camp in 1954 after watching a bench on the sidelines collapse under Bingaman's weight, Lions head coach Buddy Parker claimed that the middle guard weighed closer to 400 pounds than 300. But with no scale at the team's facility capable of accurately weighing Bingaman, Parker had to convince him to drive to a local grain company in Ypsilanti, Michigan, where he weighed in at 349½ pounds.

After shedding some of his excess weight, Bingaman helped the Lions capture their third consecutive division title in 1954, earning in the process the last of his three First-Team All-Pro nominations. But shortly after celebrating his 29th birthday the following offseason, Bingaman chose to announce his retirement, saying at the time that it was "getting tougher every year to get in shape."

Bingaman, who, in addition to recording an unknown number of sacks and tackles, intercepted two passes and recovered nine fumbles during his 80-game professional career, took a job working in public relations for Goebel Brewing Company in Detroit following his playing days. Bingaman also owned a bar in Detroit that he sold in 1959, just before he became defensive line coach of the Lions under George Wilson. Bingaman spent the next five years in that position presiding over a group that included "Fearsome Foursome" members Alex Karras, Roger Brown, Darris McCord, and Sam Williams, before being relieved of his duties as part of a purge of assistant coaches after the Lions compiled a record of 7–5–2 in 1964. After working as an NFL scout for one year, Bingaman spent four seasons serving as an assistant on the coaching staff of the Miami Dolphins, during which time he began to experience serious health problems.

Although Bingaman reduced his weight to 225 by shedding 86 pounds over a four-month span in 1963, he eventually put most of the weight back on. Bingaman began dieting again after he suffered congestive heart failure early in 1968. But less than two years later, he collapsed on the sidelines during a Dolphins game. Revived with a shot of adrenaline after medics failed to detect a pulse or heartbeat for three minutes, Bingaman was subsequently diagnosed as having suffered "an irregularity of the heartbeat which caused him to go into temporary shock." After accepting a less strenuous position as a college scout for Miami, Bingaman lived another year, before dying in his sleep from a heart attack at the age of 44 on November 20, 1970.

242 THE 50 GREATEST PLAYERS IN DETROIT LIONS HISTORY

CAREER HIGHLIGHTS

Best Season

Bingaman made his greatest overall impact in 1953, when he helped lead the Lions to a regular season record of 10–2 and their second consecutive NFL championship by serving as the anchor of the league's No. 2 ranked defense, with his exceptional play gaining him Pro Bowl and consensus First-Team All-Pro recognition.

Memorable Moments/Greatest Performances

Bingaman anchored a Lions defense that allowed just 106 yards of total offense and forced eight turnovers during a 45–7 rout of the Packers in the 1950 regular-season opener.

In addition to serving as the centerpiece of a defense that limited the Rams to just 39 yards rushing during a 17–14 Lions win on October 3, 1952, Bingaman recorded the first of his two career interceptions.

Bingaman and his defensive mates did an even better job against Pittsburgh on November 9, 1952, holding the Steelers to –3 yards on the ground during a 31–6 Lions win.

Bingaman and his cohorts turned in another dominant performance on November 6, 1954, yielding just 69 yards of total offense to the Colts during a 27–3 Lions win.

Notable Achievements

- Three-time division champion (1952, 1953, and 1954).
- Two-time NFL champion (1952 and 1953).
- Two-time Pro Bowl selection (1951 and 1953).
- Three-time First-Team All-Pro selection (1951, 1953, and 1954).

41

JERRY BALL

An outstanding interior defensive lineman who spent the first six years of his career starting for the Lions at nose tackle, Jerry Ball proved to be one of the NFL's premier players at his position during his time in Detroit. A dominant run-stuffer who drew double-team blocking on virtually every play, Ball did a superb job of either bringing down opposing ball-carriers himself or making it easier for his teammates to register tackles near the line of scrimmage. A solid pass-rusher as well, Ball once recorded nine sacks in a season, with his exceptional all-around play earning him three Pro Bowl selections and two All-Pro nominations.

Born in Beaumont, Texas, on December 15, 1964, Jerry Lee Ball spent his early years living with his grandparents after his mother and father divorced. Although Ball loved his grandparents, he later expressed regret that he had no one younger with whom to share his love of sports, saying, "I kind of have a complex about that. My grandparents supported me, but they were older and couldn't come to many events. I didn't play catch with my dad. I'd win a football game, and there wouldn't be anybody waiting for me, so I'd just get on the bus."

An excellent all-around athlete, Ball starred in baseball, basketball, football, and track and field (shot put) at predominantly black Hebert High School, which merged with the area's mostly white school prior to the start of his senior year to form Westbrook High. Continuing to excel in all four sports following the merger, Ball proved to be especially proficient on the gridiron, where his exceptional play at fullback, defensive end, and linebacker helped lead the Bruins to the 1982 Texas 5A championship.

Despite his athletic achievements, Ball looked back at his time at Westbrook High with mixed emotions. Claiming that the constant bickering of his teammates' parents threatened to derail the school's march to the state football title after the team got off to an 0–3 start, Ball recalled that all the players, black and white, got together and told their elders to leave them

Jerry Ball earned three Pro Bowl selections and two All-Pro nominations during his six seasons in Detroit.

alone and let them play, saying, "That changed me. That was my first exposure to politics in action."

Having earned First-Team All-State honors on defense and All-District honors at three different positions, Ball received a football scholarship to SMU, where, after adding 40 pounds onto his frame, he moved to nose tackle. Excelling at his new post, Ball gained All-SWC recognition three times and made All-America twice while also being named a finalist for the Lombardi and Outland trophies in each of his final two seasons.

Selected by the Lions in the third round of the 1987 NFL Draft with the 63rd overall pick, Ball immediately laid claim to the starting nose tackle job on his arrival in Detroit, after which he earned All-Rookie honors by registering one sack and 36 tackles. Improving on those numbers the

JERRY BALL **245**

following season, Ball recorded two sacks and 68 tackles, before gaining Pro Bowl, First-Team All-NFC, and unofficial All-Pro recognition from both *Pro Football Weekly* and the Newspaper Enterprise Association in 1989 by recording 73 tackles and a team-high nine sacks.

Serving as the centerpiece of the Lions' 3–4 defense, the 6'1", 330-pound Ball lined up extremely close to the line of scrimmage, almost touching the opposing center's helmet with his own. Blessed with a rare combination of size, strength, and quickness, Ball forced opposing teams, whom he referred to as "victims," to assign him multiple blockers on almost every play, sometimes occupying as many as three offensive linemen. Claiming that no center in the league had the ability to block Ball one-on-one, teammate Chris Spielman stated, "It's impossible. If the center tries to, Jerry will make every play, and the center will end up three yards in the backfield." And with Ball drawing so much attention to himself, his defensive mates often found themselves free to make tackles, as Spielman suggested when he said, "He creates a lot of havoc."

Fellow Lions defensive tackle Lawrence Pete also had high praise for his teammate, saying, "He's just relentless. Everything is can-do with him. I don't think there's anybody else at 300 pounds who can do what he can do."

So good against the run that teams often ran away from him, Ball did an exceptional job of clogging up the middle, frequently bringing down opposing running backs in the offensive backfield. Meanwhile, Ball possessed the quickness to pursue ball-carriers from sideline to sideline and apply pressure up the middle to opposing quarterbacks.

Recognized as the finest nose tackle in the NFC by 1990, Ball earned Pro Bowl, First-Team All-Conference, and Second-Team All-Pro honors by recording 50 tackles and two sacks. But prior to the start of the campaign, Ball began to rub some people in the front office the wrong way when he refused to attend training camp while holding out for more money. Settling his contract dispute shortly before the regular season got underway, Ball rejoined the team, prompting Lions head coach Wayne Fontes, who nicknamed him the "Mayor" one year and the "Governor" the next because of his larger-than-life persona and vocal leadership, to tell reporters, "Any time you get a guy of Jerry Ball's caliber, it upgrades the position. Jerry Ball's an All-Pro lineman. It's a great plus to have him report to camp and play this game."

Performing extremely well once more in 1991, Ball again gained Pro Bowl, All-NFC, and All-Pro recognition despite missing the final three games of the season after being injured by a then-legal chop block that later prompted the NFL to institute the "Jerry Ball Rule," which outlawed such maneuvers. Also experiencing differences with Lions defensive line coach

246   THE 50 GREATEST PLAYERS IN DETROIT LIONS HISTORY

Lamar Leachman during the season, Ball found objectionable the "off-color racial jokes" the latter made during the team's practices in the South, stating at one point during the campaign, "I've complained about it, but he keeps doing it. One day, he told me he respects me as a player. I said that's not what I want, I want to be respected as a human. I want to win a championship, and to do that, we have to have harmony on and off the field."

Ball remained in Detroit for one more year, registering 43 tackles, recording two and a half sacks, and recovering three fumbles, one of which he returned for a touchdown, before being traded to the Cleveland Browns for a third-round draft pick prior to the start of the 1993 campaign. Ball, who, in his six seasons with the Lions, recorded 306 tackles, 18½ sacks, and one safety; forced one fumble and recovered six others; and scored one touchdown, ended up spending one year with the Browns, three with the Raiders, and three with the Vikings, before announcing his retirement at the end of 1999 with career totals of 557 tackles, 32½ sacks, 12 fumble recoveries, five forced fumbles, one interception, and two touchdowns.

Since retiring from football, Ball has become a successful businessman, starting a Detroit-based clothing company licensed by the NFL called Ice Box Sportswear that he continues to own and operate.

LIONS CAREER HIGHLIGHTS

Best Season

Although Ball earned consensus First-Team All-Pro honors in 1991 by registering 36 tackles and two sacks for a Lions team that finished first in the NFC Central Division with a record of 12–4, he turned in a more dominant performance in 1989, when he established career-high marks with 73 tackles, nine sacks, and three fumble recoveries.

Memorable Moments/Greatest Performances

Ball recorded two sacks in one game for the first of two times in his career during a 31–22 win over the Packers on November 12, 1989.

Ball accomplished the feat again during a 27–17 win over the Bears on December 10, 1989.

Ball registered a safety when he brought down Eric Dickerson in the end zone during a 33–24 victory over the Indianapolis Colts on September 22, 1991.

Ball contributed to a 31–17 win over the Vikings on September 13, 1992, by recording a sack and returning a fumble 21 yards for a touchdown.

Notable Achievements

- Scored one defensive touchdown.
- Led Lions with nine sacks in 1989.
- Led Lions defensive linemen in tackles twice.
- 1991 division champion.
- Three-time Pro Bowl selection (1989, 1990, and 1991).
- 1991 First-Team All-Pro selection.
- 1990 Second-Team All-Pro selection.
- Three-time First-Team All-NFC selection (1989, 1990, and 1991).

42

EDDIE MURRAY

Nicknamed "Steady Eddie" for the consistency he displayed during his time in Detroit, Eddie Murray proved to be one of the NFL's most reliable placekickers over the course of a 19-year pro career that included stints with seven different teams. Having most of his finest seasons for the Lions from 1980 to 1991, Murray scored more than 100 points four times and successfully converted more than 90 percent of his field goal attempts on three separate occasions, en route to establishing himself as the second-leading scorer in franchise history. A member of teams that won two NFC Central Division titles, Murray gained Pro Bowl and All-Pro recognition twice each, before receiving the additional honor of being named to the Lions 75th Anniversary All-Time Team in 2008.

Born in Halifax, Nova Scotia, on August 29, 1956, Edward Peter Murray moved with his family at a young age to Victoria, British Columbia, where he competed in soccer, track, cricket, and rugby while attending Spectrum Community High School. Following his graduation, Murray spent a year operating a forklift in a lumberyard while also playing junior football for the Saanich Hornets of the Lower Island Junior Varsity League.

Discovered by Tulane University head coach Larry Smith while at Saanich, Murray accepted a football scholarship to the New Orleans school, where he went on to shatter nearly every Green Wave record for placekicking, including highest field goal percentage (.616) and most field goals (45), extra points (84), and points scored (219). A four-time First-Team All-South Independent selection, Murray also gained honorable mention All-America recognition in each of his final two seasons, prompting the Lions to select him in the seventh round of the 1980 NFL Draft with the 166th overall pick. Also claimed by the Hamilton Tiger-Cats in the third round (26th overall) of that year's Canadian Football League (CFL) Draft, Murray chose to remain in the United States and begin his pro career in Detroit.

Eddie Murray ranks second in franchise history in scoring.

Performing extremely well his first year in the league after beating out veteran kicker Benny Ricardo for the starting job, Murray earned NFL All-Rookie, Pro Bowl, First-Team All-NFC, and First-Team All-Pro honors by successfully converting 64.3 percent of his field goal attempts, finishing third in the league with 116 points scored, and topping the circuit with 27 field goals, which represented a single-season franchise record at the time. Murray subsequently punctuated his outstanding rookie campaign by kicking five field goals in the Pro Bowl, earning in the process game MVP honors.

250 THE 50 GREATEST PLAYERS IN DETROIT LIONS HISTORY

Continuing to provide the Lions with solid kicking the next two seasons, Murray led the NFL with 121 points scored in 1981, before successfully converting 11 of his 12 field goal attempts (91.7 percent) during the strike-shortened 1982 campaign.

Among the NFL's most accurate kickers, the 5'10", 177-pound soccer-style kicking Murray also possessed one of the league's stronger legs, which became evident in 1983, when he successfully converted three of his four field goal attempts from more than 50 yards out.

However, after setting a new NFL playoff record (since broken) by kicking a 54-yard field goal in the second quarter of the Lions' 1983 NFC divisional round playoff game matchup with the 49ers, Murray experienced the most disappointing moment of his career when he narrowly missed a 43-yard attempt in the final seconds of regulation, dooming his team to a 24–23 defeat.

Putting his critical miss behind him, Murray remained one of the NFL's better kickers from 1984 to 1987, performing especially well in 1985, when, in addition to ranking among the league leaders with 26 field goals, 109 points scored, and a field goal percentage of 83.8, he set a franchise record by successfully converting 12 straight field goal attempts. Even better in 1988 and 1989, Murray missed just two of his 42 field goal attempts over the course of those two seasons, posting in the process identical field goal percentages of 95.2, which tied the NFL record for highest field goal accuracy. But after being accorded Pro Bowl and Second-Team All-Pro honors in the second of those campaigns, Murray failed to perform at the same level in 1990, when a hip injury that forced him to sit out five contests adversely affected his kicking. Continuing to struggle somewhat in 1991, Murray successfully converted only 67.9 percent of his field goal attempts, prompting the Lions to release him after they moved up several spots in the second round of the 1992 NFL Draft to select fellow kicker Jason Hanson.

Recalling his feelings on being informed of his release, Murray said, "At the time I was released, I felt that, given how long I was there, that I deserved to be told that they were thinking about that, so I could prepare myself for that. But all of a sudden, it happened. When you trade up, you want that kid, whatever position it is. Just 48 hours later, I was released, without even being given a chance to compete for the job. The rug and everything else were pulled out from under me. My world started to topple."

Murray, who left Detroit having kicked 244 field goals and 381 extra points, scored a total of 1,113 points, and successfully converted just over 75 percent of his field goal attempts, subsequently played for both the

Kansas City Chiefs and Tampa Bay Buccaneers in 1992, before signing with the Dallas Cowboys, with whom he won the NFL championship in 1993. Murray then split the remainder of his career between the Cowboys, Philadelphia Eagles, Washington Redskins, and Minnesota Vikings, briefly retiring in both 1996 and 1998, before leaving the game for good following the conclusion of the 2000 campaign with career totals of 352 field goals, 538 extra points, and 1,594 points and a lifetime field goal percentage of 75.5.

Following his playing days, Murray returned to the Detroit area, where he eventually became the director of donor relations in southeastern Michigan for the HOPE Network, a faith-based health care nonprofit organization whose mission includes mental health and autism awareness.

LIONS CAREER HIGHLIGHTS

Best Season

Murray had his two highest-scoring seasons as a member of the Lions in 1980 and 1981, tallying 116 points in the first of those campaigns, before leading the league with 121 points in the second. But while Murray scored fewer points (96) in 1989, he proved to be far more accurate, successfully converting 95.2 percent of his field goal attempts (20 for 21) for the second straight time (he posted marks of 64.3 percent in 1980 and 71.4 percent in 1981).

Memorable Moments/Greatest Performances

Murray earned NFL Special Teams Player of the Week honors for the first time by converting all five of his field goal attempts during a 29–7 win over the Packers on September 14, 1980, with the longest of his kicks covering 43 yards.

Murray gave the Lions a 27–24 victory over the Cowboys on November 15, 1981, by driving the ball through the uprights from 47 yards out in the closing moments.

Murray tallied nine of the 11 points the Lions scored during an 11–0 win over Tampa Bay in the opening game of the 1983 regular season, successfully converting field goal attempts of 29, 48, and 38 yards.

Murray gave the Lions a 23–20 overtime victory over the Packers on November 20, 1983, by kicking his third field goal of the game, with this one coming from 37 yards out.

252   THE 50 GREATEST PLAYERS IN DETROIT LIONS HISTORY

After kicking a 46-yard field goal during regulation, Murray gave the Lions a 27–24 win over Atlanta on September 9, 1984, by driving the ball through the uprights from 48 yards out in overtime.

Murray proved to be the difference in a 19–9 win over the Packers on November 20, 1988, successfully converting all four of his field goal attempts, the longest of which came from 42 yards out.

Murray earned NFL Special Teams Player of the Week honors for the second time by successfully converting field goal attempts of 33, 43, 35, and 36 yards during a 33–7 victory over Tampa Bay on December 17, 1989.

Murray earned that distinction again by kicking four field goals during a 40–27 win over Denver on November 22, 1990, with the longest of his kicks coming from 45 yards out.

Murray gave the Lions a 17–14 win over Buffalo in the final game of the 1991 regular season by connecting on a 21-yard field goal in overtime.

Notable Achievements

- Scored more than 100 points four times, topping 120 points once.
- Converted more than 90 percent of field goal attempts three times, topping 95 percent twice.
- Led NFL in points scored once, field goals made once, and field goal percentage twice.
- Ranks among Lions career leaders with 1,123 points scored (2nd), 244 field goals made (2nd), and 381 extra points made (2nd).
- Two-time division champion (1983 and 1991).
- Member of 1980 NFL All-Rookie Team.
- Three-time NFL Special Teams Player of the Week.
- Two-time Pro Bowl selection (1980 and 1989).
- 1980 First-Team All-Pro selection.
- 1989 Second-Team All-Pro selection.
- Three-time First-Team All-NFC selection (1980, 1988, and 1989).
- Pro Football Hall of Fame All-1980s Second Team.
- Named to Lions 75th Anniversary All-Time Team in 2008.

43

MEL GRAY

Widely considered to be one of the greatest return men of all time, Mel Gray spent six of his 12 NFL seasons in Detroit, amassing more yards on special teams than any other player in franchise history. A member of the Lions from 1989 to 1994, Gray returned five kickoffs and two punts for touchdowns, en route to accumulating a total of almost 7,000 kickoff- and punt-return yards that places him well ahead of anyone else in team annals. A major contributor to Lions squads that won two division titles, Gray gained Pro Bowl and All-Pro recognition four times each during his time in the Motor City, before being further honored by being named to the Lions All-Time Team in 2019.

Born in Williamsburg, Virginia, on March 16, 1961, Melvin Junius Gray starred in multiple sports at Lafayette High School, excelling as a running back in football and a sprinter in track and field, tying the school record in the 100-meter dash as a sophomore, before earning a spot on the All-Peninsula District Track Team for the 200-meter dash his senior year.

Failing to receive any scholarship offers, Gray enrolled at Coffeyville Community College, a small school located in Coffeyville, Kansas, that claims membership in both the Kansas Jayhawk Community College Conference and the National Junior College Athletic Association. Starting at halfback for the Red Ravens the next two seasons, Gray spent his freshman year sharing the backfield with future Heisman Trophy winning fullback Mike Rozier on a team that earned a No. 2 ranking in the NJCAA poll by posting a perfect 11–0 record. Taking over as the team's feature back the following year, Gray rushed for 1,397 yards and scored 20 touchdowns, earning in the process First-Team All-Jayhawk Conference and Little All-America honors.

Subsequently recruited heavily by both the University of Pittsburgh and Purdue University, Gray elected to transfer from Coffeyville to Purdue at the end of his sophomore year. Performing extremely well for the Boilermakers the next two seasons, Gray gained a total of 1,765 yards on the ground, amassed 2,202 yards from scrimmage, and scored 16 touchdowns,

Mel Gray amassed more yards on special teams than any other player in franchise history.

with his outstanding play his senior year gaining him Second-Team All-Big Ten recognition.

Selected by the Chicago Blitz in the seventh round of the 1984 USFL Draft with the 133rd overall pick, Gray headed west when Chicago traded him to the Los Angeles Express prior to the start of the regular season. Displaying his varied skill set his first year as a pro, Gray helped the Express advance to the playoffs by rushing for 625 yards, gaining another 288 yards on 27 pass receptions, amassing 332 kickoff-return yards, and scoring four touchdowns. Gray spent one more year in Los Angeles, accumulating 830 all-purpose yards in 1985, before joining the New Orleans Saints, who had selected him in the second round of the 1984 NFL Supplemental Draft of USFL and CFL players, when the less established league folded in August 1986.

Used primarily by New Orleans as a kickoff- and punt-returner the next three seasons, Gray performed admirably in that role, amassing nearly

3,000 all-purpose yards and scoring twice on special teams. Nevertheless, the Saints chose not to protect Gray following the conclusion of the 1988 campaign, leaving him feeling dejected and unwanted.

Recalling his feelings at the time, Gray said, "For me, it was kind of scary. I was very excited about being in New Orleans. I had a good time. I was starting to find some success under [special teams coordinator] Joe Marciano. . . . To find myself being put on Plan B . . . it was almost like being cut. You don't know what's going to happen. You don't know if the next team is going to pick you up."

Ultimately signed by the Lions as a Plan B free agent, Gray found his deal and new home very much to his liking, remembering, "After leaving New Orleans, with a minimum salary, coming to Detroit at the time it was a very lucrative contract for a special teams player. I took advantage of it."

Despite missing six games due to injury his first year in the Motor City, Gray had a solid season for the Lions, amassing 785 all-purpose yards, 716 of which came on special teams, and finishing second in the league with an average of 26.7 yards per kickoff return. Establishing himself as the NFL's finest return man the following year, Gray earned Pro Bowl and All-Pro honors for the first of three straight times by leading the league with 1,300 kickoff- and punt-return yards. Gray followed that up by leading the NFL with 1,314 kickoff- and punt-return yards and averages of 25.8 yards per kickoff return and 15.4 yards per punt return in 1991, before topping the circuit with 1,181 kickoff- and punt-return yards in 1992.

Extremely dangerous once he got his hands on the football, the 5'9", 167-pound Gray possessed outstanding speed, superior quickness, and tremendous open-field running ability. Capable of stopping on a dime and then accelerating quickly before his opponent had a chance to react, Gray did a superb job of evading would-be tacklers, with former Cincinnati Bengals defensive back Solomon Wilcots saying, "His thing was speed. . . . Coaches were screaming, 'Everybody hustle to the ball. Everybody get to him. We need 11 guys to tackle him.' And you would all come walking over to the sideline saying, 'What happened? We prepared for this guy, but we just couldn't stop him from getting to the end zone.'"

A fearless runner, who, despite his smallish frame, often ran into piles of players with abandon, Gray displayed little regard for his body, with longtime Detroit sportscaster James Samuelson stating, "Watching Mel Gray made me realize that the greatest attribute a kick-returner can have— and he had it—was fearlessness. Where you collect the ball, you just pick a hole, and you go. And if you get hit, you get hit hard and you are down. But if you burst through that hole, you are gone."

256   THE 50 GREATEST PLAYERS IN DETROIT LIONS HISTORY

Longtime Lions beat writer Tom Kowalski added, "The amazing thing about Mel Gray was that he never lost that fearlessness. A lot of returners in this league do it for a year or two. It's the special ones like Mel Gray who do it year-after-year-after-year. That is really hard to do."

Claiming that he acquired his toughness while playing running back under Melvin Jones, his head coach in high school, Gray stated, "He started me on the right track. To play in his backfield, you had to be fearless. You can't be afraid to run the ball up into the crowd. I took that along with me to college and the NFL."

Gray added, "I took some hits. Little dings and bruises. You have to keep coming back. You've got to be physically tough as well as mentally tough. When you enjoy it, you make it that much better."

Following an injury-marred 1993 season that saw him amass "only" 885 all-purpose yards, Gray garnered Pro Bowl and All-Pro honors for the final time in 1994 by finishing third in the league with 1,509 kickoff- and punt-return yards while also topping the circuit with three kickoff-return TDs and an average of 28.4 yards per kickoff return. A free agent at the end of the year, Gray signed with the Houston Oilers, with whom he spent most of the next three seasons, before announcing his retirement following the conclusion of the 1997 campaign after appearing in three games with the Philadelphia Eagles. Over the course of 12 NFL seasons, Gray scored nine times on special teams and amassed 10,250 kickoff-return yards, 2,753 punt-return yards, and 13,279 all-purpose yards. During his time in Detroit, Gray scored seven touchdowns and accumulated 7,040 all-purpose yards.

Following his playing days, Gray did some substitute teaching, before eventually getting involved in the real estate business in the Houston area. Ranked fifth by the NFL Network on that station's 2009 list of the Top 10 Return Aces of All-Time, Gray looks back favorably on his time in the Motor City, saying, "It definitely was the highlight of my career. Everything was perfect for me. The location. The surroundings. The players. The fans. I had success on top of it. Those six years in Detroit defined my career."

LIONS CAREER HIGHLIGHTS

Best Season

Gray had the finest season of his career in 1994, when, in addition to amassing 1,509 kickoff- and punt-return yards, he set single-season franchise records that still stand by returning three kickoffs for touchdowns and averaging 28.4 yards per kickoff return.

Memorable Moments/Greatest Performances

Gray scored what proved to be the game-winning points of a 21–17 victory over the Packers on December 15, 1991, when he returned a punt 78 yards for a touchdown midway through the fourth quarter.

Gray gave the Lions an early 7–0 lead over the Vikings on September 13, 1992, when he returned a punt 58 yards for a touchdown in the first quarter of a 31–17 win.

Although the Lions ultimately suffered a 27–23 defeat at the hands of the Tampa Bay Buccaneers on September 27, 1992, Gray gave them a 23–20 fourth-quarter lead when he returned a kickoff 89 yards for a touchdown.

Gray contributed to a 30–10 victory over the Seattle Seahawks on October 17, 1993, by returning a kickoff 95 yards for a touchdown.

Gray lit the scoreboard again when he returned a kickoff 102 yards for a touchdown during a 21–16 win over the Bears on October 23, 1994.

Gray scored the first points the Lions tallied during a 38–30 loss to the Packers on November 6, 1994, when he returned a kickoff 91 yards for a touchdown.

Gray earned NFC Special Teams Player of the Week honors by returning a kickoff 98 yards for a touchdown during a 41–19 pasting of the Vikings on December 17, 1994.

Notable Achievements

- Returned five kickoffs and two punts for touchdowns.
- Amassed more than 1,000 all-purpose yards four times, topping 1,500 yards once.
- Led NFL in kickoff-return yards once, kickoff- and punt-return yards three times, kickoff-return average twice, and punt-return average once.
- Ranks fourth in NFL history with 10,250 kickoff-return yards, 13,003 kickoff- and punt-return yards, and six kickoff-return touchdowns.
- Holds Lions career records for most kickoff-return yards (5,478) and kickoff-return touchdowns (5).
- Ranks among Lions career leaders with 1,427 punt-return yards (2nd) and 7,040 all-purpose yards (6th).
- Holds Lions single-season records for most kickoff-return touchdowns (3 in 1994) and highest kickoff-return average (28.4 in 1994).

THE 50 GREATEST PLAYERS IN DETROIT LIONS HISTORY

- Two-time division champion (1991 and 1993).
- 1994 Week 16 NFC Special Teams Player of the Week.
- Four-time Pro Bowl selection (1990, 1991, 1992, and 1994).
- Three-time First-Team All-Pro selection (1990, 1991, and 1994).
- 1992 Second-Team All-Pro selection.
- Four-time First-Team All-NFC selection (1989, 1990, 1991, and 1994).
- Pro Football Hall of Fame All-1990s Second Team.
- Named to Lions 75th Anniversary All-Time Team in 2008.
- Named to Lions All-Time Team in 2019.

44

JOHNNIE MORTON

Part of an outstanding Lions receiving corps that also included Herman Moore, Brett Perriman, and Germaine Crowell at various times, Johnnie Morton spent eight years in Detroit serving as a key contributor to teams that made four playoff appearances. A member of the Lions from 1994 to 2001, Morton recorded the third-most receptions and receiving yards of any player in franchise history despite playing second fiddle to Moore much of his time in the Motor City. An extremely consistent wideout who amassed more than 1,000 receiving yards in four out of five seasons at one point, Morton also established himself as one of the franchise's career leaders in several other offensive categories, before departing for Kansas City following the conclusion of the 2001 campaign.

Born in Torrance, California, on October 7, 1971, Johnnie James Morton Jr. grew up just off the Pacific coast, some 15 miles southwest of Los Angeles. The son of an African American father and Japanese American mother, Morton attended a Japanese elementary school for three years, before entering the public school system. Eventually enrolling at South High School in Torrance, Morton excelled in multiple sports for the Spartans, performing well enough on the gridiron to earn a scholarship to USC.

A four-year starter for the Trojans at wide receiver, Morton broke 12 USC team and Pacific-10 Conference records for receptions and receiving yards, ending his career with 201 receptions, 3,201 receiving yards, and 23 touchdown catches. Particularly outstanding his senior year, Morton gained consensus First-Team All-America recognition by catching 78 passes, amassing 1,373 receiving yards, and scoring 12 touchdowns.

Expected to go early in the 1994 NFL Draft, Morton gathered with his agent, Leigh Steinberg, in an effort to pare down his list of possible destinations, recalling, "We made a list of the teams that I was most likely to be drafted by, maybe I'd be drafted by, and no chance. The Lions were in the last category—no chance."

Johnnie Morton ranks third in franchise history in receptions and receiving yards.
Courtesy of George A. Kitrinos

Morton's assumption seemed logical since not only did the Lions need help on defense, but they already had Herman Moore and Brett Perriman on board. Nevertheless, they ended up selecting him in the first round with the 21st overall pick, with Morton later saying, "I was in shock. Why would they pick me? It ended up being the best moment in my life."

Seeing very little action as a rookie, Morton made just three receptions for 39 yards and one touchdown, making his biggest contribution on special teams, where he returned a kickoff 93 yards for a TD.

Looking back on his first year as a pro, Morton stated, "It was probably the most frustrating football year of my life. I was coming off a really great year [at USC]. I wanted to come in and make a huge splash in Detroit."

So despondent that he approached Lions chief operating officer Chuck Schmidt at one point during the campaign about the possibility of being traded, Morton eventually came to look more favorably on his situation after he spoke with Ron Hughes, the team's longtime head of player personnel.

Recalling his conversation with Hughes, Morton said, "He came up to me one day at my locker. He was a straight up guy. He'd just give you the straight truth. That's it, whether you liked it or not. . . . He told me, 'You're going to play a lot. Just be patient. I promise you; we wouldn't have drafted you if we didn't have big plans for you.'"

Assuming a far more prominent role on offense his second year in the league, Morton helped the Lions score 436 points and advance to the playoffs as a wild card by making 44 receptions for 590 yards and eight touchdowns while serving as a slot receiver alongside Moore and Perriman. Continuing his solid play in 1996, Morton caught 55 passes, amassed 714 receiving yards, and scored six touchdowns, before beginning an outstanding five-year run during which he posted the following numbers after displacing Perriman as the team's No. 2 receiver prior to the start of the 1997 season:

1997: 80 receptions, 1,057 receiving yards, 6 touchdown receptions
1998: 69 receptions, 1,028 receiving yards, 2 touchdown receptions
1999: 80 receptions, 1,129 receiving yards, 5 touchdown receptions
2000: 61 receptions, 788 receiving yards, 3 touchdown receptions
2001: 77 receptions, 1,154 receiving yards, 4 touchdown receptions

Eventually establishing himself as the Lions' top wideout, Morton led the team in receptions twice and receiving yards three times. Blessed with good speed, soft hands, and excellent moves, the 6', 190-pound Morton proved to be a precise route runner who did an outstanding job of creating separation between himself and his defender and gaining yards after the catch. A fierce competitor, Morton never shied away from going over the middle of the field or diving to make contested catches in traffic, with former Lions head coach Bobby Ross once praising him by saying, "He can make the 'pro catch.'"

Meanwhile, as Morton's status within the organization grew, he came to embrace the football environment in Detroit, stating, "It was the people, and just the passion. I grew up on the West Coast. Sports aren't taken as seriously. I remember going to Lakers games. It was almost like a club to them. They [the fans] were making an appearance. . . . In Detroit, it was something I'd never been accustomed to. There's so much passion around sports. That was huge. . . . The fans poured their heart out to the team. They lived and died with the team. It was so cool. They've been Lions fans their entire lives. Their kids have Lions gear. It's a totally different atmosphere. I grew to love and appreciate that."

262   THE 50 GREATEST PLAYERS IN DETROIT LIONS HISTORY

Feeling as he did about the Lions and the Motor City, Morton hoped to remain in Detroit when he became a free agent at the end of 2001. But with the Chiefs offering him far more money, he had little choice but to go to Kansas City.

Expressing his elation following the signing of Morton, Chiefs head coach Dick Vermeil said, "He would come in here and be the top receiver on the team. He would add another degree of explosiveness to our offense. We need to score more points. He could make the plays to help us do that."

Morton, who, during his time in Detroit, made 469 receptions; amassed 6,499 receiving yards, 6,642 yards from scrimmage, and 7,249 all-purpose yards; caught 35 TD passes; and scored 36 touchdowns, ended up spending three years in Kansas City and another in San Francisco, before retiring following the conclusion of the 2005 campaign with career totals of 624 receptions, 8,719 receiving yards, 43 touchdown catches, and 44 touchdowns.

After retiring from football, Morton did some modeling work and briefly became involved with mixed martial arts, before running afoul of the law in 2012, when he received a sentence of two years' probation for lying to a grand jury during a criminal probe of his California business associate, money launderer Neang Chhorvann. After claiming during a 2009 testimony that he did not have any business dealings with Chhorvann, Morton later acknowledged that he had given him more than $2 million to invest for him.

Since that time, though, Morton has helped rebuild his reputation by remaining active in several charitable organizations, including D.A.R.E., Athletes and Entertainers for Kids, the Kansas City School for the Blind, and Big Brothers of America.

Even though Morton spent the last four years of his career playing in other cities, he says that his heart remained in Detroit, stating, "I felt like this was my town. I was excited to go to a new stadium [Ford Field in 2002]. I felt like I helped put the foundation down, put the bricks down. . . . I just never saw myself playing anywhere but Detroit. Ask anyone. I'm an ex-Lion."

LIONS CAREER HIGHLIGHTS

Best Season

Although Morton posted extremely comparable numbers in 1999 and 2001, we'll go with the 1997 season since, in addition to making 80 receptions and amassing 1,057 receiving yards, he scored six touchdowns and placed in the league's top 10 in a major statistical category for the only time in his career (he finished ninth in receptions).

Memorable Moments/Greatest Performances

Morton scored the first touchdown of his career when he gathered in an 18-yard pass from Dave Krieg during a 41–19 win over the Vikings on December 17, 1994.

Although the Lions lost to Miami, 27–20, in the 1994 regular-season finale one week later, Morton scored on special teams when he returned a kickoff 93 yards for a touchdown.

Morton went over 100 receiving yards for the first time as a pro when he made seven receptions for 102 yards and one touchdown during a 44–38 win over the Vikings on November 23, 1995.

Morton helped lead the Lions to a 35–16 victory over the Bears on September 22, 1996, by making seven receptions for 174 yards and two touchdowns, the longest of which covered 62 yards.

Morton again torched the Chicago defensive secondary on November 27, 1997, making seven receptions for 120 yards and one touchdown during a 55–20 Lions win, with his TD coming on a 50-yard connection with Scott Mitchell.

Morton starred in defeat on December 7, 1997, making nine receptions for 171 yards and one touchdown during a 33–30 loss to the Dolphins.

Although the Lions suffered a 31–27 defeat at the hands of the Bears on October 4, 1998, Morton collaborated with quarterback Charlie Batch on a career-long 98-yard scoring play.

Morton gave the Lions a 31–27 victory over the St. Louis Rams on November 7, 1999, when he gathered in a 12-yard touchdown pass from Gus Frerotte with just 28 seconds left in regulation.

Notable Achievements

- Recorded 80 receptions twice.
- Surpassed 1,000 receiving yards four times.
- Amassed more than 1,000 all-purpose yards five times.
- Returned one kickoff for a touchdown.
- Recorded longest reception in NFL in 1998 (98 yards).
- Led Lions in receptions twice and receiving yards three times.
- Ranks among Lions career leaders with 469 receptions (3rd), 6,499 receiving yards (3rd), 35 touchdown receptions (tied for 4th), 36 touchdowns (tied for 8th), 6,642 yards from scrimmage (6th), and 7,249 all-purpose yards (4th).

45

AMON-RA ST. BROWN

One of the NFL's most consistently productive receivers the past four seasons, Amon-Ra St. Brown has excelled for the Lions at wideout ever since he first arrived in Detroit in 2021. A three-time Pro Bowler who has also earned two All-Pro nominations, St. Brown has surpassed 100 receptions and 1,000 receiving yards three times each, en route to establishing himself as one of the franchise's career leaders in both categories. Detroit's top pass-catcher in each of the last four seasons, St. Brown has played a key role in the Lions' return to prominence, serving as arguably the most potent offensive weapon on teams that have won two division titles.

Born in Anaheim Hills, California, on October 24, 1999, Amon-Ra Julian Heru J. St. Brown grew up with his two older brothers in the Golden State, although he also spent a considerable amount of time in Germany. The son of a German mother, Miriam Steyer, and an American father, John Brown, who twice won the Mr. Universe title as an amateur bodybuilder, Amon began weight training with his brothers at an early age at the urging of his dad, who placed great importance on his sons developing into exceptional athletes. Meanwhile, St. Brown's mom made certain that her sons also did well in school and received exposure to different cultures, teaching them how to speak both German and French.

Eventually emerging as a star on the gridiron at Mater Dei High School in Santa Ana, California, St. Brown made 72 receptions for 1,320 yards and 20 touchdowns his senior year, prompting USC to offer him a football scholarship. Continuing to excel at wideout for the Trojans, St. Brown posted three-year totals of 178 receptions, 2,270 receiving yards, and 16 touchdown catches, earning First-Team All-Pac-12 honors during the COVID-shortened 2020 campaign by leading the conference with 41 receptions and seven TD catches.

Praising St. Brown for the versatility he displayed during his time at USC, former Trojans head football coach Clay Helton stated, "There are only a few kids who can play on the inside and outside at that level, and

Amon-Ra St. Brown has surpassed 100 receptions and 1,000 receiving yards in each of the past three seasons.

Amon-Ra proved he was one of them. He had the wiggle to find open grass inside yet also the strength, power, speed, and route-running ability to win one-on-one matchups outside."

Choosing to forgo his final year of college, St. Brown declared himself eligible for the 2021 NFL Draft, where the Lions ended up selecting him in the fourth round with the 112th overall pick. Falling as far as he did in the draft due to a poor showing at the NFL Scouting Combine, St. Brown, who originally expected to be chosen during the latter stages of the first round, posted the 49th-fastest 40-yard dash time among wide receivers. Nevertheless, Lions GM Brad Holmes, who had previously scouted Cooper Kupp for the Los Angeles Rams, remained undeterred, telling Jeffrey

266   THE 50 GREATEST PLAYERS IN DETROIT LIONS HISTORY

Becker of *The Athletic*, "It was easy to envision with Amon-Ra because we were around Kupp. I'm not saying he's Kupp, but watching him play, he reminded me of Kupp and Robert Woods. They aren't the fastest, but they are very quick and sudden, explosive in a short area, and physical."

The 16th wideout taken in that year's draft, St. Brown entered the NFL with a huge chip on his shoulder, telling the NFL Network some three years later, "I actually still think about it. I actually have my goals written down in my notebook; what I want to achieve every year. So, what I want to achieve this year, going into the season, my personal goals, and then right below that I have the 16 receivers written down, where they went to college right below that. And so, I read that whole list three times before I go to practice every day. It's something I'll never forget. Something I make sure I'm always reminded of."

St. Brown also recalled his initial reaction to being selected by the Lions, saying, "I remember getting drafted and seeing the 313 [area code]. I said 'expletive.' The one team I told my brother I do not want to go to is Detroit. I wanted to go to the Packers and play with him [Equanimeous St. Brown] and Aaron [Rodgers], go to the Chiefs and play with Mahomes, Cowboys, any big team with a good quarterback. I saw the 313, and I said, 'It's over with. I don't know what I'm gonna do. It's gonna be in the middle of nowhere. The team isn't good. I probably know two players on the roster.' It was terrible. And me going in the fourth round—it was all bad. I mean, looking back, I was hot, like, when I got drafted, I wasn't excited. I was mad at the situation."

Despite his reservations about joining a Lions team with a recent history of losing, St. Brown performed extremely well in his first NFL season, making 90 receptions for 912 yards, amassing 973 yards from scrimmage, and scoring six touchdowns, one of which came on a 26-yard run. Even better the next two seasons, St. Brown earned Pro Bowl honors in 2022 by making 106 receptions for 1,161 yards and six touchdowns, before gaining Pro Bowl and All-Pro recognition the following year by ranking among the league leaders with 119 receptions, 1,515 receiving yards, and 10 TD catches.

Although the 6', 202-pound St. Brown lacks top-end speed, he is very quick, is a precise route-runner, does an excellent job of finding the "soft spot" in the zone, and catches the ball well in tight coverage, with Lions quarterback Jared Goff calling him "the friendliest target I've ever thrown to."

In discussing the special connection that has developed between Goff and St. Brown, Lions head coach Dan Campbell said, "Those two have been clicking now for four years—really three and a half; it started about halfway through that '21 season, and it's just built from there. If you're a quarterback, we've got a dang good one, but it's easy to throw to a guy like St. Brown because he gets open, he's got body control, balance, he can separate, he's got quickness, he's got play speed, strong hands. They've done it well enough that they can think without speaking. They know each other, what they're getting ready to do, and all that. So, it's special, and they make each other better."

Meanwhile, after initially dreading coming to Detroit, St. Brown has come to very much enjoy his time in the Motor City, saying, "I don't think I'd be able to do what I've done on any other team. Like I've said, the people, the organization, the coaches, the players, this city, the fans. I didn't know coming here what kind of fans they had here."

St. Brown continued, "I knew, for the most part, it was a losing franchise. I didn't think the fans were like this. I thought it would just be whatever. But I remember my rookie year, the fans were at almost every game. We weren't winning any games, and they were still there supporting us. Just from then on, I knew what kind of fans they had here, the people of this city. And that's something I really appreciate as a player because things happen in sports, you have losing seasons, you have winning seasons, but to feel loved and supported by your fans is great. That's what Detroit city fans are like."

After signing a four-year, $120 million contract extension with the Lions prior to the start of the 2024 season that will likely keep him in Detroit through at least the end of 2028, St. Brown earned his third straight Pro Bowl selection and second All-Pro nomination by making 115 receptions for 1,263 yards and 12 touchdowns. St. Brown will enter the 2025 campaign with career totals of 430 receptions, 4,851 receiving yards, and 33 TD catches, all of which place him extremely high in team annals.

CAREER HIGHLIGHTS

Best Season

St. Brown had the finest season of his young career in 2023, when he gained Pro Bowl and First-Team All-Pro recognition by finishing second in the NFL with 119 receptions while also placing in the league's top five with 1,515 receiving yards and 10 touchdown receptions, with his 119 catches representing the third-highest single-season total in franchise history.

Memorable Moments/Greatest Performances

St. Brown made 10 receptions for 86 yards and one touchdown during a 29–27 win over the Vikings on December 5, 2021, with his 11-yard connection with Jared Goff on the game's final play giving the Lions their first win of the season.

St. Brown earned NFC Offensive Player of the Week honors by making nine receptions for 116 yards and two touchdowns during a 36–27 win over Washington on September 18, 2022.

St. Brown contributed to a 40–14 victory over Jacksonville on December 4, 2022, by making 11 receptions for 114 yards and two touchdowns.

St. Brown helped lead the Lions to a 20–6 win over Tampa Bay on October 15, 2023, by making 12 receptions for 124 yards and one TD, which came on a 27-yard hookup with Jared Goff.

St. Brown played a huge role in a 41–38 victory over the Los Angeles Chargers on November 12, 2023, finishing the game with eight receptions for 156 yards and one touchdown.

St. Brown contributed to a 30–20 win over the Vikings in the final game of the 2023 regular season by making seven receptions for 144 yards and one touchdown, which came on a career-long 70-yard connection with Jared Goff.

St. Brown had another big game against the Vikings on October 20, 2024, when he caught eight passes for 112 yards and one touchdown during a 31–29 Lions win.

St. Brown contributed to a 52–6 rout of the Jacksonville Jaguars on November 17, 2024, by making 11 receptions for 161 yards and two touchdowns, which came on connections of 27 and nine yards with Jared Goff.

St. Brown starred in defeat on December 15, 2024, when, in addition to scoring a touchdown on a 66-yard hookup with Jared Goff during a 48–42 loss to the Buffalo Bills, he established career-high marks in receptions (14) and receiving yards (193).

Notable Achievements

- Has surpassed 100 receptions three times, topping 90 catches another time.
- Has surpassed 1,000 receiving yards three times, topping 1,500 yards once.
- Has scored at least 10 touchdowns twice.
- Has finished second in NFL in receptions twice.

- Has finished third in NFL in receiving yards and touchdown receptions once each.
- Has led Lions in receptions and receiving yards four times each.
- Ranks among Lions career leaders with 430 receptions (4th), 4,851 receiving yards (6th), and 33 touchdown receptions (7th).
- Two-time division champion (2023 and 2024).
- 2022 Week 2 NFC Offensive Player of the Week.
- Three-time Pro Bowl selection (2022, 2023, and 2024).
- Two-time First-Team All-Pro selection (2023 and 2024).
- Two-time First-Team All-NFC selection (2023 and 2024).

46

PAUL NAUMOFF

One of the better players on mostly mediocre Lions teams, Paul Naumoff spent his entire 12-year NFL career in Detroit, often failing to receive the recognition he deserved due to the lack of overall success experienced by the ball club. A somewhat undersized linebacker who started on the left side on the Lions' defense in each of his last 11 seasons in the Motor City, Naumoff earned the respect of his teammates and coaches with his consistently excellent play and ability to take the field each week. Known perhaps more than anything for his tremendous durability, Naumoff missed just two games his entire career, at one point appearing in 142 consecutive contests. A one-time team MVP on defense, Naumoff also earned one Pro Bowl selection and two All-NFC nominations, before retiring following the conclusion of the 1978 campaign with more games played to his credit than all but two players in franchise history to that point.

Born in Columbus, Ohio, on July 3, 1945, Paul Peter Naumoff received his introduction to organized football in high school, starring on both sides of the ball for the powerhouse Eastmoor Academy teams. Following his graduation, Naumoff enrolled at the University of Tennessee, where he spent the next three seasons manning three different positions.

After seeing very little action as a backup wide receiver his sophomore year, Naumoff moved to defensive end the following season, when he helped lead the Vols to an 8–1–2 record, a No. 7 ranking in the final AP poll, and a victory over Tulsa in the 1965 Bluebonnet Bowl. Despite his strong play at end, Naumoff volunteered to move to linebacker prior to the start of the ensuing campaign after teammate Tom Fisher lost his life in a car accident. Displaying a natural affinity for his new post, Naumoff gained First-Team All-SEC and consensus First-Team All-America recognition while serving as co-captain of a Vols team that compiled a record of 8–3 and surrendered just 99 points to the opposition all year. Experiencing the most memorable moment of his college career during Tennessee's 18–12 win over Syracuse in the 1966 Gator Bowl, Naumoff made a jarring tackle

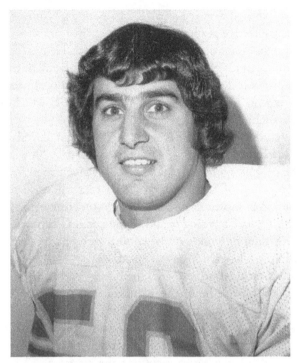

Paul Naumoff appeared in 142 consecutive games for the Lions.

of fullback Larry Csonka late in the final period that helped preserve the victory. Recalling his former teammate's huge hit years later, Nick Showalter stated during a 2010 interview, "You could hear every pad and every part of a Riddell helmet crush. Those helmets had a special sound to them."

Subsequently selected by the Lions in the third round of the 1967 NFL Draft with the 60th overall pick, Naumoff spent his first season in Detroit playing on special teams and seeing limited duty on defense while serving as the primary backup for starting linebackers Mike Lucci, Wayne Walker, and Ernie Clark. Displacing Clark as the starter at left-outside linebacker the following year, Naumoff began a string of eight straight seasons in which he started every game at that post.

Performing well alongside Lucci and Walker from 1968 to 1972, Naumoff helped form an outstanding linebacking corps that helped the Lions finish second in the NFC Central Division five straight times and allow the second-fewest points of any team in the league in both 1969 and 1970. The swiftest of the three, Naumoff did an excellent job of pursuing opposing ball-carriers from sideline to sideline and dropping into pass coverage.

272 THE 50 GREATEST PLAYERS IN DETROIT LIONS HISTORY

Although somewhat undersized at 6'1", 215 pounds, Naumoff also proved to be extremely effective at plugging the hole against the run and shedding blockers. Since the Lions did not begin recording tackle numbers until well after Naumoff began his career, it is not known how many times he brought down the opposition during his 12 seasons in Detroit. However, he is on record as having made 21 stops during a 1975 contest, which remains the single-game franchise record.

Eventually stepping out of the shadows of Lucci and Walker, Naumoff earned Pro Bowl and First-Team All-NFC honors in 1970, when he served as one of the central figures on a defense that helped the Lions compile a regular-season record of 10–4 that earned them a wild-card playoff berth. Although the Lions subsequently suffered a 5–0 defeat at the hands of the Dallas Cowboys in the opening round of the postseason tournament, Naumoff registered their only sack of the contest when he tackled quarterback Craig Morton for a 16-yard loss.

Naumoff continued to provide the Lions with consistently strong play from his left-outside linebacker position for eight more years, earning Second-Team All-NFC and team MVP honors on defense in 1975, before announcing his retirement following the conclusion of the 1978 campaign due to a foot injury that posed the risk of permanent damage had he elected to further extend his playing career. Over the course of 12 NFL seasons, Naumoff recorded six interceptions, seven fumble recoveries, 20½ sacks, and an unknown number of tackles that likely would place him among the franchise's all-time leaders. Naumoff also appeared in 168 out of 170 contests, missing just one game in each of his last two seasons, with his 168 game appearances placing him third in franchise history, behind only Wayne Walker and Dick LeBeau, at the time of his retirement.

Following his playing days, Naumoff opened a beer distributorship in Tennessee that he continued to operate for many years, until finally retiring to private life. Naumoff lived until August 17, 2018, when he passed away at his home in the Knoxville suburb of Lenoir City at the age of 73.

CAREER HIGHLIGHTS

Best Season

The Lions' strong showing in 1970 helped Naumoff earn his lone Pro Bowl and First-Team All-NFC nominations. But he performed slightly better individually in 1975, when, in addition to picking off two passes and recovering a fumble, he recorded a career-high six and a half sacks, earning in the process Second-Team All-NFC honors.

Memorable Moments/Greatest Performances

Naumoff recorded the first of his six career interceptions during a 42–0 mauling of the Bears on September 22, 1968.

Naumoff helped anchor a defense that allowed just 96 yards of total offense during a 28–0 shutout of the Rams on December 14, 1969.

Naumoff and his cohorts turned in another dominant performance on October 28, 1973, yielding just 63 yards of total offense during a 34–0 victory over the Packers.

Naumoff set a single-game franchise record that still stands by recording 21 tackles during a 21–10 win over the Cleveland Browns on November 9, 1975.

Notable Achievements

- Missed just two games entire career, at one point appearing in 142 consecutive contests.
- Holds franchise single-game record for most tackles (21 vs. Cleveland on November 9, 1975).
- Tied for 12th in franchise history with 168 games played.
- Lions 1975 team MVP on defense.
- 1970 Pro Bowl selection.
- 1970 First-Team All-NFC selection.
- 1975 Second-Team All-NFC selection.

47

AIDAN HUTCHINSON

One of the NFL's brightest young stars, Aidan Hutchinson has spent the past three seasons helping to restore the Lions to prominence. The defensive leader of a team that has won two division titles, Hutchinson has provided the Lions with consistently excellent play from his post at left end while also setting an example for his teammates with his tenacity and tremendous work ethic. A one-time Pro Bowler who has also earned one First-Team All-NFC nomination, Hutchinson has led the Lions in sacks in each of his first three years in the league despite sustaining a serious leg injury midway through the 2024 campaign that brought his season to a premature end.

Born in Plymouth, Michigan, on August 9, 2000, Aidan Joseph Bernardi Hutchinson grew up with his two older sisters some 25 miles west of Detroit. The son of Chad Hutchinson, a former All-American defensive lineman at the University of Michigan who later spent three years playing in the NFL, and 1988 Miss Michigan Teen USA beauty pageant winner Melissa Sinkevics, young Aidan spent two years competing in dance with his sisters, later crediting the experience with helping him improve his agility and coordination.

After playing lacrosse throughout grade school, Hutchinson began competing in tackle football as well once he reached the seventh grade. Recalling that his former charge demonstrated his relentless nature every time he stepped onto a middle school field, Hutchinson's eighth-grade coach Jeff Falcon recounted, "He never gave up on plays. Players on the teams we'd play would come up to him after the games and tell him, 'Hey, nice job.'"

Continuing to compete in both sports at Divine Child High School in Dearborn, Michigan, Hutchinson gradually developed into a star on the gridiron, gaining All-State recognition as a defensive end while splitting his time on offense between the line and tight end. An excellent student

Aidan Hutchinson has served as a key figure in the Lions' return to prominence.
Courtesy of All-Pro Reels Photography

as well, Hutchinson earned honor roll status with his outstanding work in the classroom.

Choosing to follow in his father's footsteps, Hutchinson accepted a football scholarship to the University of Michigan, where he ended up surpassing his dad in terms of his athletic achievements. After seeing limited action as a freshman, Hutchinson recorded 68 tackles and four and a half sacks his sophomore year, before missing most of the ensuing campaign with an injury. Returning with a vengeance in 2021, Hutchinson earned All-America honors, gained recognition as the 2021 Woodson-Nagurski Big Ten Defensive Player of the Year, and garnered a runner-up finish in the Heisman Trophy voting by registering 14 sacks, breaking in the process the existing single-season school record of 11 previously set by his father

276   THE 50 GREATEST PLAYERS IN DETROIT LIONS HISTORY

in 1992. Continuing to excel in the classroom as well, Hutchinson earned Academic All-Big Ten honors in each of his final three years at Michigan.

Selected by the Lions with the second overall pick of the 2022 NFL Draft, Hutchinson expressed his joy to have been chosen by his hometown team after hearing his name called, telling reporters, "To the city, just know I'm going to give it my all. . . . It was the Lions all the way. The whole draft process, I wanted them to pick me."

Making an immediate impact in his first NFL season, Hutchinson helped the Lions improve their record from 3–13–1 to 9–8 by recording nine and a half sacks, 52 tackles, three interceptions, and two fumble recoveries, earning in the process a spot on the NFL All-Rookie Team and a runner-up finish in the NFL Defensive Rookie of the Year voting. Even better in 2023, Hutchinson gained Pro Bowl and First-Team All-NFC recognition by registering 11½ sacks and 51 tackles, forcing three fumbles and recovering two others, and picking off one pass for a Lions team that won its first division title in 30 years and came within one game of advancing to the Super Bowl.

Blessed with a rare combination of size, speed, strength, and agility, the 6'7", 270-pound Hutchinson possesses an explosive first step that frequently allows him to gain an immediate advantage over his blocker. While Hutchinson also defends the run extremely well, he is known more for his ability to apply pressure to opposing quarterbacks by employing a wide variety of moves that include a ferocious chop-and-spin maneuver. A relentless pass-rusher, Hutchinson received high praise for his tremendous determination from three-time Pro Bowl defensive end Simeon Rice, who said, "He's just tenacious from a skill standpoint. He has a belief in himself. He has a desire to be great. You can look at that. He wants to make every play. He wants to make every sack. He wants to be special. And now he's got the skill set. What I see that he brings is counters. Not only can he get off the ball, but he's got countermoves, and that's rare because I looked at him this week and I was like, 'He knows what he's doing.' . . . You've got [Nick] Bosa—he's one way. He gets there, but he's got one way. This kid has different little countermoves that work for him."

Los Angeles Rams offensive guard Kevin Dotson also spoke of Hutchinson's commitment to getting to the quarterback, saying, "He has a high motor and so it's something that you can't give up on the play. . . . Even if you block him once, twice in a play, if you're not blocking the whole time while the quarterback has the ball, he can make something happen."

Chicago Bears left tackle Braxton Jones expressed similar sentiments when he stated, "He doesn't stop. A lot of guys will get blocked for the first two seconds and then they kind of throttle it down. Aidan is always working in the pocket. . . . He has the motor that some cats don't. That's where he exposes some tackles."

Claiming that Hutchinson's confidence in his own abilities also works in his favor, private NFL coach/defensive line expert Eddy McGilvra said, "Obviously, Aidan has physical tools that you can't teach. The speed, size, frame and sudden twitch are just different. But I believe why he's so good and only getting better is because he's confident. His confidence is growing, and he's starting to get deeper into his bag of moves. When I got with Aidan for his draft process he wouldn't even try and spin a certain direction because he only had one spin side. Now look at him. He's a mad man."

Suggesting that Hutchinson's training regimen, superior conditioning, and attention to detail have also helped him develop into one of the league's top players at his position, Pittsburgh Steelers wide receiver Roman Wilson said of his former Michigan teammate, "He's someone that's detail-oriented, lives in the weight room, and is just built. A freak. Just a natural born leader as well with great energy in the locker room. I feel like the only way I can describe him is someone that only really cares about football and getting better at football."

Meanwhile, Hutchinson's private strength coach David Lawrence said of his pupil, "The thing with him is his daily habits. A lot of guys are gifted, but he really works at the little things in the offseason. He's meticulous with his sleep, stretching, nutrition. . . . It's a full-time job, 24/7, 365 for him. He's all in. He's completely dialed in. I've worked with over 100 professional and Olympic athletes and he's definitely in the top 10 in terms of focus and completely all-in on being as good as he can be."

Hutchinson got off to a tremendous start in 2024, recording seven and a half sacks and 19 tackles in the first five games of the regular season, before breaking his left leg while bringing down Dak Prescott behind the line of scrimmage during a 47–9 rout of the Dallas Cowboys in week 6. Carted off the field on a stretcher after having his leg placed in an air cast, Hutchinson, who doctors subsequently diagnosed as having a fractured tibia and fibula, underwent immediate surgery that forced him to miss the rest of the season. Fortunately, Hutchinson is expected to be fully healthy by the start of the 2025 campaign, which he will enter with career totals of 28½ sacks, 122 combined tackles, 30 tackles for loss, four interceptions, four forced fumbles, and four fumble recoveries.

THE 50 GREATEST PLAYERS IN DETROIT LIONS HISTORY

CAREER HIGHLIGHTS

Best Season

Hutchinson had the best season of his young career in 2023, when, in addition to recording 11½ sacks, 51 combined tackles, 36 solo stops, and 14 tackles for loss, he forced three fumbles and recovered two others and registered 33 hits on opposing quarterbacks.

Memorable Moments/Greatest Performances

Hutchinson starred during a 36–27 win over Washington on September 18, 2022, recording the first three sacks of his career and registering five solo tackles, two of which resulted in a loss.

Hutchinson gained recognition as NFC Defensive Player of the Week by intercepting a pass and recovering a fumble during a 31–18 win over the Giants on November 20, 2022.

Hutchinson earned that distinction again by recording two sacks and forcing a fumble during a 20–6 win over Atlanta on September 24, 2023.

Hutchinson starred in defeat in week 17 of the 2023 regular season, registering three sacks, five solo tackles, four tackles for loss, and one forced fumble during a 20–19 loss to Dallas.

Hutchinson helped lead the Lions to a 24–23 victory over the Rams in the wild card round of the 2023 NFC playoffs by recording two sacks and four solo tackles, two of which resulted in a loss.

Although the Lions suffered a 20–16 defeat at the hands of the Tampa Bay Buccaneers on September 15, 2024, Hutchinson performed magnificently, recording four and a half sacks, one forced fumble, and four solo tackles, all of which resulted in a loss.

Notable Achievements

- Has finished in double digits in sacks once.
- Two-time division champion (2023 and 2024).
- Member of 2022 NFL All-Rookie Team.
- Finished second in 2022 NFL Defensive Rookie of the Year voting.
- Two-time NFC Defensive Player of the Week.
- September 2024 NFC Defensive Player of the Month.
- 2023 Pro Bowl selection.
- 2023 First-Team All-NFC selection.

48

FRANK RAGNOW

A versatile lineman capable of playing either center or guard, Frank Ragnow has proven to be one of the NFL's finest interior offensive linemen since he arrived in Detroit in 2018. An outstanding run-blocker and excellent pass-protector, Ragnow has helped anchor an offensive line that has gradually developed into the best in all of football over the past few seasons, with his exceptional all-around play earning him four Pro Bowl selections and three All-Pro nominations. A superior leader as well, Ragnow, who is known for his ability to play through injuries, inspires his teammates with his mental and physical toughness, which has made him one of the most respected members of Lions teams that have won two division titles.

Born in Victoria, Minnesota, on May 17, 1996, Frank Ragnow grew up some 20 miles southwest of Minneapolis, where he shared an extremely close relationship with his parents, saying, "I'm just so proud of the way I was raised and my upbringing."

Especially close to his father, Ragnow recalled, "My dad was my best friend. I'm sure every kid says that, but my dad—He was my biggest fan, my biggest supporter, a great dad and my best friend."

Developing into a star on the gridiron at Chanhassen High School, Ragnow, whom ESPN evaluated as a four-star athlete, received a No. 24 ranking among all offensive tackles in the nation his senior year. Excelling in track and field as well, Ragnow earned a second-place finish in the shot put in the Class AA State Finals with a throw of 57'6¼".

Recruited by several major colleges as graduation neared, Ragnow fielded offers from schools such as Wisconsin, Vanderbilt, Minnesota, Ohio State, and Florida State, before ultimately choosing to attend the University of Arkansas on a football scholarship. A four-year starter for the Razorbacks, Ragnow spent three seasons manning the center position and another playing right guard, going his entire college career without allowing a single sack. Displaying his ability to play through adversity, Ragnow performed

Frank Ragnow has helped anchor the Lions' offensive line for the past seven seasons.

well despite losing his father to a heart attack in 2016 and learning that his mother had been diagnosed with cancer during his sophomore year.

Impressed with Ragnow's superior play at the collegiate level, the Lions selected him in the first round of the 2018 NFL Draft with the 20th overall pick, making him the first center and the second interior offensive lineman to hear his name called. Displaying his love and devotion to his parents at a press conference held shortly thereafter, Ragnow said, "My dad's not here, but I'm very excited to take care of my mom, because I had an amazing childhood. . . . To be able to give back to my mom—I wish I could give back to my dad and go fishing with him and everything—but to be able to give back to my mom and my family, it means the world."

When asked about his style of play, Ragnow stated, "I think I just play football. I take a lot of pride in the way that I play, how hard I play. I take a lot of pride in finishing guys, and I just think that's very important."

Meanwhile, in evaluating his team's first pick of the draft, new Lions head coach Matt Patricia said, "We've got a guy that's smart, tough . . . and can help us run the ball and help us protect our quarterback, and someone that can play a couple different positions inside, so we're excited. This is a guy with great traits, great character, hard worker, everything that we're about. Blue-collar type of guy that we know is just going to make us tougher up front."

Claiming that the Lions had found their center of the future, Ragnow's offensive line coach at Arkansas, Kurt Anderson, said of his former protégé, "He is about as natural a center as you're gonna find. . . . He sees the big picture, he sees the rotation of the secondary, how that adjusts things up front, gets you into the right call."

Despite Anderson's comments, the Lions chose to move Ragnow to left guard prior to the start of his rookie season to take full advantage of his quickness and athleticism. Starting every game at that post his first year in the league, Ragnow performed well for a team that finished last in the NFC North with a record of 6–10, before being shifted back to his more natural position of center the following year. Although the Lions won a total of just 11 games over the course of the next three seasons, Ragnow established himself as one of the league's top centers, gaining Pro Bowl and Second-Team All-Pro recognition in 2020.

Signed to an extension by the Lions following the conclusion of the 2020 campaign, Ragnow received high praise at the time from Detroit GM Brad Holmes, who said in a statement, "Frank is a foundational piece of what we're building in Detroit, and he is everything that we're looking for in a Lion. Frank plays the game the right way and has dedicated himself to improving his craft each season. We are ecstatic to come to this agreement and to have Frank be a leader on our team for years to come."

Big and strong at 6'5", 310 pounds, Ragnow plays the game with tremendous physicality, a trait he claims he developed during his youth, saying, "To be an offensive lineman, you don't get much of the glory. You don't get much of anything else. You've got to love football. I love that part of the game. It's just kind of been what drew me to the game. I've always been the bigger kid. I was the double-striper, when I was little, I wasn't able to touch the ball. So, that's what you kind of really have to fall in love with, and that's what I've always been in love with."

282   THE 50 GREATEST PLAYERS IN DETROIT LIONS HISTORY

Extremely athletic, Ragnow possesses the quickness to hold up equally well in pass-protection or run-blocking, making him arguably the most versatile center in the league, as one NFL scout suggested when he said, "He can run the whole line, great communicator, takes pressure off the quarterback, athletic enough to pull, can play guard if you need. Some centers can't do that. He's probably the most versatile center right now."

After missing just three games his first three years in the league, Ragnow sat out much of the 2021 campaign with a badly injured toe he sustained during a 24–14 loss to the Bears in week 4. Although Ragnow continued to be plagued by injuries that included a fractured cartilage in his throat, a sprained knee, a sprained ankle, and a torn meniscus, he missed a total of just three games the next two seasons, prompting Lions head coach Dan Campbell to say, "This guy, he's as throwback as they get. He will play through any injury and will himself to go."

In discussing his willingness to take the field at much less than 100 percent, Ragnow stated, "I just take a lot of pride in being out there with the guys, being out there for the city. They signed me to the extension a few years ago, and I want to be fulfilling that. I don't want to be the guy who gets paid and is not doing that stuff. I want to be out there and finding a way to win."

With the Lions experiencing a resurgence under Campbell the past three seasons, Ragnow has received more recognition than ever before, earning four consecutive Pro Bowl nominations and three Second-Team All-Pro selections. Meanwhile, Ragnow, who established in 2022 the Rags Remembered Foundation to assist children who have experienced the loss of parents and other loved ones, remains one of the emotional leaders of a team that ranks among the best in the NFL.

Following completion of this work's text, Ragnow announced his retirement on June 2, 2025.

CAREER HIGHLIGHTS

Best Season

Ragnow performed exceptionally well for the Lions in 2020, when he did not allow a single sack in 929 snaps, earning in the process Pro Bowl and All-Pro honors for the first time and a No. 3 ranking from Pro Football Focus among NFL centers. But Ragnow also gained Pro Bowl and All-Pro recognition in 2023, when, in addition to yielding just one sack and incurring only three penalties, he helped the 12–5 Lions finish fifth in the league with 2,311 yards rushing. Factoring everything into the equation, Ragnow had his finest all-around season in 2023.

Memorable Moments/Greatest Performances

Ragnow's superior blocking at the point of attack helped the Lions gain 248 yards on the ground and amass 457 yards of total offense during a 32–21 win over the Miami Dolphins on October 21, 2018.

Ragnow anchored an offensive line that enabled the Lions to amass 504 yards of total offense during a lopsided 41–10 victory over the Bears on January 1, 2022, with 265 of those yards coming on the ground and the other 239 through the air.

Ragnow helped the Lions rush for 200 yards and accumulate a total of 533 yards on offense during a 41–38 win over the Los Angeles Chargers on November 12, 2023.

Notable Achievements

- Two-time division champion (2023 and 2024).
- Four-time Pro Bowl selection (2020, 2022, 2023, and 2024).
- Three-time Second-Team All-Pro selection (2020, 2023, and 2024).

49

TERRY BARR

A versatile player who started for the Lions on both sides of the ball at different times, Terry Barr spent his entire nine-year NFL career in Detroit, performing well as a wide receiver on offense and a cornerback on defense as well as a return man on special teams. Moving to wideout in 1961 after spending his first few years in the Motor City serving as a member of the Lions' defensive secondary, Barr experienced his greatest success at that post, earning a pair of Pro Bowl and All-Pro nominations by surpassing 50 receptions and 1,000 receiving yards twice each. The NFL leader in touchdown catches in 1963, Barr established himself as one of the Lions' career leaders in that category, before retiring at only 29 years of age due to a badly injured knee.

Born in Grand Rapids, Michigan, on August 10, 1935, Terry Albert Barr grew up with his nine siblings on the city's east side, where he starred in football, basketball, and track at Central High School, winning back-to-back state championships in the 440-yard dash in 1952 and 1953. Offered an athletic scholarship to the University of Michigan after earning All-State honors in both football and track his senior year at Central High, Barr spent three seasons playing halfback on offense and cornerback on defense for Michigan head coach Bennie Oosterbann. A standout at both positions, Barr performed particularly well in his final two seasons, accounting for more than 1,600 yards of total offense, with his strong play his junior year helping the Wolverines earn a No. 12 ranking in the final AP poll.

Selected by the Lions in the third round of the 1957 NFL Draft with the 36th overall pick, Barr spent his first year in Detroit playing mostly on special teams, amassing 186 punt- and kickoff-return yards for the eventual NFL champions. Although Barr continued to return punts and kickoffs the following year, he assumed a far more prominent role on defense, recording three interceptions after laying claim to the starting right cornerback job, with his strong play gaining him unofficial Second-Team All-Pro recognition from the *New York Daily News*.

Terry Barr led the NFL with 13 touchdown receptions in 1963.

With Yale Lary moving from safety to cornerback prior to the start of the 1959 campaign, Barr saw less playing time on defense in each of the next two seasons. But, in addition to amassing more than 500 yards on special teams, Barr began to gradually transition to the offensive side of the ball, seeing some action at both wide receiver and running back.

Shifted to flanker full-time in 1961, Barr had a solid first season at his new post, catching 40 passes, amassing 630 receiving yards, and tying for the team lead with six touchdown receptions. Unfortunately, Barr missed much of the ensuing campaign after sustaining a knee injury in week 6 that forced him to undergo season-ending surgery. Nevertheless, he provided a glimpse of what lay ahead by making 25 receptions for 425 yards and three touchdowns in his six starts.

Fully recovered by the start of the 1963 season, Barr established himself as one of the NFL's top wideouts, earning Pro Bowl, Second-Team All-Pro, and First-Team All-Western Conference honors by ranking among the league leaders with 66 receptions and 1,086 receiving yards while also topping the circuit with 13 touchdown catches. Continuing his outstanding play in 1964, Barr again gained Pro Bowl and Second-Team All-Pro recognition by making 57 receptions, finishing second in the league with 1,030 receiving yards, and placing fourth in the circuit with nine TD catches.

Combining with split end Gail Cogdill to form arguably the NFL's top wide receiver tandem, the 6', 190-pound Barr managed to post excellent numbers even though the Lions found themselves being hampered by mediocre quarterback play his entire time in Detroit. Blessed with outstanding speed, Barr proved to be one of the league's top deep threats, averaging at least 18 yards per reception on three separate occasions and recording seven touchdown receptions of more than 50 yards over the course of his career. Also known for his soft hands, Barr received high praise for his ability to gather in the football from Cogdill, who stated, "I don't think Terry ever dropped a ball."

Meanwhile, Joe Schmidt said of his longtime teammate, "He delivered a lot of great, big plays for the Detroit Lions during the time that he played."

Barr performed well over the first half of the 1965 season, making 24 receptions for 433 yards and three touchdowns through week 7. But after reinjuring his knee during a 31–7 win over the Los Angeles Rams on October 31, Barr had to sit out the rest of the year. Choosing to announce his retirement following the conclusion of the campaign, Barr ended his playing career with 227 receptions, 3,810 receiving yards, 35 touchdown catches, 151 rushing yards, two rushing TDs, and 37 total touchdowns scored on offense. He also intercepted five passes on defense, amassed a total of 917 yards on special teams, returned one kickoff for a touchdown, and accumulated a total of 4,974 all-purpose yards.

Following his playing days, Barr became a successful businessman in suburban Detroit, operating an insurance agency in partnership with former Lions teammates Joe Schmidt and Nick Pietrosante for several years, before purchasing in 1971 a Southfield, Michigan–based company he renamed Terry Barr Sales, L.L.C., which serviced the automotive industry. Barr also later served as chairman of Libralter Plastics (an automotive industry supplier), owned a restaurant, and ran a manufacturing operation. Barr lived until May 28, 2009, when he died at his home in Bloomfield Hills, Michigan, at the age of 73 following a long battle with Alzheimer's disease.

On learning of his passing, University of Michigan athletic department spokesperson Bruce Madej issued a statement that read, "We feel a great loss today with the passing of Terry Barr. More than just being a part of sports in the state of Michigan, he was a true gentleman. He epitomized what it meant to be a sportsman. He was a great representative of the University of Michigan."

Meanwhile, one of Barr's three sons, Terrence Barr, said, "He'd been ill for some time, for a number of years. We had a lot of time to prepare for this. . . . I already miss him. . . . He's in a better place. That's no way to live. It's a nasty disease."

CAREER HIGHLIGHTS

Best Season

Although Barr also performed exceptionally well the following year, he had his finest all-around season in 1963, when he established career-high marks with 66 receptions, 1,086 receiving yards, 1,095 yards from scrimmage, and a league-leading 13 touchdown catches.

Memorable Moments/Greatest Performances

Barr recorded the first of his five career interceptions during a 31–10 win over the 49ers on November 17, 1957.

Barr contributed to a 59–14 rout of the Browns in the 1957 NFL Championship Game by returning an interception 19 yards for a touchdown.

Barr scored on special teams when he returned a kickoff 86 yards for a touchdown during a 41–24 victory over the Los Angeles Rams on October 26, 1958.

Barr tallied his first points on offense when he registered a 32-yard touchdown run during a 45–21 win over the Chicago Cardinals on December 6, 1959.

Barr contributed to a lopsided 45–14 victory over the Cardinals on November 12, 1961, by making four receptions for 113 yards and one touchdown, which came on a 40-yard connection with Jim Ninowski.

Barr helped lead the Lions to a 29–20 win over the Baltimore Colts on September 30, 1962, by making six receptions for a career-high 165 yards and one touchdown, which covered 80 yards.

288 THE 50 GREATEST PLAYERS IN DETROIT LIONS HISTORY

Barr had a big day against the 49ers on November 3, 1963, making 10 receptions for 135 yards and three touchdowns during a convincing 47–7 Lions win.

Barr helped the Lions forge a 17–17 tie with the Rams on September 19, 1964, by making seven receptions for 109 yards and two touchdowns, the longest of which covered 46 yards.

Barr helped the Lions begin the 1965 campaign on a positive note by making seven receptions for 133 yards and one touchdown during a 20–0 win over the Rams in the regular-season opener.

Notable Achievements

- Surpassed 50 receptions and 1,000 receiving yards twice each.
- Returned one kickoff for a touchdown.
- Led NFL with 13 touchdown receptions in 1963.
- Finished second in NFL with 1,030 receiving yards in 1964.
- Finished third in NFL with 66 receptions in 1963.
- Led Lions in receptions and receiving yards twice each.
- Ranks among Lions career leaders with 35 touchdown receptions (tied for 4th) and 38 touchdowns (7th).
- 1957 division champion.
- 1957 NFL champion.
- 1963 Week 9 NFL Player of the Week.
- Two-time Pro Bowl selection (1963 and 1964).
- Two-time Second-Team All-Pro selection (1963 and 1964).
- 1963 First-Team All-Western Conference selection.

50
DARRIS MCCORD

The third member of the Lions' famed "Fearsome Foursome" defensive line to make our list, Darris McCord spent his entire 13-year career in Detroit, providing consistently excellent play from his left end position. Although often overshadowed by perennial Pro Bowl linemates Alex Karras and Roger Brown, McCord performed extremely well in his own right, applying constant pressure to opposing quarterbacks while also excelling against the run. A durable player who missed just two games his entire career, McCord started 168 out of 170 contests from 1955 to 1967, earning his lone Pro Bowl nomination in 1957, when he helped lead the Lions to their last NFL championship.

Born in Franklin, Tennessee, on January 4, 1933, Darris Paul McCord moved with his family to Detroit at an early age after his father landed a good-paying factory job in the Motor City. McCord subsequently spent most of his formative years living in Michigan, briefly attending Cass Tech High, before returning to Tennessee, where he starred on the gridiron for three seasons at Franklin High School.

Following a one-year stint at the Battle Ground Military Academy, McCord accepted a football scholarship to the University of Tennessee, where he spent the next three seasons playing under head coaches Robert Neyland and Harvey Robinson. A member of the 1952 Volunteers team that earned a No. 8 ranking in the final AP poll, McCord, who played tackle on both sides of the ball, gained First-Team All-America recognition as a senior for his outstanding two-way play.

In discussing McCord's contributions to the school's football program, the *Tennessee Football Media Guide* said of him, "Captained the 1954 squad that went 4–6 under second-year coach Harvey Robinson. The tackle played on both sides of the offensive and defensive lines after Robinson switched back to the old two-way player system. . . . Robinson looked for leadership from McCord and found it in a steady blocker on the offensive

Darris McCord served as a member of the Lions' original "Fearsome Foursome" defensive line.

end and a brute tackler in contrast. His hard work and grit earned him All-America status from the Football Writers Association of America in 1954 before embarking on a professional career."

Selected by the Lions in the third round of the 1955 NFL Draft with the 36th overall pick, McCord spent his first pro season playing right tackle on offense, before being shifted to the defensive side of the ball prior to the start of the 1956 campaign. Alternating between end and tackle the next three seasons, McCord performed well at both posts, before moving to left defensive end full-time in 1959 after Alex Karras laid claim to the spot immediately next to him.

Establishing himself as one of the NFL's better players at his position over the course of the next several seasons, the 6'4", 250-pound McCord served as a key member of a Lions defense that consistently ranked among

DARRIS MCCORD **291**

the league's best, although the team's offense, unfortunately, failed to perform at the same level. Joined by left tackle Karras, right tackle Roger Brown, and right end Sam Williams on a line that became known as the "Fearsome Foursome," McCord developed tremendous chemistry with his linemates, particularly Karras, recalling years later, "We could almost read each other's mind. When I went one way, he knew how I was going, and I knew how he was going. So, as you know, the Fearsome Foursome worked tremendously well together in a relationship like that."

Although the NFL did not begin recording sacks as an official statistic until well after McCord retired, pro football researchers later credited him with an "unofficial" total of 38.5 sacks, which does not include any he recorded prior to 1960. A good pass-rusher who brought down opposing quarterbacks behind the line of scrimmage as many as eight times in a season, McCord contributed to a defense that registered two of the top four single-season sack marks in franchise history (50 in 1964 and 49 in 1965).

Extremely effective against the run as well, McCord drew praise for the totality of his game from former Lions wide receiver Gail Cogdill, who also claimed that his longtime teammate failed to receive the recognition he deserved when he said, "We always had a good defense. We had Roger Brown and Alex Karras at the tackles. The two guys who never really got the credit, but who I thought were as good as anyone in the league, were Sammy Williams and Darris McCord, our ends. They were always left off the all-star teams. But Williams and McCord were always there, always doing their job. They didn't really get beat that much. They didn't get run over. You look back and say, 'Why didn't they get the recognition?' We had a 'Fearsome Foursome,' but Williams and McCord were seldom recognized as part of that foursome."

Mike Lucci also spoke of his former teammate's ability to excel against both the run and the pass when he stated, "It was amazing how many times it was him that got to the quarterback first, or the one who was leaping over a block."

McCord continued to start for the Lions at left defensive end until the end of the 1967 season, when he announced his retirement. In addition to his 38.5 career sacks, McCord recorded three interceptions and a pair of safeties, recovered nine fumbles, and scored one touchdown.

Following his playing days, McCord operated an engineering business in Detroit for many years, before eventually retiring to private life. Diagnosed with pancreatic cancer in March 2013, McCord lived another seven months, finally succumbing to the disease on October 9, 2013, when he died at his home in Bloomfield Hills, Michigan, at the age of 80.

Recalling his former linemate on learning of his passing, Roger Brown said, "Darris was kind of quiet. He wasn't a yeller or cursing people out or

292　THE 50 GREATEST PLAYERS IN DETROIT LIONS HISTORY

talking about their mother or anything like that. He was just a quiet, good player, and you knew he would hold up his side."

Meanwhile, Lions president Tom Lewand issued a statement that read, "Darris will not only be remembered as a cornerstone to the Lions' great Fearsome Foursome defensive line of the 1960s, but also as someone who made many positive contributions to the Detroit community over the last five decades."

CAREER HIGHLIGHTS

Best Season

McCord recorded an unofficial total of eight sacks in 1961 that represented his highest single-season mark. But he earned Pro Bowl honors for the only time in his career in 1957, when he helped the Lions capture the NFL championship, making that his most impactful season.

Memorable Moments/Greatest Performances

McCord contributed to an 18–6 victory over the Packers on November 28, 1957, by recording a safety when he sacked quarterback Babe Parilli in the end zone.

McCord registered a sack of Y. A. Tittle during the Lions' 31–27 victory over the 49ers in the 1957 playoff game to determine the Western Division champion.

In addition to sacking quarterback Zeke Bratkowski in the end zone for a safety during a 12–3 win over the Rams on November 4, 1962, McCord helped anchor a defense that allowed just 124 yards of total offense.

McCord scored the only touchdown of his career when he recovered a fumble in the end zone during a 38–10 win over the Browns on December 8, 1963.

Notable Achievements

- Missed just two games entire career, starting 168 out of 170 contests.
- Scored one defensive touchdown.
- 1957 division champion.
- 1957 NFL champion.
- 1957 Pro Bowl selection.

SUMMARY AND HONORABLE MENTIONS
(THE NEXT 25)

Having identified the 50 greatest players in Detroit Lions history, the time has come to select the best of the best. Based on the rankings contained in this book, the members of the Lions' all-time offensive and defensive teams are listed below. Our squads include the top player at each position, with the offense featuring the two best wide receivers, running backs, tackles, and guards, as well as the top quarterback, tight end, center, and a third-down back. Meanwhile, the defense features two ends, two tackles, three linebackers, two cornerbacks, and a pair of safeties. Special teams have been accounted for as well, with a placekicker, punter, kickoff returner, and punt returner also being included.

OFFENSE		DEFENSE	
Player	Position	Player	Position
Matthew Stafford	QB	Robert Porcher	LE
Barry Sanders	RB	Alex Karras	LT
Billy Sims	RB	Doug English	RT
Dutch Clark	3rd-Down RB	Al "Bubba" Baker	RE
Charlie Sanders	TE	Joe Schmidt	LB
Calvin Johnson	WR	Chris Spielman	LB
Herman Moore	WR	Wayne Walker	LB
Lou Creekmur	LT	Lem Barney	LCB
Harley Sewell	LG	Jack Christiansen	SS
Alex Wojciechowicz	C	Yale Lary	FS
Ox Emerson	RG	Dick LeBeau	RCB
Lomas Brown	RT	Yale Lary	P
Jason Hanson	PK	Mel Gray	PR
Mel Gray	KR		

SUMMARY AND HONORABLE MENTIONS

Although I limited my earlier rankings to the top 50 players in Lions history, many other fine players have donned the team's colors through the years, some of whom narrowly missed making the final cut. Following is a list of those players deserving of an honorable mention. These are the men I deemed worthy of being slotted into positions 51 to 75 in the overall rankings. Where applicable and available, the statistics they compiled during their time in Detroit are included, along with their most notable achievements while playing for the Lions.

51—GEORGE CHRISTENSEN (OT/G; 1931–1938)

Notable Achievements

- 1935 division champion.
- 1935 NFL champion.
- Two-time First-Team All-Pro selection (1933 and 1934).
- Four-time Second-Team All-Pro selection (1931, 1932, 1935, and 1936).
- Pro Football Hall of Fame All-1930s Team.

52—DARIUS SLAY (DB; 2013–2019)

Lions Numbers

19 Interceptions, 265 Interception-Return Yards, 1 Interception-Return Touchdown, 347 Tackles, 1 Sack, 1 Forced Fumble, 2 Fumble Recoveries.

Notable Achievements

- Led NFL with eight interceptions and 26 passes defended in 2017.
- Finished fourth in NFL with 107 interception-return yards in 2018.
- Led Lions in interceptions four times.
- Three-time NFC Defensive Player of the Week.
- Three-time Pro Bowl selection (2017, 2018, and 2019).
- 2017 First-Team All-Pro selection.
- 2017 First-Team All-NFC selection.

53—DICK STANFEL (G; 1952–1955)

Notable Achievements

- Three-time division champion (1952, 1953, and 1954).
- Two-time NFL champion (1952 and 1953).
- Two-time Pro Bowl selection (1953 and 1955).
- Two-time First-Team All-Pro selection (1953 and 1954).
- Pro Football Reference All-1950s Second Team.
- Pro Football Hall of Fame All-1950s Team.
- Named to Lions All-Time Team in 2019.
- Inducted into Lions Ring of Honor in 2009.
- Inducted into Pro Football Hall of Fame in 2016.

54—BRETT PERRIMAN (WR; 1991–1996)

Lions Numbers

428 Receptions, 5,244 Receiving Yards, 25 Touchdown Receptions, 173 Rushing Yards, 5,417 Yards from Scrimmage, 5,591 All-Purpose Yards.

Notable Achievements

- Surpassed 100 receptions once, topping 90 receptions another time.
- Surpassed 1,000 receiving yards twice.
- Topped 1,500 yards from scrimmage once.
- Led Lions in receptions twice and receiving yards once.
- Ranks among Lions career leaders in receptions (5th), receiving yards (4th), and yards from scrimmage (9th).
- Two-time division champion (1991 and 1993).
- 1995 Week 13 NFC Offensive Player of the Week.

55—GOLDEN TATE (WR; 2014–2018)

Lions Numbers

416 Receptions, 4,741 Receiving Yards, 22 Touchdown Receptions, 139 Rushing Yards, 4,880 Yards from Scrimmage, 5,093 All-Purpose Yards.

Notable Achievements

- Surpassed 90 receptions four times.
- Surpassed 1,000 receiving yards three times.
- Led Lions in receptions four times and receiving yards twice.
- Ranks among Lions career leaders in receptions (6th) and receiving yards (8th).
- 2014 Pro Bowl selection.

56—NICK PIETROSANTE (RB; 1959–1965)

Lions Numbers

3,933 Yards Rushing, 134 Receptions, 1,323 Receiving Yards, 5,256 Yards from Scrimmage, 5,424 All-Purpose Yards, 28 Rushing TDs, 2 TD Receptions, 30 TDs, 4.2 Rushing Average.

Notable Achievements

- Surpassed 1,000 yards from scrimmage twice.
- Averaged more than five yards per carry twice.
- Led NFL with an average of 5.9 yards per carry in 1959.
- Led Lions in rushing four times.
- Ranks among Lions career leaders in rushing yards (5th), rushing touchdowns (4th), and yards from scrimmage (10th).
- 1959 *Sporting News* NFL Rookie of the Year.
- Named to Lions All-Time Team in 2019.

57—JIM GIBBONS (WR/TE; 1958–1968)

Career Numbers

287 Receptions, 3,561 Receiving Yards, 20 Touchdown Receptions.

Notable Achievements

- Finished fourth in NFL with 51 receptions in 1960.
- Led Lions in receptions three times and receiving yards once.
- Three-time Pro Bowl selection (1960, 1961, and 1964).

58—SHAUN ROGERS (DT; 2001–2007)

Lions Numbers

29 Sacks, 355 Tackles, 6 Forced Fumbles, 9 Fumble Recoveries, 1 Interception, 2 Touchdowns.

Notable Achievements

- Led Lions with seven sacks in 2007.
- Led Lions defensive linemen in tackles twice.
- Member of 2001 NFL All-Rookie Team.
- Finished third in 2001 NFL Defensive Rookie of the Year voting.
- Two-time NFC Defensive Player of the Week.
- Two-time Pro Bowl selection (2004 and 2005).
- 2004 Second-Team All-Pro selection.

59—DEXTER BUSSEY (RB; 1974–1984)

Career Numbers

5,105 Yards Rushing, 193 Receptions, 1,616 Receiving Yards, 6,721 Yards from Scrimmage, 6,832 All-Purpose Yards, 18 Rushing TDs, 5 TD Receptions, 23 TDs, 4.2 Rushing Average.

Notable Achievements

- Surpassed 1,000 yards from scrimmage three times.
- Finished second in NFL with an average of 5.0 yards per carry in 1980.
- Led Lions in rushing four times.
- Ranks among Lions career leaders in rushing yards (3rd), yards from scrimmage (5th), and all-purpose yards (7th).

60—DON DOLL (DB/PR/KR; 1949–1952)

Lions Numbers

26 Interceptions, 464 Interception-Return Yards, 2 Interception-Return Touchdowns, 10 Fumble Recoveries, 162 Punt-Return Yards, 808 Kickoff-Return Yards, 1,461 All-Purpose Yards.

Notable Achievements

- Recorded more than 10 interceptions twice.
- Amassed more than 100 interception-return yards twice.
- Recorded four interceptions vs. Chicago Cardinals on October 23, 1949.
- Led NFL with 301 interception-return yards and 536 kickoff-return yards in 1949.
- Finished second in NFL in interceptions twice and yards per kickoff return once.
- Led Lions in interceptions twice.
- Holds single-season franchise records for most interceptions (12 in 1950) and most interception-return yards (301 in 1949).
- Ranks among Lions career leaders in interceptions (8th) and interception-return yards (7th).
- 1952 division champion.
- 1952 NFL champion.
- Three-time Pro Bowl selection (1950, 1951, and 1952).
- 1949 First-Team All-Pro selection.
- 1951 Second-Team All-Pro selection.
- Named to Lions 75th Anniversary All-Time Team in 2008.
- Named to Lions All-Time Team in 2019.

61—ACE GUTOWSKY (RB; 1932–1938)

Spartans/Lions Numbers

3,077 Yards Rushing, 3 Receptions, 64 Receiving Yards, 3,141 Yards from Scrimmage, 20 Touchdowns, 3.6 Rushing Average, 249 Passing Yards, 3 Touchdown Passes.

Notable Achievements

- Led NFL with 857 yards from scrimmage in 1936.
- Finished second in NFL in rushing yards once and rushing touchdowns twice.
- 1935 Western Division champion.
- 1935 NFL champion.
- Five-time Second-Team All-Pro selection (1932, 1934, 1936, 1937, and 1938).

62—ALTIE TAYLOR (RB; 1969–1975)

Lions Numbers

4,297 Yards Rushing, 173 Receptions, 1,523 Receiving Yards, 5,820 Yards from Scrimmage, 6,115 All-Purpose Yards, 24 Rushing TDs, 6 TD Receptions, 30 TDs, 3.7 Rushing Average.

Notable Achievements

- Surpassed 1,000 yards from scrimmage once.
- Led Lions in rushing three times.
- Ranks among Lions career leaders in rushing yards (4th), rushing touchdowns (tied for 8th), yards from scrimmage (7th), and all-purpose yards (9th).

63—GREG LANDRY (QB; 1968–1978)

Lions Numbers

12,451 Passing Yards, 80 TD Passes, 81 Interceptions, 54.8 Pass Completion Percentage, 73.4 QBR, 2,502 Rushing Yards, 19 Rushing Touchdowns.

Notable Achievements

- Completed more than 60 percent of passes twice.
- Posted touchdown-to-interception ratio of better than 2–1 once.
- Posted passer rating above 90.0 once.
- Ran for more than 500 yards twice.
- Ran for nine touchdowns in 1972.
- Finished third in NFL with 18 touchdown passes in 1972.
- Ranks among Lions career leaders in pass completions (6th), passing yards (5th), and touchdown passes (4th).
- Two-time NFL Offensive Player of the Week.
- 1976 NFL Comeback Player of the Year.
- 1971 Pro Bowl selection.
- 1971 First-Team All-NFC selection.

64—KEITH DORNEY (OT/G; 1979–1987)

Notable Achievements

- 1983 division champion.
- Member of 1979 NFL All-Rookie Team.
- 1982 Pro Bowl selection.
- Two-time First-Team All-NFC selection (1981 and 1985).
- 1982 Second-Team All-NFC selection.

65—MIKE COFER (LB/DE; 1983–1992)

Career Numbers

511 Tackles, 62.5 Sacks, 1 Interception, 10 Fumble Recoveries.

Notable Achievements

- Recorded at least 10 sacks twice.
- Led Lions in sacks four times.
- Ranks among Lions career leaders in sacks (tied for 5th) and tackles (6th).
- Two-time division champion (1983 and 1991).
- 1984 Week 8 NFL Defensive Player of the Week.
- 1988 Pro Bowl selection.
- 1988 Second-Team All-Pro selection.
- Two-time Second-Team All-NFC selection (1988 and 1990).

66—JAHMYR GIBBS (RB; 2023–2024)

Career Numbers

2,357 Yards Rushing, 104 Receptions, 833 Receiving Yards, 3,190 Yards from Scrimmage, 26 Rushing Touchdowns, 5 Touchdown Receptions, 31 Touchdowns, 5.5 Rushing Average.

Notable Achievements

- Rushed for 1,412 yards in 2024.
- Has amassed more than 1,000 yards from scrimmage twice.
- Has scored more than 10 touchdowns twice.

SUMMARY AND HONORABLE MENTIONS **301**

- Scored four touchdowns vs. Minnesota Vikings on January 5, 2025.
- Led NFL with 16 rushing touchdowns and 20 touchdowns in 2024.
- Finished third in NFL with 1,929 yards from scrimmage in 2024.
- Holds Lions single-season record for most touchdowns (20 in 2024).
- Tied with Barry Sanders for Lions single-season record for most rushing touchdowns (16 in 2024).
- Ranks among Lions career leaders in rushing touchdowns (tied for 5th).
- Two-time division champion (2023 and 2024).
- Member of 2023 NFL All-Rookie Team.
- 2024 Week 18 NFC Offensive Player of the Week.
- Two-time Pro Bowl selection (2023 and 2024).

67—DAVID HILL (TE; 1976–1982)

Lions Numbers

245 Receptions, 3,054 Receiving Yards, 23 Touchdown Receptions.

Notable Achievements

- Surpassed 50 receptions once.
- Led Lions in receptions once and receiving yards twice.
- Member of 1976 NFL All-Rookie Team.
- Two-time Pro Bowl selection (1978 and 1979).

68—ROCKY FREITAS (OT; 1968–1977)

Notable Achievements

- Started 112 consecutive games from 1969 to 1976.
- 1972 Pro Bowl selection.
- 1972 Second-Team All-Pro selection.
- Two-time Second-Team All-NFC selection (1970 and 1972).

69—STEPHEN BOYD (LB; 1995–2001)

Career Numbers

575 Tackles, 6.5 Sacks, 3 Interceptions, 6 Forced Fumbles, 6 Fumble Recoveries, 1 Touchdown.

302 SUMMARY AND HONORABLE MENTIONS

Notable Achievements

- Recorded more than 100 tackles four times.
- Led Lions in tackles four times.
- Ranks fifth in Lions history in career tackles.
- 1997 Week 1 NFC Defensive Player of the Week.
- 1998 Week 13 NFL Defensive Player of the Week.
- November 1998 NFC Defensive Player of the Month.
- Two-time Pro Bowl selection (1999 and 2000).
- 2000 Second-Team All-Pro selection.

70—MATT PRATER (K; 2014–2020)

Lions Numbers

179 Field Goals, 231 Extra Points, 768 Points, 84.4 Field Goal Percentage.

Notable Achievements

- Scored more than 100 points six times, topping 120 points twice.
- Converted more than 85 percent of field goal attempts four times, surpassing 90 percent once.
- Holds franchise record for longest field goal made (59 yards twice).
- Ranks third in franchise history in points scored, field goals made, and extra points made.
- Seven-time NFC Special Teams Player of the Week.
- Two-time NFC Special Teams Player of the Month.
- 2016 Pro Bowl selection.

71—PAT STUDSTILL (WR/PR/KR/P; 1961–1967)

Lions Numbers

153 Receptions, 2,452 Receiving Yards, 15 TD Receptions, 716 Punt-Return Yards, 1,924 Kickoff-Return Yards, 5,097 All-Purpose Yards, 1 Kick-off-Return TD, 16 TDs, 7,925 Punting Yards, 42.4-Yard Punting Average.

Notable Achievements

- Surpassed 60 receptions and 1,000 receiving yards once each.
- Amassed more than 1,000 all-purpose yards twice.

- Led NFL with 1,266 receiving yards in 1966.
- Finished second in NFL with 67 receptions in 1966.
- Led NFL with 457 punt-return yards and average of 15.8 yards per punt return in 1962.
- Led NFL in total punting yards and punting average once each.
- Recorded longest punt in NFL in 1967 (78 yards).
- Holds franchise record for longest touchdown reception (99 yards).
- Two-time Pro Bowl selection (1965 and 1966).
- 1966 First-Team All-Pro selection.
- Two-time First-Team All-Western Conference selection (1966 and 1967).

72—MEL FARR (RB; 1967–1973)

Career Numbers

3,072 Yards Rushing, 146 Receptions, 1,374 Receiving Yards, 4,446 Yards from Scrimmage, 26 Rushing Touchdowns, 10 Touchdown Receptions, 36 Touchdowns, 4.2 Rushing Average.

Notable Achievements

- Amassed 1,177 yards from scrimmage in 1967.
- Scored 11 touchdowns in 1970.
- Rushed for 197 yards vs. Minnesota Vikings on November 12, 1967.
- Finished second in NFL with nine rushing touchdowns in 1970.
- Led Lions in rushing three times and receptions once.
- Ranks among Lions career leaders in rushing yards (8th) and rushing touchdowns (tied for 5th).
- 1968 Week 5 NFL Offensive Player of the Week.
- 1967 NFL Offensive Rookie of the Year.
- 1967 UPI and *Sporting News* NFL Rookie of the Year.
- Two-time Pro Bowl selection (1967 and 1970).
- 1970 Second-Team All-NFC selection.

73—CHARLIE ANE (OT/C; 1953–1959)

Notable Achievements

- Missed just one game entire career, appearing in 83 of 84 contests.
- Three-time division champion (1953, 1954, and 1957).

304 SUMMARY AND HONORABLE MENTIONS

- Two-time NFL champion (1953 and 1957).
- Two-time Pro Bowl selection (1956 and 1958).
- 1956 Second-Team All-Pro selection.

74—JAMES JONES (RB; 1983–1988)

Lions Numbers

3,452 Yards Rushing, 285 Receptions, 2,318 Receiving Yards, 5,770 Yards from Scrimmage, 23 Rushing Touchdowns, 10 Touchdown Receptions, 33 Touchdowns, 3.6 Rushing Average.

Notable Achievements

- Amassed more than 1,000 yards from scrimmage three times.
- Surpassed 50 receptions twice.
- Led Lions in rushing and receptions three times each.
- Ranks among Lions career leaders in rushing yards (6th), rushing touchdowns (10th), and yards from scrimmage (8th).
- 1986 Week 1 NFC Offensive Player of the Week.

75—JIM ARNOLD (P; 1986–1993)

Lions Numbers

22,893 Punting Yards, 42.7-Yard Punting Average.

Notable Achievements

- Led NFL in total punting yards once.
- Finished second in NFL in total punting yards and punting average once each.
- Ranks second in franchise history in total punting yards.
- Two-time division champion (1991 and 1993).
- 1989 Week 10 NFL Special Teams Player of the Week.
- 1993 Week 18 NFC Special Teams Player of the Week.
- Two-time Pro Bowl selection (1987 and 1988).
- 1987 First-Team All-Pro selection.
- 1988 Second-Team All-Pro selection.
- Two-time First-Team All-NFC selection (1987 and 1988).
- Named to Lions 75th Anniversary All-Time Team in 2008.

GLOSSARY

ABBREVIATIONS AND STATISTICAL TERMS

C: Center.

COMP %: Completion percentage. The number of successfully completed passes divided by the number of passes attempted.

DB: Defensive back.

DE: Defensive end.

DT: Defensive tackle.

FS: Free safety.

G: Guard.

INTS: Interceptions. Passes thrown by the quarterback that are caught by a member of the opposing team's defense.

KR: Kickoff returner.

LB: Linebacker.

LCB: Left cornerback.

LE: Left end.

LG: Left guard.

LOLB: Left-outside linebacker.

LT: Left tackle.

MLB: Middle linebacker.

NT: Nose tackle.

OT: Offensive tackle.

P: Punter.

PK: Placekicker.

PR: Punt returner.

QB: Quarterback.

QBR: Quarterback rating.

RB: Running back.

RCB: Right cornerback.

RE: Right end.

RG: Right guard.

ROLB: Right-outside linebacker.

RT: Right tackle.

SS: Strong safety.

ST: Special teams.

TD PASSES: Touchdown passes.

TD RECS: Touchdown receptions.

TDS: Touchdowns.

TE: Tight end.

WR: Wide receiver.

BIBLIOGRAPHY

BOOKS

Canning, Whit. *Doak Walker: More Than a Hero*. Carrollton, TX: Masters Press, 1997.

Herskowitz, Mickey. *The Golden Age of Pro Football: A Remembrance of Pro Football in the 1950s*. New York: Macmillan, 1974.

Jones, Danny. *More Distant Memories: Pro Football's Best Ever Players of the 50's, 60's, and 70's*. Bloomington, IN: AuthorHouse, 2006.

Merlo, Dennis. *The Loneliest Lions Fan: Sixty Years of a Fan's Frustration*. Conneaut Lake, PA: Page Publishing, 2022.

Pasche, Paula. *100 Things Lions Fans Should Know & Do before They Die*. Chicago: Triumph Books, 2012.

———. *Game of My Life Detroit Lions: Memorable Stories of Lions Football*. New York: Sports Publishing, 2015.

Plimpton, George. *Paper Lion: Confessions of a Last-String Quarterback*. New York: Harper & Row, 1966.

Sanders, Charlie. *Charlie Sanders's Tales from the Detroit Lions*. Champaign, IL: Sports Publishing, 2005.

Zwerneman, Brent. *Game of My Life: 25 Stories of Aggie Football*. Champaign, IL: Sports Publishing, 2003.

WEBSITES

ESPN.com
https://sports.espn.go.com

Newsday.com
https://www.newsday.com

NYDailyNews.com
https://www.nydailynews.com/new-york

NYTimes.com
https://www.nytimes.com

Pro Football Talk from nbcsports.com
https://profootballtalk.nbcsports.com

SpTimes.com
https://www.sptimes.com

StarLedger.com
https://www.starledger.com

SunSentinel.com
https://articles.sun-sentinel.com

The Players, online at Profootballreference.com
https://www.pro-football-reference.com/players